Fourth - Generation Systems

Fourth - Generation Systems

Their scope, applications and methods of evaluation

UNICOM

APPLIED INFORMATION TECHNOLOGY REPORTS

Edited by **Simon Holloway**

CHAPMAN AND HALL

LONDON · NEW YORK · TOKYO · MELBOURNE · MADRAS

UK	Chapman and Hall, 11 New Fetter Lane, London EC4P 4EE
USA	Van Nostrand Reinhold, 115 5th Avenue, New York NY10003
JAPAN	Chapman and Hall Japan, Thomson Publishing Japan, Hirakawacho Nemoto Building, 7F, 1–7–11 Hirakawa-cho, Chiyoda-ku, Tokyo 102
AUSTRALIA	Chapman and Hall Australia, Thomas Nelson Australia, 480 La Trobe Street, PO Box 4725, Melbourne 3000
INDIA	Chapman and Hall India, R. Sheshadri, 32 Second Main Road, CIT East, Madras 600 035

First edition 1990

© 1990 Unicom Seminars Ltd

Printed in Great Britain by T. J. Press (Padstow) Ltd., Padstow, Cornwall

ISBN 0–412–37910–4   0–442–31199–0 (USA)

British Library Cataloguing in Publication Data
Fourth generation systems : their scope, applications and
methods of evaluation.
1, Computer systems
I. Holloway, Simon
004

ISBN 0–412–37910–4

Library of Congress Cataloguing-in-Publication Data
available

CONTENTS

NEW PRODUCTS: THE VENDOR'S DETAILS

APPENDICES

INTRODUCTION

Introduction

FOURTH-GENERATION SYSTEMS: THEIR SCOPE, APPLICATION AND METHODS OF EVALUATION

Simon Holloway
DCE Information Management Consultancy Limited

Many organizations which use management information systems are now aware that computer systems constructed using third generation languages such as COBOL and Fortran can be more effectively produced and maintained using modern productivity-enhancing tools. These tools have been given various names, including fourth-generation languages (4GLs), application generators, or more recently fourth-generation systems (4GSs). The term fourth generation is open to a wide variety of meanings − no two definitions ever have quite the same implications. True 4G implies that all phases of application design and development are catered for, not just the coding phase, which is after all a relatively small proportion of the total effort involved in developing and maintaining a major application system.

There is, however, one central theme common to all definitions of 4G environment, and that is significant improvements in productivity over conventional methods of writing application software (again "conventional methods" is open to different interpretations depending on the individual user site, but is generally taken to be a high-level language such as COBOL or PL/1 together with file handlers for either sequential file structures or network/hierarchical databases).

The prime purpose of 4G software must be to assist the DP community to respond to genuine user requirements in such a way as to make it unnecessary for a user to attempt to seek alternative solutions. A method of achieving a gain in productivity is to narrow the gap between the forms of system description intelligible to the business manager, and the forms of system description usable by the systems designer. The latter can be narrowed by the use of 4G systems that employ standard logical constructs and avoid the need for complex database navigation. The gap can also be narrowed from the business manager's end, starting with systems specification. Firstly the overall structure of the system can be defined using graphical techniques, such as structure diagrams and data-flow diagrams. This stage can also by further improved by the use of the appropriate design-aid software. Next the prototyping techniques. This will not only allow the user to see what is actually going to be the end product, but also provides automatic production of associated documentation. Finally, it is possible to describe the logical process necessary to move from input to output using a language that is very close to English.

4GSs have been found appropriate for a large class of commercial applications, and allow rapid system development. In some cases such development can be extremely fast, which permits a significant change in the methodology used. The use of prototyping promotes more effective discussions between clients and system implements, whilst at the same time reducing the cost of development.

This book contains papers presented at two seminars:-

- 4GSs: their scope, application and methods of evaluation, presented by Unicom Seminars Limited in London in December 1987.

- 4GSs and their impact on software development and DP organizations, presented by the Belgian Institute for Automatic Control (BIRA) in Ghent in June 1988.

The book surveys the current state of the art for 4GSs, in terms of their scope, application and methods of evaluation. One additional chapter has been added that was not presented at these seminars. This provides further information on the subjects of information-resource dictionaries.

To achieve the flexibility and ease-of-use needs of today's DP professional, the vast majority of 4G products are formulated on a relational DBMS. The flat file structure with its independence of column and new position, coupled with simple manipulation (select, project and form) provide the necessary foundation stone on which to build. Two chapters in this book look at RDBMS and their role with 4G products. Gardarin looks at the strategies and tools needed to develop large-scale applications using relational DBMSs. He stresses the importance of database design task. A new class of database design tools have been developed based on expert systems; Gardarin uses the SECSI product as an example of what these products can achieve.

To aid the development and maintenance of systems, the generation products have taken to heart the use of an integrated data dictionary. In the main, the data dictionaries of 4G products can be described as active, that is, information about the program, screen or report is automatically captured and recommended in the data dictionaries, when it is created, maintained or deleted. The problem that has arisen is that the 4G product dictionaries only support the physical world of that product (the programs and physical data structure). There is little or no support for the work of the analyst in capturing the conceptual world. This has led to organizations no longer having just one data dictionary, but two or more. There is then a problem of sharing information between these data dictionaries and it becomes a much harder task to manage. The answer is to produce an international standard for data dictionaries. ANSI have developed a proposal. Emerson in his paper discusses the need for this standard, and how Pansophic have use the ANSI proposal to solve the problem of interchange of information.

4GSs can be viewed not just as a single product, but a well-integrated set of tools. To understand how to select the most appropriate toolset for an organization, it is essential to understand the different types of 4GSs and their associated features. Johnson reviews the software development process, highlighting areas where there are opportunities for significant cost savings. He then analyses the characteristics of 4GSs, describing their components and their impact on application development. Sharkey looks at those features of a 4GS, which distinguish it from its competitors, by analysing the various building blocks that are found in typical products. Wilcox describes the nature and inherent architecture of 4GLs and application generators. He comes to the conclusion that while 4GLs provide productivity in commercial DP, application generators have wider scope of applicability. Bander reviews the 4G marketplace and, by looking at the design and marketing of these products, puts forward reasons for the large differences in functionality of 4G products.

It is important to choose the right tool for your organization to use. Selection criteria are needed to help evaluate the best product. The chapters by Martland, Toller and Windsor describe various selection criteria lists that have been drawn up. Martland looks at the major factors which affect the selection of a 4GS. Windsor

3

describes the process that his company has evolved for its customers to evaluate, select and try out 4GS products.

The introduction of 4GSs also affects the techniques used to develop application systems. Prototyping, whilst not being dependent on 4GSs, is more readily possible. There is therefore a need for DP departments when choosing 4GSs to consider the effect on their current development methods. Jeffreys analyses some of the problems encountered using prototyping, and describes how the ISE methodology has solved the problem of costing. Porter outlines some methods that can form the basis for sound development of 4GSs and database systems.

For complete success with 4GSs, it has become apparent that it is not just having the right set of software tools and development techniques to achieve the required productivity gains, it is also necessary to have the right organizational structure. The use of prototyping, in particular, changes the relationship and roles of analysts and coders, as well as affecting the role of the end user in the development process. Scott looks at how organizations need to plan for the introduction of 4GSs and their effect on the organization. Holloway reviews the organizational implications caused by 4GSs, by looking at the factors that effect the successful use of these products. He concludes with a proposal for the organizational structure needed to succeed in the 1990s.

When evaluating software, one useful technique is to hear what users of particular products have to say. This book provides some useful user experience stories. Lennox reviews the use his company has made of ICL's QuickBuild, Oracle and the Pick development environment. He outlines the selection criteria used to decide which product to use for a given application, and then compares the similarities and differences of the products. Butler describes the selection process his company went through to choose a 4GS. His chapter contains the selection criteria used and the weighting factors applied. Williams discusses the use of ICL's QuickBuild product set to support strategic information systems development. He puts forward a strategy for the use of 4GSs. Verbraak describes the experiences of his company in using Pansophic's Telon product. De Niel provides an overview of Cortex's CorVision and Application Factory products, and then describes the experiences his company has had using these products. Geubelle focuses on the impact of on-line transaction development processing on application development. He describes the needs that 4GSs must meet to satisfy this type of development, and concludes by showing how Sybase can be used to support it.

The book concludes with chapters from software vendors describing some of the newer 4GS products on the market. These include Progen, Powerhouse, Progress, PRO-IV, Infoexec, AND Natural 2.

4GSs are here to stay. The good products have proved that they are able to replace COBOL and Fortran usage. To achieve the full measure of productivity, it is necessary not only to use these products with the right development methodology, but also to evolve the right organizational structure. For those organizations, who are review their development strategy, it is necessary to carry out a detailed and careful evaluation of the products available.

RELATIONAL DBMS
DESIGN

Chapter 1
STRATEGIES AND TOOLS FOR DEVELOPING LARGE-SCALE APPLICATIONS USING RELATIONAL DBMS

Mokrane Bouzeghoub, Georges Gardarin, Elisabeth Metais
Inria and Paris VI University

1   INTRODUCTION

One of the most important tasks a relational DBMS user or administrator has to perform is the database design (Batini, 1985). By design, we mean the activity of structuring the enterprise information in well-specified relational schemas which may be implemented in relational systems. Historically, researchers and designers have separated the static and dynamic aspects of database design. By static aspects, one means the design of data structures (i.e. relations and views) and time-independent integrity constraints (i.e. domain, keys, referential constraints ...). The dynamic aspects describe the actions operating on these data structures and the sequence of transactions modifying the database from one consistent state to another. In this chapter, we shall concentrate on static aspects although we would try to encompass the whole database design process and consider dynamic aspects when necessary.

Relational (or non-relational) database design is a very important task because good design is the necessary condition for good usage of the database, both from a semantics point of view and for performance reasons. Misunderstandings in relation or attribute meanings are generally due to poor design. Bad performances are also often due to poor design. The main aspects which make database design difficult are the following:

1. **Size of the application:** The difficulty of the design increases with the size of the application. Designing small databases is quite easy but structuring several hundred objects, relationships and constraints without computer aids is always a hard task, especially for people whose profession is not specialist in database design.

2. **Modelling choices (abstraction, classification):** Objects may be classified into categories with respect to their inherent properties (physical aspect) or their functional characteristics. Consequently, the problem is to find the most invariant attributes and classes.

3. **Relative perception of the real world:** The real world may be reported in different ways with respect to the designers' perceptions: several database schemas may describe the same reality. The problem is to characterize the best schema and to find a methodology to build and to choose the best one.

4. **Availability of information:** The designer cannot often get a detailed description of objects because of the lack of knowledge about the application. However the design must start with incomplete and imperfect knowledge.

5. **Evolutivity:** As the design is based on a fuzzy universe of discourse, new information may arise and may entail changes in the definition of classes, relationships and constraints. These changes must be integrated without reconsidering all the modelling phases.

In this chapter, we propose an approach to design relational databases. This approach is based on a methodology and a supporting tool, namely the SECSI expert system. While the methodology is rather classical, the design tool is based on techniques used in artificial intelligence. The SECSI expert system aims at combining various categories of knowledge coming both from relational theory, semantic data modelling (Brodie, 1984), artificial intelligence and software engineering. This expert system which was first built at University of Paris VI is now marketed by INFOSYS, a French company.

The chapter is organized as follows. Section 2 presents an overview of the design methodology. Section 3 details the expert system approach, its objectives, its structure and the knowledge involved. Section 4 presents the SECSI system architecture. Finally, section 6 shows an example of SECSI session.

2   A TYPICAL DESIGN METHODOLOGY

- Capture and abstraction of user requirements;

- integration of external views;

- normalization of conceptual relations;

- optimization of the internal schema.

The design process is sketched in Figure 1.1. It is a strength of most relational systems that they allow the database administrator dynamically to add or remove views, relations, attributes, integrity constraints and indexes. Thus iterative design must be supported and backtracking to a previous phase must be possible.

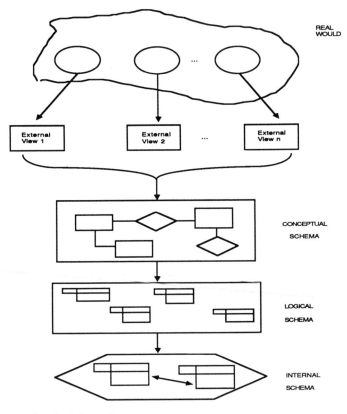

Figure 1.1   A sketch of the design process.

2.1 Capture and abstraction of user requirements

A top-down design of a relational database starts with user interviews and observations. By looking at existing forms, by questioning end users, by analysing the enterprise organization and the information flows, it is possible to capture the user requirements and to divide them in more or less independent contexts. Abstracting from these limited portions of the information system leads to a formal representation of the objects, their properties and interrelationships, and the activities involving those objects (Sevcik, 1981). Thus, a representation of each portion of the modelled enterprise may be done bringing out an external schema with static and dynamic aspects in a chosen formalism (e.g. entity-relationship diagrams). The appropriate selection of details of the enterprise to model depends on the transactions the user has in mind and more generally on the database purpose. It is not an easy task and many iterations are generally necessary. As output, the first phase of the database design, which is probably the most informal one, must deliver a set of external views both for the static characteristics (i.e. the data descriptions) and the main dynamic aspects (i.e. a first specification of the typical transactions). In summary, the abstraction of user requirements may be defined as the phase of the design process which consists in determining and formalizing external views, using a specific external data model.

2.2 Integration and synthesis of external views

The next phase in the design is the integration of the various database views. A union of the views is not sufficient because similar concepts may be described in different views. It is necessary to understand precisely the meaning of each object and attribute, and to isolate objects and attributes having similar or different meanings. Similar objects must be integrated. Functional dependencies are useful information in understanding the semantics of an object or an attribute. Also, knowing the most important processes which intend to act upon objects facilitates object comprehension and comparisons. The integration phase terminates with the elaboration of a first global schema of the database in some formalism, for example the entity-relationship model or even a richer semantics-data model. In summary, view integration may be defined as the phase of the design process which consists in elaborating a unique, coherent and non-redundant global conceptual schema by integrating all the various external views.

2.3 Conceptual relation design and normalization

This phase starts with the previous conceptual schema, performs a first transformation in relations and then applies dependency theory to improve the schema. The purpose is to reduce data redundancy and to avoid update anomalies. The non-loss decomposition method yields molecular relations, which cannot be decomposed further on without loss of information. Although it is theoretically a well-founded method, the normalization process which is described below is so tedious to apply that many database designers do not bother. Schema normalization can be defined as the phase of the design process which aims at obtaining molecular relations representing without loss of information unique facts, concepts or events, in order to avoid data redundancy and update anomalies.

2.4 Optimization and internal schema design

This last phase involves specifying the physical representation of the database. The basis for optimization is the knowledge of the most frequent transactions. This knowledge derives from the dynamic aspect of modelling. The logical and physical design are generally based on cost models which are system-dependent. As joins are generally cost operations, they are avoided by implementing natural joins of relations with associated integrity constraints; this process is known as **schema denormalization.** Schema denormalization is the optimization process which aims at determining the most suitable joins of normalized relations to implement in the internal schema. Denormalization is necessary to avoid costly join. However, too much denormalization leads to data redundancy: relations become large and selections are then costly. To avoid too many joins and over long selections, a compromise must be elaborated at the level of the internal schema. Also, integrity constraints on the internal schema relations must be generated during the denormalization process to control data redundancy: a good system should enforce these integrity constraints, thus avoiding update anomalies.

Finally, file organizations and access paths such as relation clustering, hashing methods and indexes must be chosen. This is part of the physical design. **Physical design** is the optimization process which aims at choosing file organizations, access methods, indexed attributes and record clusterings for the implemented relations. Let us point out that physical design is, at least in theory, the only sub-phase which is system-dependent.

3 A NEW CLASS OF DATABASE DESIGN TOOLS: EXPERT SYSTEMS

3.1 Overview of existing tools

We distinguish three categories of tools. These tools are characterized by the methodology and the models that they support.

The first category consists of manual tools which are generally based on semantic models like the entity-relationship model hen 76 or the semantic hierarchy model. In these tools, all the design choices are left to the database administrator (DBA); the methodology offers a few guidelines for validating the design Hammer 81. These tools are very interesting for small applications but inapplicable with large ones.

The second category of tools provides a set of algorithms built upon the relational model. Such tools provide programs deriving a normalized relational schema from a set of attributes and dependencies (Beeri, 1979), (Zaniolo, 1981). This approach is one of the best formalized but unfortunately, this approach ignores natural objects such as hierarchies, entities and relationships.

The third category consists of a set of interactive programs designed to aid manual methods. These tools could be considered as a combination of manual tools and algorithmic tools. They often call for CAD techniques. Interactions between the users and the system are question-answering oriented (Tardieu, 1984) (Atzeni, 1981) or graphics-language oriented (Chan, 1980). This approach is static because computer aids are programmed once and for all, hence it is difficult to modify or add design rules. But this remains an interesting approach if we combine it with the new developments in knowledge representation.

Because of the insufficiencies of the existing tools, we proposed a new integrated knowledge-based tool for helping the user in the difficult process of database design (Bouzeghoub, 1984). Several tools are now built following a similar approach, among them Tucherman (1985) and Rolland (1986).

3.2 Main characteristics of expert systems for database design

An expert system is a specialized software tool which solves a problem as well as a human expert does. Thus, in our area, we would like to replace the database designer by an expert system. To achieve such an objective, we first have to **constitute a complete knowledge base** including theoretical algorithms and rules, and experimental knowledge in the database design process. Second, we must **provide an interactive methodological environment** which accepts incomplete specifications, provides the same reasoning as a human expert, permits backtracking to any design step, uses a question-answering system and can infer from examples. Third, it is desirable that our expert system be **an open tool** which can learn and integrate new theoretical and experimental rules. The system must also transfer its expertise through its use, via explanation of its design rules and through justification of its results. Finally, the expert system must **provide end-user friendly interfaces;** for this purpose, we propose to offer several external languages: a declarative language, a graphical interface and a quasi-natural language.

3.3 Different levels of expertise

The expertise of the system lies in three categories:

1. **Theoretical knowledge**: This knowledge coincides with the design concepts (models, rules, facts) and the design methodology (advice, reasoning). Theoretical knowledge is composed of algorithms, rules and heuristics.

   - Algorithms: some parts of the design process are well isolated and formalized, and have already been expressed by many efficient algorithms, such as normalization algorithms, cost evaluation of transactions and access paths optimization.

12

- Rules: correspond to some known or admitted expertise as in normalization (Armstrong's inference rules), view integration rules, mappings rules and consistency enforcement rules.

- Heuristics: may be abusive interpretations of the real world, or assumptions in some value distributions, or simplification of the correlation between attributes and between constraints.

2. **Specific domain knowledge:** For each application domain (insurance, banking, medicine, travel), there is some common terminology, managerial rules and skills which represent the specific know-how of the domain. This know-how can be represented either by general behaviour rules or by general predefined structures. This knowledge is stored in the system knowledge base and reused, when appropriate, during the design process.

3. **Specific application rules:** Within a specific application domain, there are some properties which characterize each application (e.g. reservation in a given travel agency). These properties are described by facts and rules which constitute the detailed specification of the application.

3.4   Knowledge representation

As usual, the system supports two types of knowledge: facts and rules. To represent these two types of knowledge, we utilize two different representation models: a semantic network to represent facts and production rules to represent the design process and application-behavioural constraints.

The semantic network is defined by a set of typed nodes (attributes, values of attributes, entities, instances of entities) and a set of typed arcs with their corresponding inverse (aggregation arcs (a/p), association arcs (r/o), classification arcs (c/i), generalization arcs (g/s), equivalence arcs (e)).

To enhance the semantics of this model, additional constraints are defined: domains, unicity, union and intersection of classes, cardinalities, functional dependencies, roles.

3.5   Reasoning mechanism

Each step of the design methodology consists either of:

1.   Proving hypothesis, for example, "is a view redundant to another one?", "is a dependency derivable from a set of given dependencies?";

2.   or transforming a specification from one given form to another. For example, the transformation from an external description into a semantic net schema and then to a first normal form relational schema.

These two principles lead to the use of a combination of two inference mechanisms: **backward chaining** to prove hypotheses and **forward chaining** to apply transformation rules. The transition from one mechanism to another is controlled by meta-rules.

4   THE SECSI SYSTEM ARCHITECTURE

The system aims to infer from a high-level description of the real world a relational schema composed of a set of normalized relations with their keys and a set of virtual relations with the corresponding deriving queries. The overall architecture is portrayed in Figure 1.2, and explained hereafter.

4.1   The knowledge base

The knowledge base is composed of two parts: a rule base and a fact base.

The rule base is created and updated by the design expert. This base contains general rules such as normalization rules; but also specific rules which can be system-dependent or even application-dependent. General design rules are grouped into the DESIGN module which is composed of two parts: the RUN part yields a normalized relational schema from an application description, and the EXPLAIN part brings out explanations about the produced schema and the applied rules.

The fact base is designed by the database administrator. It contains compiled specifications describing the application. These compiled specifications are represented by a semantic network. For more details on this network, see Bouzeghoub (1985 and 1986).

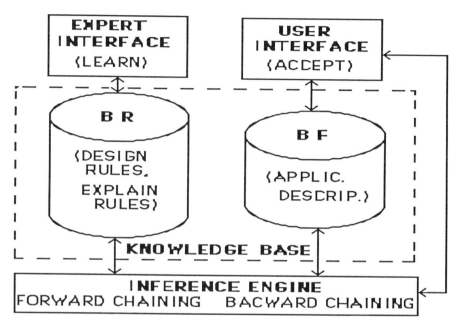

Figure 1.2 An overview of SECSI architecture.

4.2   The external interfaces

The external interfaces are composed of two modules:

1.   The expert interface (LEARN) allows the expert to introduce and update the design rules. Such rules are introduced either using a graphical interface or as production rules written directly in PROLOG. This interface has also to check the consistency of the rule base.

2.   The user interface (ACCEPT) helps the DBA to fill in and to modify the base of facts. Three languages are offered to the end-user: a restricted natural language (ACCEPT-NATURAL), a simple declarative language (ACCEPT-SHORT) and a graphical language (ACCEPT-GRAPHICS). The DBA supplies the description of his application in one or all of these languages. An interactive parser processes the given description and

15

generates a specific semantic network portraying the application. Finally, a documentation service is provided to the end-user (HELP-USER) and to students who wish to learn some aspects of database design (HELP-STUDENT).

4.3   The inference engine

The inference engine is a program composed of the basic mechanisms which permit to manage and apply the rules in the rule base. These basic mechanisms are represented by the two following statements: proof (goal) and apply (sequence of rules). The first statement applies the design rules in a backward chaining to prove a given goal. The second statement transforms the current workspace in forward chaining by applying the sequence of rules given as arguments. These two statements are embedded in a hierarchy of meta-rules which describe the design methodology.

5   AN EXAMPLE OF A SECSI SESSION

This section shows a sample of a SECSI session.

5.1   Description of the application

Describing the application in a comprehensible manner is an important problem in database design. To be more flexible we allow the database administrator to describe his application either in a formal declarative language or in a restricted subset of natural language.

> > SECSI VERS_1,INFOSYS,1986

SECSI	> HELLO!WHICH TRANSACTION DO YOU WANT: (ACCEPT/DESIGN/HELP/LEARN/END)?
USER	< ACCEPT.
SECSI	> PLEASE ENTER THE DESCRIPTION OF YOUR APPLICATION.
USER	< STUDENTS AND TEACHERS ARE PERSONS.
	< A STUDENT IS ENROLLED IN A COURSE AT A GIVEN DATE.

	< A PERSON HAS A NAME
	< AN EMPLOYEE HAS A SSN AND A SALARY.
	< A TEACHER HAS A TEL AND AN ADDRESS.
	< A PROFESSOR IS RESPONSIBLE FOR A COURSE.
	< STAFF AND TEACHER ARE EMPLOYEES.
	< A PERSON IS A STUDENT.
SECSI	> YOU ARE CREATING A CYCLE OF GENERALIZATIONS:
	A STUDENT IS A PERSON
	A PERSON IS A STUDENT
	> DO YOU WANT TO RETRACT?
USER	< RETRACT THE LAST.
	....
	< STOP.
SECSI	> WHAT IS THE NAME OF THIS APPLICATION?
USER	< UNIVERSITY.

5.2 Acquisition of constraints

The previous description is parsed and checked in order to preserve consistency, and finally validated. Then, SECSI asks the user some questions about additional information. Some questions may concern constraints on the attributes, such as the number of possible values of an attribute for one given entity, the cardinalities of associations and functional dependencies.

1. Cardinalities of aggregations:

SECSI	> COULD ANY TEACHER HAVE SEVERAL ADDRESSES?
USER	< YES.
SECSI	> COULD ANY TEACHER HAVE SEVERAL TEL?
USER	< YES.
SECSI	> IS THIS THE TEL DEPENDENT ON THE ADDRESS?
USER	< ?.
SECSI	> I MEAN FOR EACH ADDRESS
	IS THERE ONLY ONE TEL?
USER	< NO.
SECSI	> AND REVERSELY?
USER	< YES.
SECSI	> FOR EACH SALARY IS THERE ONE OR SEVERAL
	EMPLOYEES?

USER   < !.
SECSI   > OK:I WILL GENERATE DEFAULT ANSWERS.

         ...

2. Cardinalities of associations:

SECSI   > MAY EACH PROFESSOR BE RESPONSIBLE FOR ONLY ONE,
           OR SEVERAL COURSES?
USER   < ONE.
SECSI   > MAY EACH COURSE HAVE ONLY ONE OR SEVERAL
           RESPONSIBLES?
USER   < ONE.
SECSI   > DOES A COURSE EXIST WITHOUT A RESPONSIBLE?
USER   < NO.
USER   < /.
SECSI   > WHAT NEW ASSERTION DO YOU WANT TO ENTER?
USER   < A TEACHER MAY BE RESPONSIBLE FOR SEVERAL COURSES.

3. Functional dependencies:

There is a particular interaction between constraints. Hence, from cardinalities of
aggregations and associations, the system generates some functional and
multivalued dependencies. To complete this set of dependencies, the system utilizes
heuristics based on examples to avoid useless questions.

SECSI   > PLEASE, WOULD YOU GIVE ME SOME EXAMPLES OF
           TUPLES OF THE RELATION TEACHER
           (SSN, NAME, ADDRESS, TEL)
USER   < 1234 DUPONT PARIS 222477
         < 1235 DUPONT MARSEILLE 662532
         < 2500 DURAND GRENOBLE   886542
         < 3000 PERRIER LYON   274078
         < 1112 PERRIER LYON   157109

SECSI   > THUS THE FOLLOWING DEPENDENCIES ARE NOT VALID:
NAME   -- > ADDRESS
NAME   -- > TEL
ADDRESS   -- > NAME
(NAME,ADDRESS) -- > TEL
(NAME,ADDRESS) -- > SSN

18

5.3 Mapping of the semantic network to the relational schema

After the constraint acquisition phase, the system proceeds to the simplification and the transformation of the semantic network generated previously in a normalized relational schema.

SECSI   > STEP1:REMOVING GENERALIZATION HIERARCHIES.
           > GENERALIZATION HIERARCHIES WILL BE REMOVED
           AND REPLACED BY NEW ATTRIBUTES:
           > IN THE RELATION TEACHER, A NEW ATTRIBUTE IS
           CREATED.ITS NAME IS TEACHER. ROLE
           AND ITS DOMAIN IS (PROFESSOR,INSTRUCTOR)
           ...

As generalization hierarchies cannot be easily represented in the relational model, they are removed and replaced either by new attributes, or virtual relations and deriving queries. For example, the system has chosen the concept of TEACHER for both INSTRUCTORS and PROFESSORS. At the end of this step, we obtain an entity-relationship schema, and the system completes the step.

SECSI   > STEP 2: REMOVING MULTIVALUED ATTRIBUTES.
           > ADDRESS AND TEL ARE REMOVED FROM TEACHER AND
           CONSTITUTE A NEW 1NF RELATION.
           > DO YOU GIVE A NAME TO THIS NEW RELATION?
USER   < LOCATION
SECSI   > OTHER ENTITIES ARE IN 1NF.

SECSI   > STEP3:REMOVING ASSOCIATION ARCS:
           > ASSOCIATION ARCS ARE REMOVED AND REPLACED BY
           REFERENTIAL INTEGRITY CONSTRAINTS.

SECSI   > STEP4, NORMALIZATION PROCESS:
           ONLY BASE RELATIONS ARE NORMALIZED.

At the end of this step, we obtain a set of relations in first normal form. The 4NF normalization process is based on functional and multivalued dependencies. This process is embedded in step 3. It is based both in synthesizing algorithms and decomposition algorithms.

5.4 The obtained results

When the redesign process is terminated, we obtain the following results:

1. A set of basic relations in 4FN and the various keys of these relations. In the example below, key attributes are underlined. Notice that in the results some new attributes appear (e.g. teacher.role and stu.number) which were not in the initial description. They have been created to replace some concepts which don't exist in the relational model such as generalization or association. Other attributes have been created during the normalization process (e.g. tea_ssn).

    ++RELATIONS
    ENROLLED (CLA-NUMBER COU-NAME STU-NUMBER DATE)
    TEACHER (DEP-NAME SALARY NAME SSN TEA-ROLE AGE)
    STAFF (DEP-NAME SALARY NAME SSN)
    STUDENT (NAME NUMBER SSN)
    COURSE (TEA-SSN ROOM DAY NAME HOUR)
    ADDRESS-TEL-TEACHER (TEA-SSN TEL ADDRESS)

2   A set of virtual relations and the definition of the corresponding relational queries which permit to derive them from the database implemented relations.

    ++VIRTUAL RELATIONS
    PERSON = UNION(STUDENT AME,NSS, TEACHER AME,NSS, STAFF AME,NSS)
    DIR_OF-LABO = REST(JOIN(STAFF,
                TEACHER/STAFF.SSN = TEACHER.SSN)
                /TEACHER.ROLE = "DIR_OF_LABO")
                EMPLOYEE = UNION(TEACHER(SSN,SALARY,
                STAFF(SSN,SALARY)

3. A set of constraints like domain, referential and other general semantic constraints have been generated by the mapping rules and the normalization process. Other constraints have been introduced by the end-user.

++DOMAIN CONSTRAINTS
TEACHER.ROLE = {DIR_OF_LABO,INSTRUCTOR,PROFESSOR}
COURSE.NAME = {AI,DB,MATH}

++ REFERENTIAL AND INCLUSION CONSTRAINTS
ENROLLED.CLA-NUMBER = CLASS.NUMBER
ENROLLED.CLA-NAME = CLASS.NAME
ENROLLED.STU-NUMBER = STUDENT.NUMBER
CLASS.COU-NAME = COURSE.NAME
ADDRESS-TEL-TEACHER.TEA-SSN = TEACHER.SSN

++OTHER SEMANTIC INTEGRITY CONSTRAINTS
CLASS.TEA-SSN = TEACHER.SSN = = >
          TEACHER.ROLE = "INSTRUCTOR"
COURSE.TEA-SSN = TEACHER.SSN = = >
       TEACHER.ROLE = "PROFESSOR"

This last constraint means that a course is given only by a teacher who is a professor.

5.5 Documentation and explanation

At any time, the user can stop the dialogue (by answering "!")and the system generates default answers. The user can also answer "?" if he doesn't understand, the question is then reformulated in another way or some help appears on the screen. To change a previous specification, the user can type "/" and SECSI will ask him to enter what he wants to change. Sometimes, the end-user (the DBA) may be surprised by the results given by SECSI because he doesn't understand them (constraints, virtual relation), or because they seem different from his perception of the reality. SECSI can explain the choice of permanent or virtual relations or any object appearing in the results.

USER   < WHY IS A PERSON A VIRTUAL RELATION?

SECSI   < (1)YOU HAD INTRODUCED PERSON AS AN ENTITY
          °HAVING THE ATTRIBUTES SSN NAME
          °GENERIC OF STUDENT TEACHER STAFF
          (2)THE FOLLOWING STRUCTURE (TO WHICH THIS OBJECT
          BELONGS)HAS BEEN
TRANSFORMED AS FOLLOWS:

```
                    PERSON ─────────────────┐
                ┌──────────────┬─────────┐  │
                │              │         │  NAME SSN
            STUDENT        STAFF    TEACHER
               │            ║         ║   │   │
           NUMBER           ║         ║  TEL ADDRESS
                            ║         ║
            ENROLLED        ║         ║
                            ║         ║
                          RESPONSIBLE
```

          > KNOWING THAT:
          °THERE ARE MORE THAN 3 ATTRIBUTES IN
           SPECIFICS:NUMBER, TEL AND ADDRESS
          °SPECIFICS ARE INVOLVED IN 2 ASSOCIATIONS:
           ENROLLED AND RESPONSIBLE
          °THE SPECIFICS STAFF AND TEACHER HAVE ANOTHER
           GENERIC: EMPLOYEE
          > I HAVE APPLIED THIS TRANSFORMATION:
          °THE GENERIC PERSON HAS BEEN SUPPRESSED
          °THE SPECIFICS BECAME BASE RELATIONS
          °PERSON IS NOW A VIRTUAL RELATION AND ITS DERIVING
           RULE IS EXPRESSED IN THE RESULTS.

6   CONCLUSION

In this chapter, we have described a design methodology and an expert-system-based tool for database design. Compared to the existing tools, the proposed one seems more suitable for database design in the sense that it takes advantage of both theoretical development and practical experience. With future development of deductive databases and knowledge bases, this approach is more adequate to integrate new concepts and new design rules. We think that only powerful expert systems will efficiently handle the complexity introduced by these new developments. The ability to justify several design choices and to explain reasoning alternatives is one of the important features of expert systems; it makes them attractive for complex problems.

The sample of the SECSI session shown in this paper illustrates only the logical design process. The corresponding product is written in PROLOG and runs on PC and SUN machines. It includes more than 1000 PROLOG clauses with the declarative and natural interfaces, about 60 logical design rules and a few explanation rules. Currently, we are developing other versions for view integration and physical design.

7   REFERENCES

Atzeni (1981), Atzeni C., Lenzerini M., Villanellei F. "INCOD: A System for Conceptual Design of Data and Transactions in the E_R Model," (Intl. conf. on ERA P.P.CHEN ed. ER institute 81).

Batini (1985), Batini C. and CERIS, "Database Design: Methodologies, tools and environments", panel session, ACM SIGMOD 1985.

Beeri (1979), Beeri C. And Bernstein P.A. "Computational problems related to the design of normal form relation schemas", ACM Transactions On Database Systems, March 1979.

Bouzeghoub (1984), Bouzeghoub M. And Gardarin G. "The design of an expert system for database design", Intl.Workshop on New Applications of Databases, Cambridge (UK), Sept. 1983. Published in *New Applications of Databases*, Academic Press, Gardarin & Gelenbe eds. 1984.

Bouzeghoub (1985), Bouzeghoub M., Gardarin G., Metais E. "Database Design Tools: an Expert System Approach" VLDB Conf. Stockholm August 1985.

Bouzeghoub (1986), Bouzeghoub M. "SECSI: Un systeme expert en conception de systemes d'informations", These de Doctorat de l'Universite Pierre et Marie Curie (Paris VI), mars 1986.

Brodie (1984), Brodie M., Mylopoulos J.,Schmidt Y. "On Conceptual Modelling: Perspectives from Artificial Intelligence, Databases and Programming languages. Springer-Verlag, NY 1984.

Chan (1980), Chan E.F., Lockovsky F.H. "A graphical database design aid using the E-R model", Int.Conf. on ERA. Chen Ed., North-Holland, 1980.

Chen (1976), Chen P.P. "The Entity Relationship Model Toward a Unified View of Data", (ACM TODS VI, N1, March 1976).

Hammer (1981), Hammer N. And Mcleod D. "Database Description with SDM: A Semantic Data Model", (ACM TODS VI, N3, Sep 81).

Reiner (1986), Reiner D.S. "Database Design — Theory and Practice", 12th Very Large Data Bases Tutorials, Kyoto, Japan, August 1986.

Rolland (1986), Rolland C. Proix C., "OICSI, an Expert System for DB Design", IFIP World Computer Congress, DUBLIN, Sept. 1986, pp 241-250.

Sevcik (1981), Sevcick K. "Data Base System Performance Prediction Using An Analytical Model", 7th Very Large Data Bases Conf., Cannes, France, Sept. 1981, pp 182-198.

Tardieu (1984), Tardieu H., Nanci D., Pascot D. "Conception d'un systeme d'information", Editions d'Organisation, Paris, 1984.

Tucherman (1985), Tucherman L., Furtado A. And Casanova M. "A Tool for Modular Database Design", VLDB Conf. Stockholm, 1985.

Zaniolo (1981), Zaniolo C., Melkanoff M.M: "On the design of relational database schemata", ACM-TODS, VI, N1; March 1981.

DATA
DICTIONARY
STANDARDIZATION

Chapter 2

Use of the Proposed ISO/ANSI Standard Information Resource Dictionary System for Multi-Vendor Software Integration

E. James Emerson
Pansophic Systems, Inc.

1   INTRODUCTION

In 1979, "Managing the Crises in Data Processing" written by Richard L. Nolan appeared in *Harvard Business Review*. Nolan identified six stages of DP growth that all DP organizations pass through to reach "maturity".

Nolan's discussion of these stages centres on the effects that these stages have on:

- the types of applications that have been developed;

- the degree to which data is managed and controlled; and

- the level to which application integration has been achieved using database management system (DBMS) technology.

This chapter explores the evolution of dictionary systems technology using, as a framework, the six stages of DP growth identified by Nolan. Nolan's paper discusses applications, data, and DBMS. This chapter discusses the analogous dictionary areas of meta-applications, meta-data and dictionary systems.

Meta-applications are used by the MIS department to control and manage hardware and software resources and to develop applications. Such meta-applications include compilers, editors, DBMS, application generators, and job scheduling systems.

The concept of meta-data is more difficult to define. Strictly speaking, it is information about data. For example, John Doe's social-security number is a data element. Information about that data element would include the fact that a

25

social-security number is a nine-digit numeric field. For the purpose of this paper, meta-data is defined, somewhat more loosely, as any data used in the support of meta-applications.

A dictionary system is a special purpose DBMS for the storage and maintenance of meta-data. This term is used instead of the more traditional term of "data dictionary system" in order to imply that it can be used for the control and management of any information resource (e.g. programs, transactions, disk drives) and is not limited to data objects only.

Growth processes	Stage I Initiation	Stage II Contagion	Stage III Control	Stage IV Integration	Stage V Data Administration	Stage VI Maturity
Applications portfolio	Functional cost reduction applications	Proliferation	Upgrade documentation and restructuring of existing applications	Retrofitting existing applications using data base technology	Organization Integration of applications	Application integration "mirroring" information flows
DP organization	Specialization for technological learning	User-oriented programmers	Middle management	Establish computer utility and user account teams	Data Administration	Data Resource Management
DP planning and control	Lax	More lax	Formalized planning and control	Tailored planning and control systems	Shared data and common systems	Data resource strategic planning
User awareness	"Hands off"	Superficially enthusiastic	Arbitrarily held accountable	Accountability learning	Effectively accountable	Acceptance of joint user and data processing accountability
Dictionary systems	"Controlled" copy libraries and element catalogues	Stand-alone data dictionaries	Data dictionaries integrated with DBMS	Multiplicity of proprietary data dictionary systems	Standard Information Resource Dictionary Systems	Standard Information Resource Dictionary Methodologies

Table 2.1 Six stages of data processing growth.

26

2 SIX STAGES OF DICTIONARY SYSTEMS GROWTH

In Nolan's article, he included an exhibit that mapped various growth processes to the six stages of growth. This exhibit has been duplicated in Table 2.1 with the addition of a new growth process entitled Dictionary systems.

Stage I

In stage I, when the very first applications for an organization are being developed, the DP manager begins to realize that his data definitions are inconsistent and not well controlled. Initially, this problem may be addressed with carefully controlled copy libraries that contain "official" versions of a company's file and record definitions and, perhaps, standard subroutines for critical functions. If control down to the element (field) level is desired, the installation may develop its own element-cataloguing system to keep track of the rapidly growing set of elements. This element-catalogue system is, in essence, a primitive but effective dictionary system.

Stage II

In stage II, applications begin to proliferate at a high rate. In an attempt to regain control of an ever worsening situation, a DP organization might invest in a stand-alone dictionary system. In this stage, the stand-alone data dictionary is used primarily as a documentation tool. Because the stand-alone data dictionary is so isolated from the day-to-day activities of the DP organization, however, these dictionaries are rarely, if ever, used to the extent that is originally planned. Many fall into total disuse during this stage.

Stage III

In stage III, database technology may be introduced for use in the development of certain key applications. Many DBMSs come with their own integrated data dictionary that must be used to define application databases, records, elements, transactions and so on. These data dictionaries may also be well integrated with other application development tools provided by the same vendor (eg report writers, application generators, or 4GLs). In this stage, the DBMS dictionaries begin to meet the promises of dictionary technology because they become integrated with some of the day-to-day activities of the DP organization.

Stage IV

In stage IV, the DP environment usually becomes very complex. The wide variety of applications that have been implemented are also of varying ages. With this variance in age comes a wide variance in the technologies employed. A DP organization at this stage, then, is usually characterized by having multiple DBMSs, application-development systems, data dictionaries, report writers and so on installed and in use. It is not that unusual to have multiple technologies applied to the implementation of a single application.

DP organizations can go along for a long while in this stage. They find it very difficult, however, to go forward to subsequent stages, and the high level of application integration that characterizes them, without first integrating the meta-applications on which they depend around an information-resource dictionary system.

Stage V

In stage V, a standard Information Resource Dictionary System (IRDS) has been installed and the integration of the meta-applications that support the integration of regular applications has been completed. This integration is achieved through the design and implementation of a common schema (data model) for the IRDS. By adopting a common data model for all meta-applications, they can share all of the meta-data that they employ and begin truly to support the newly integrated applications that use their widely variant technologies.

During this stage, both applications and meta-applications are tightly integrated. Applications are tightly integrated through the design and implementation of a corporate data model and through attentive data administration. While these applications employ a multitude of technologies and designs, they are integrated by the corporate data model through which they communicate.

Meta-applications are tightly integrated through the design and implementation of a corporate, and cross-vendor, meta-data model and through attentive meta-data administration. While these meta-applications employ a multitude of technologies and designs, and come from many different vendors, they are integrated by the corporate meta-data model through which they communicate.

Stage VI

In stage VI, this integration is refined further. Through the application of consistent methodologies and techniques, regular applications begin to "resemble" one another or develop a common "style". The boundaries between applications so well integrated seem to disappear and it is as if there is really only one application that "mirrors" the corporation's "personality" and unique way of doing business.

Meta-applications are usually supplied by many different vendors and, thus, are unlikely ever to reach this stage of "seamless" integration. This is also probably true for applications software supplied by many outside vendors. By agreeing on certain key methodologies, however, meta-application software from multiple vendors can be very tightly integrated. Such methodologies might include common paradigms for information-resource inventory control, change management, and configuration management.

3   THE IRDS STANDARD

In order to progress from stage IV into subsequent stages, the installation of a standard IRDS is required. The term "IRDS" is the name given to a standard for dictionary systems that is currently under development at both the national and international level.

Before 1983, two separate efforts were underway to develop a standard for information-resource dictionary systems. The US National Bureau of Standards (NBS) was working on a Federal Information Processing Standard (FIPS), and technical committee X3H4 of the American National Standards Institute (ANSI) was working on a draft proposed American National Standard (dpANS).

In 1983, these groups merged their efforts and completed the development of an IRDS standard in 1986. This standard has undergone two American public reviews required for final acceptance by ANSI, and should become an American National Standard in late 1988 or early 1989.

In January of 1987, this same standard was accepted as a draft proposed standard by the International Standards Organization (ISO). Specifically, it was accepted by technical committee 97, subcommittee 21, working group 3 (TC97/SC21/WG3) of ISO. It has undergone one international review by the member bodies of participating countries. However, it is not likely to become an international standard for several years.

The IRDS defined by this standard is a specialized DBMS for the control and management of information resources and for the support of information-management tools. It uses the entity-relationship model as its paradigm for the contents of the dictionary and its schema. It is fully extensible allowing any types of entities, relationships or attributes to be defined and maintained.

The fact that it employs a specific type of data model and that it is fully extensible makes it a powerful and expandable DBMS for the MIS department and the meta-applications that it employs. It provides special features unique to this environment, however, with its life-cycle management control features, versioning capabilities, and specialized key structures.

Four different interfaces are defined by the standard:

- Services Interface — a programmatic interface, invoked via a given language's external call mechanism, which allows full use of the IRDS from within a program;

- Command Language Interface — a command interface intended to be the primary batch interface to the IRDS;

- Panel Interface — a panel oriented interface intended to be the primary online interface to the IRDS;

- IRD to IRD Interface — a specialized interface that allows different IRDS implementations to exchange dictionary and schema information

Because the services interface supports all of the functionality of the IRDS, all of the other interfaces can be implemented as meta-applications on top of it.

4   INTEGRATION OF META-APPLICATIONS

To progress forward into stages V and VI not only requires the installation of a standard IRDS. It also requires that the meta-applications in use by the DP organization integrate around it. This is a difficult task.

In integrating meta-applications around an IRDS, there are several primary goals:

- control of an inventory of all information resources — hardware, software, networks, data and so on;

- support for all meta-applications used in the support of the MIS department including editors, compilers, DBMSs, data and process modelling tools, application-development systems, 4GLs, project-planning systems, and so on;

- change-management capabilities;

- configuration-management capabilities; and

- standards-definition and enforcement.

The IRDS defined by the ISO/ANSI standard is a sound foundation for the attainment of these goals.

Without an IRDS, today's environment makes attainment of these goals a difficult task: each meta-application has its own proprietary "dictionary" and communication links to allow these dictionaries to share common meta-data are not easily developed.

Some vendors have attempted to solve this problem by providing an entire family of meta-applications integrated around their own proprietary DBMS and dictionary. This approach has met with limited success but assumes that all applications are exclusively developed and supported using that single vendor's products. This is rarely the case.

This problem becomes even more difficult in large DP installations that have a mix of hardware environments, during the later stages of growth. That is, they have mainframes for corporate-level computing, minicomputers for departmental computing, and microcomputers for personal computing. The current trend is to create applications where processing and data are shared among all of these levels. No single vendor has yet developed a set of meta-applications that support this kind of application. Thus, applications must be created using tools from several different vendors.

On top of all this, it is extremely unlikely that a vendor, attempting to provide such an all-encompassing set of meta-applications, would succeed equally at all levels. The vendor specializing in support of a particular environment or meta-application will be likely to provide better tools than the vendor attempting to provide everything for all environments.

5   PANSOPHIC'S INTEGRATION STRATEGY

Pansophic Systems is a vendor of systems software that has been in business since 1969 when we introduced PANVALET. Since that time, Pansophic's product line has expanded to include report writers (EASYTRIEVE/PLUS), application-development systems (TELON and GENER/OL), change-management systems (CMF), graphics systems (D-PICT/Intellichart), and micro—mainframe links (PANLINK and Corporate Tie). While still emphasizing the IBM mainframe market, Pansophic has begun to expand into other hardware markets with D-PICT/Intellichart, EASYTRIEVE PLUS PC, and TELON PC.

As our product line became more diverse, we began to address the problem of product integration. For a time, we considered developing proprietary database and dictionary technology for our products. We realized, however, that this approach would not provide a basis for moving to the next stages of growth. DP organizations do not want another proprietary database and dictionary. Instead, they want a way to integrate what they have.

We feel that the only way to achieve this is to standardize around a particular database and dictionary. We looked to ANSI for guidance and found that efforts were already well underway to standardize database and dictionary technologies.

We joined each of the relevant technical committees within ANSI to learn more about this effort. One technical committee, X3H2, was developing standards for relational (SQL) and network (NDL) database systems. The other technical committee, X3H4, was developing a standard for an IRDS.

In assessing the relevance of these standards in commercial markets, we felt that the best approach would be to determine the degree to which IBM, our primary hardware market, was following them. In the database area, IBM's direct participation in X3H2 and the introduction of DB2 and SQL/DS to the marketplace was the best evidence that the SQL standard would have commercial relevance.

In the dictionary area, however, the evidence was less clear. Until recently, IBM did not participate in X3H4 even though other vendors, such as MSP and SOFTWARE/AG, have been long-term members. IBM did, however, attend every vendor workshop held by NBS and was the most vocal in its questions and comments. IBM also responded to the first public review of the standard and was the only commenting organization, outside of committee members, to explain and defend their comments in person to the X3H4 committee. In September 1987, IBM joined X3H4 in order to determine the requirements for making their "repository" compliant with the standard. We now feel confident that IBM's "repository" will closely adhere to the ANSI IRDS Standard and that the IRDS standard will soon have definite commercial relevance.

Based on this research, a strategy for Pansophic began to unfold. The keystone of this strategy is a facility we call the Pansophic Resource Dictionary (PAN/RD). This facility is our implementation of the ISO/ANSI IRDS standard. While our long-term goal in the IBM mainframe environment is to integrate our products around IBM's repository, we feel that we need our own facility to support other hardware environments and to provide an IRDS to the IBM mainframe environment sooner than IBM's repository.

To ensure the portability of PAN/RD to all hardware environments, we are developing it in Pascal and using SQL as the supporting DBMS. We are ensuring the portability of our Pascal code by developing cross-compiler technology for other hardware environments. By choosing SQL as the supporting DBMS, we are also ensuring portability as there are very few major hardware environments that do not already have an available SQL implementation. To guarantee this, we have entered into an arrangement with Relational Technology, vendors of the INGRES DBMS, to provide a limited version of their SQL DBMS to our customers if they do not already have one.

To facilitate the integration of other vendor's products with ours, PAN/RD will have an open architecture. The interfaces will follow the IRDS standard and will be published. The specific IRDS data model employed by our products will also be published. Customers will be able to purchase the right to use these interfaces and the data models and they will be made available on an OEM basis for other vendors to use even if our other products are not involved.

Developing the PAN/RD software alone is not sufficient to attain the degree of meta-application integration called for by stages V and VI. For this reason, we are doing research in two areas. First, we are developing a cross-product meta-data model that, when implemented in PAN/RD, will support their integration by allowing several products to share meta-data. Second, we are attempting to generalize the methodologies employed by our Change Management Facility (CMF) product in the areas of inventory control, change management, and configuration management. This will allow us to integrate those methodologies into PAN/RD to provide the associated functions for all types of information resources.

Throughout this research, we will submit the relevant portions to ISO and ANSI as base documents for further standardization efforts. We have already done this by providing our design for the PAN/RD services interface as a base document for review and eventual standardization. This document has been accepted and refined within both ISO and ANSI and is well on its way to becoming a new part of the IRDS standard.

6   SUMMARY

The stages of growth exhibited by applications, data, and database systems are also exhibited by meta-applications, meta-data and dictionary systems. Further, this growth is best facilitated when the "meta" level can reach a new stage before the regular applications level. The more advanced meta-applications on the market today are in stage IV.

To go forward into subsequent stages, vendors of meta-applications must integrate around a standard IRDS by retrofitting their meta-applications to this technology. To achieve stage V, vendors of meta-applications must integrate around a standard meta-data model implemented in the IRDS. To achieve stage VI, vendors of meta-applications must integrate around a standard set of methodologies for information-resource inventory control, change management and configuration management implemented in the IRDS.

Pansophic Systems is taking a first step towards these new stages of meta-applications growth with the development of PAN/RD, an implementation of the ISO/ANSI IRDS standard. We are also conducting research into common meta-data models and common methodologies for our products. The relevant portions of this research will be provided as base documents to the standards community where appropriate.

It is only through standardization at the national and international level that meta-applications can be integrated to the degree required by the sixth stage of growth. Pansophic encourages other users and vendors to participate in this process. The more users and vendors that participate, the better and more widely accepted these standards will be.

Chapter 3

CASE TOOLS:
DOES THE ISO STANDARD IRDS PROVIDE
SUFFICIENT SUPPORT ?

Kathleen Spurr
ADC Analysis Design Consultants

1   INTRODUCTION

The use of data dictionaries as a documentation tool can be traced back to the mid-1960s [3,10]. Since then, much work has been carried out in this area, culminating in the imminent ISO Series of Standards for the IRDS (information resource dictionary system) [6]. During the same period, progress has been made in developing formal or pseudo-formal methodologies for systems analysis and design. [11,12,13,14].

It has long been recognized that data dictionaries should provide support for systems analysis and design. In 1978, Gradwell [5], gave the Data Dictionary Systems Working Party's views on this:

> The DDSWP sees a data dictionary as a tool with several major objectives.
> These are:
>
> a)   To provide facilities for documenting the information collected during all stages of a computer project; analysis, design and implementation.
>
> b)   To provide facilities that will continue to be used in the re-analysis, redesign and re-implementation that will continue after the first phase of the first project ...

In recent years, manufacturers have recognized the importance of providing automated support for analysis and design, resulting in a series of products which are known in the general category of CASE tools (computer assisted systems engineering). Examples of such products are Automate (LBMS), IEW (Arthur Young), IEF (James Martin Associates), "Software Through Pictures" (IDE) and QuickBuild (ICL). Each such CASE tool requires the support of an underlying dictionary system. In this article, we explore whether the proposed International Standard IRDS provides sufficient support for such CASE tools.

2   THE STRUCTURE OF THE IRDS

An essential feature of data dictionaries has been their capacity for storing and manipulating "meta-data" (ie data about data). Thus they distinguish between "type" occurrences and "instance" occurrences. Internationally, the IRDS Rapporteur Group have considered this to be a useful distinction, which they have applied and extended so that the current draft version of the IRDS Standard recognizes four data levels, partly to illustrate the type-instance distinction, and partly to hold other information. These levels are:

1. the fundamental level;

2. the IRD definition level;

3. the IRD level;

4. the application level;

The Application level is the level on which instances of business data are recorded. The IRD level, in addition to other information, contains the schema defining the types of data which may occur at the application level. Some, but not all, of the IRD definition level defines the types of data which may be held in the IRD. The fundamental level prescribes the types of objects about which data may be stored in the IRD Definition. Figure 3.1 illustrates the corresponding conceptual structure of the IRDS.

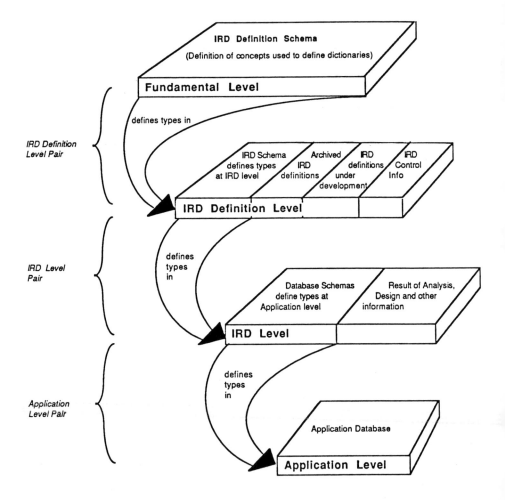

Figure 3.1 The conceptual structure of the IRDS.

Note that the type-instance pairing is identified in the form of three level pairs. Figure 3.2 gives examples of objects which may occur at each of the four levels.

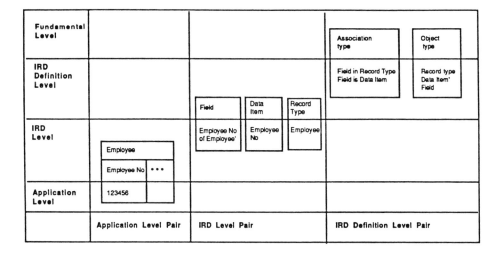

Figure 3.2 Examples of objects at each level.

Three types of service are provided, corresponding to the three types of level pair:

1. IRD definition services, acting on the IRD definition level pair.

2. IRD services, acting on the IRD level pair.

3. Application services, acting on the application level pair.

The IRDS services interface [8] describes the IRD definition services and the IRD services. These services are fairly basic in nature. For example, there exists a service to add a meta-object to the IRD definition level. This affects an IRD definition level pair. Figure 3.3 shows how the services relate to the level pairs.

Fundamental Level			IRD Definition Schema
IRD Definition Level		IRD Schema	IRD Definition Schema
IRD Level	Application Schema	IRD	
Application Level	Application		
	Application Level Pair	IRD Level Pair	IRD Definition Level Pair
	Application Services including database services and graphics services	IRD Services	IRD Definition Services

Figure 3.3 The relation of services to level pairs.

This briefly outlines essential features of the IRDS. When discussing the application of the IRDS to support CASE tools, we need first to describe characteristics of the many, varied methods for developing information systems. This is discussed in the next section.

3   METHODS FOR DEVELOPING INFORMATION SYSTEMS

Much progress has been made since the early 1970s in developing systematic techniques for analysis and design of information systems. These are well documented in [11,12,2,1]. Each technique has its own characteristics and models, which the author [15] has categorized in terms of heterarchy or hierarchy structures. This categorization is shown in Figure 3.4.

Structure of Model	Data Model	Activity Model
Heterarchy	Entity Relationship	Data Flow Function Dependency
Hierarchy	Sub-typing Generalization	Activity Decomposition Structure Charts Levelled Data Flow Diagrams

Figure 3.4 Categories of models.

In addition, the type of component being modelled may refer to:

1. whether the component is part of a logical or physical model

2. a component of the current system or a component of a proposed system

When considering techniques for systems analysis and design, it can be useful to distinguish between "components" and "models". Examples of components are entities, attributes, functions and activities. Examples of models are entity-relationship models, data flow diagrams and entity life-histories. Each model will be associated with a particular structural form (as in Figure 3.4) and will include components.

Each method has its own view of the lifecycle, which is generally expressed in the form of a series of lifecycle stages. Maddison [11] and Fitzgerald [4] give an all-embracing definition of the lifecycle as consisting of:

- a general planning or strategy stage;
- a feasibility or evaluation phase;

- an analysis phase;
- a design phase;
- an implementation phase;
- an overall review and maintenance phase;

The lifecycle phases of most methods are included in this general definition.

Thus, in providing support for a particular method, the underlying dictionary system needs to provide the facilities to enable representation of components and models in terms of the following characteristics:

1. the logical/physical nature of the component or model;

2. the place of the component or model with regard to the current system or the proposed system;

3. the position of the component or model with regard to the lifecycle phases in which it participates.

If the underlying dictionary system were relational, some of these characteristics could be described using attribute values, as in the simple representation of Figure 3.5.

COMPONENT

Name	Type	Logical/ Physical	Current/ Proposed	Lifecycle Phase
Customer	Entity	Logical	Current	Analysis
Customer -Account	Entity	Physical	Current	Analysis
Payment	Model	Logical	Current	Analysis
Purchase	Model	Logical	Current	Analysis
Customer -Record	Record	Physical	Proposed	Design
Client- Relation	Relation	Physical	Proposed	Design
Patron	Record	Physical	Proposed	Design

Figure 3.5 Examples of a relational representation of characteristics.

In addition to describing such components or models, the underlying dictionary system needs to recognize certain rules. For example, a Custom entity defined during analysis may produce several alternative design components; Customer-record, client-relation and patron. This is shown in Figure 3.6.

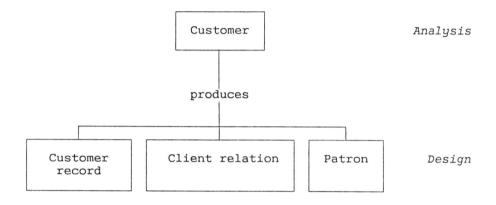

Figure 3.6 Example of alternative design components produced by an analysis entity.

4 CASE TOOLS: REQUIREMENTS FOR THE UNDERLYING DICTIONARY SYSTEM

The last 20 years have seen two separate, yet related developments in computing:-

1. The development and use of data dictionary systems and their imminent standardization.

2. The development of formal methods for analysis and design.

The marriage of these two areas has brought about the birth of a new generation of software tools, known by many practitioners as CASE tools (computer assisted systems engineering). Some of these tools are merely automated drawing aids. Other, more sophisticated tools are able to carry out consistency checks, indicate the impact of changes to the system and enforce a certain progression through the lifecycle stages. The former are described by the author [15] as "Diagram Tools". It is the latter as "Data Dictionary (or Encyclopedia) based tools". It is the latter type of CASE tool which appears to have the most potential. Data dictionary support for analysis and design is discussed by the author in [16].

Several such CASE tools are currently available. LBMS produce "Automate Plus" which is designed to support its own method, LSDM, together with the UK Government Standard method SSADM. Arthur Young (IEW) are marketing the Information Engineering Workbench (IEW), which has been developed by a consortium of Knowledgeware, James Martin, and Arthur Young. James Martin Associates have themselves been producing the Information Engineering Facility (IEF). Other examples include "Quickbuild" which has been developed by ICL and "Software through Pictures", developed by IDE. Most of these products have facilities for data modelling and activity modelling, but other features such as logical/physical modelling and progression through the lifecycle vary.

Having examined several of the CASE tools currently available on the market, it would appear that, in order to be effective, the underlying dictionary system should provide the following capabilities:

1. The facility to model complex objects corresponding to the heterarchy/ hierarchy types shown in Figure 3.4. In addition, there should be a facility to describe and enforce rules for such objects.

2. The facility to partition the dictionary in several ways, possibly corresponding to the various lifecycle stages, or the logical/physical characteristics of the system. One example of such partitioning may be found in the IEW which divides the underlying dictionary system into three: the planning workstation, the analysis workstation and the design workstation. In addition, there should be facilities to describe and enforce rules for progression between the corresponding parts of the system.

5   CASE TOOLS: IS THE IRDS SUITABLE AS A CHOICE FOR THE UNDERLYING DICTIONARY SYSTEM?

The latest version of the IRDS framework [9] allows both the IRD and the IRD definition to be partitioned. Three types of partition are allowed:

> uncontrolled;
>
> controlled;
>
> achieved.

Thus, it would seem that the IRDS does provide some facilities for partitioning. However, the latest version of the IRDS framework does not clarify the rules for movement between the associated parts.

The other essential requirement of the underlying dictionary system relates to its ability to handle complex objects. The latest version of the IRDS services interface [8] describes its data structure using the ISO Standard for SQL [7]. Thus a relational data model which includes referential integrity has been chosen. An attempt has been made towards more powerful object modelling, in that the IRDS services interface defines the terms "meta-object" and "meta-association". However, the object-modelling approach has not been pushed to its fullest extent, and the resulting model is basically relational. As such, it would appear to be no better than any other relational system when used to support CASE tools.

A clear requirement for CASE tools involves the ability to specify and enforce rules. These rules may arise due to the complex objects involved, or alternatively arise in connection with lifecycle progression. Although the IRDS services interface [8] does specify some general rules at the IRD level and the IRD definition level, these are not seen as being sufficiently powerful for the CASE tool designer. Thus, it does not appear that the IRDS can naturally reflect the object structure that CASE tools require. If the IRDS were to to be used in this context, many additional rules would have to be created before the underlying dictionary system were acceptable. The Bauhaus school of design was founded on the principle that "form ever follows function" [17]. It appears that some of the developers of the IRDS Standard had not recognized the principle that an essential function of the IRDS is to support CASE tools, thus they did not recognize that the form of the IRDS should follow object-modelling constructs.

6   CONCLUSION

Most of the existing CASE tools already require and provide the support of an underlying dictionary system. Thus, it would appear that CASE tools do not, of necessity, require the support of the ISO Standard IRDS. However, we might have expected some benefits to arise in using the IRDS for such a purpose. It would appear that we should not be over-ambitious in our expectations for the IRDS in this context. Although one would not deny that the IRDS could be used for such purposes, it would seem that in its present form it would perform no better than a relational database.

This is not intended as a criticism of the IRDS Standard, since it should be remembered that the current IRDS work originated in 1980 with developments in the American National Standards Institute. The environment for information system development was very different then. This author welcomes the imminent ISO IRDS Standards, expected to be available in draft proposal form later this year. However, in recognizing the limitations of the IRDS in providing the support that CASE tools require, we hope that more standards work will be initiated in this area. If such developments are encouraged, it may be that in another five years we may be able to provide the standard dictionary support that CASE tools require in an open systems context.

7   REFERENCES

1   Aktas, A. Z., *Structured Analysis and Design of Information Systems* (Prentice Hall) 1987.

2   Connor, D., *Information System Specification and Design Road Map* (Prentice Hall) 1985.

3   Fisher, D. L.,"Data, Documentation and Decision Tables", *Communications of the Association for Computing Machinery*, vol 9 pp 26-31, 1966.

4   Fitzgerald, G., Stokes, N. Wood, J. R. G., "Feature Analysis of Contemporary Information System Methodologies", *The Computer Journal,* vol 28 no 3, 1985.

5   Gradwell, D., "Objectives and Scope of a Data Dictionary System", *The Computer Bulletin*, December 1978.

6   Gradwell, D., "Developments in Data Dictionary Stanadard", *The Computer Bulletin*, September 1987.

7   ISO 9075, Database Language SQL and addendum 1, Database Language SQL Integrity Addendum, 1987.

8   ISO TC97/SC21/WG3 N600 "Information Resource Dictionary System, Services Interface", Working Draft, Revision 6, 29th April 1988.

9   ISO/IEC JTC1/SC21 N2642 "Information Resource Dictionary System", Framework, Working Draft, Revision 6, March 1988, available as Draft Proposal DP 10027.

10   King, P. J. H., "Some Comments on Systematics", *The Computer Journal,* vol 10, pp 116-118, 1967.

11   Maddison, R. N., (ed) *Information System Methodologies*, Wiley Heyden, 1983.

12   Olle, T. W., Sol, H. G., Verrijn-Stuart, A., (eds) *Information System Design Methodologies, A Comparative Review*, North-Holland, 1982.

13   Olle, T. W., Sol, H. G., Tully, C. J., (eds) *Information System Design Methodologies, A Feature Analysis,* North-Holland, 1983.

14   Olle, T. W., Sol, H. G., Verrijn-Stuart, A., (eds) *Information System Design Methodologies, Improving the Practice*, North-Holland, 1986.

15   Spurr, K. S., "The Use of Automated Tools during Information Systems Development" in *Proceedings of the IFIP TC8 Conference on Governmental and Municipal Information Systems, Budapest* (North-Holland) 1987.

16   Spurr, K. S., "A Data Dictionary Approach to Teaching Information Systems Analysis", *The Computer Journal*, 1988.

17   Sullivan, L., "The Tall Office Building Artistically Considered", *Lippincott's Magazine,* March 1986.

FOURTH-GENERATION SYSTEMS: FEATURES AND CHARACTERISTICS

Chapter 4
FOURTH-GENERATION TOOLS
AND
SOFTWARE DEVELOPMENT

Dr Roger Johnson
Birkbeck College, London University.

1   INTRODUCTION

In the past 20 years many branches of engineering have become large-scale
sophisticated users of computers. It is ironic that their use to support software
production has been much more modest. If any program that saves a user from
entering programs as binary digits through sense switches is a tool, then any systems
software could be regarded as tool. However, tools are more generally thought of as
"add-ons" to some basic computing system. Tools automate what programmers
would otherwise do by hand. Another feature is that the next generation of software
developers takes many of the previous generation's tools for granted. Thus over the
years compilers, source code libraries, screen painters and many other packages
have passed from the status of tools to that of standard system software.

This chapter sets out firstly to review the software development process,
highlighting areas where there are opportunities for significant cost savings. This is
followed by an analysis of the characteristics of 4GLs. Their components are then
briefly described, together with their impact on application development.

2   SOFTWARE DEVELOPMENT PROCESS

The last 20 years have seen a steady and continuous change in the relative cost of
software and hardware components of computer systems Figure 4.1 shows the way
in which the proportions have changed. It is very hard to know precisely where we
are on the curve − in particular, whether the rate of increase of software costs is

slowing down. However , there can be no question that software costs are now the predominant cost in computing projects. Consequently any significant over-run on the cost of a computer project is likely to be largely attributable to the software development process.

What is the money being spent on? Although no two projects are alike, consensus of opinion abroad would probably accept Figure 4.2 as representing a typical breakdown of effort on a DP development project.

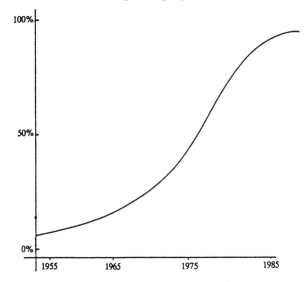

Figure 4.1   Software costs as a proportion of hardware costs.

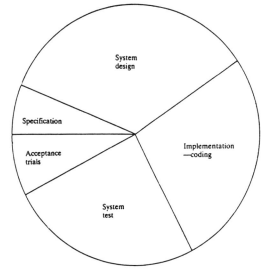

Figure 4.2   Software developments costs.

From Figure 4.2 it is apparent that the areas of design and testing are the main components of the total effort expended. It is also important to note that coding consumes a relatively small amount of effort. Many tools currently on offer in the market place are intended to reduce coding time. From Figure 4.2 we can see that the claimed benefits of such tools need careful examination. A 25% saving in coding effort has only a small impact on total project costs unless the tool also reduces either design and/or testing as well. However, the position is further influenced by the implication of Figure 4.3.

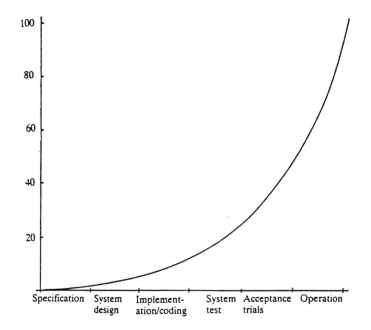

Figure 4.3 Relative cost of correcting errors at different stages.

Figure 4.3 shows that the later an error is detected, the higher the relative cost of correction. There is also evidence to suggest that over 50% of all errors are introduced during functional and system specification.

Taking Figures 4.2 and 4.3 together, it is clear that the major areas on which to concentrate are the requirements analysis and design stages since errors introduced then are extremely expensive to eradicate later. However, these phases are where an element of imprecision has traditionally been accepted by the use of prose specifications and an absence of formal methods for recording design decisions.

One other note of warning may be appropriate. Many DP installations are under pressure to reduce the timescale of the systems development cycle. Consequently, it is important to distinguish tools that will reduce the elapse time to develop a piece of software from those that only reduce the total manpower for a complete project. Some users have reported significant improvements in coding and unit testing times but little change to the duration of the total project. The reason for this seems to lie in the relatively short elapse time, involved in coding and unit testing when compared to the duration of the total project.

In summary, the need is to attack at different levels of complexity the total software development process. However, applying tools in some phases will provide a much larger return on the investment than others.

No current products support the whole design process, though, investment in support of analysis and design work is likely to produce the largest return.

3   CHARACTERISTICS OF 4GLS

The term 4GL is used to describe a software package which aims to simplify the process of developing software applications. The concept of the 4GL is reliant upon the fact that an analysis of DP applications in use today would show that a very large number of them are carrying out a small number of routine file-processing operations. For example, a common pattern is to read a record from a file, apply some comparatively simple test criteria to it to determine whether to make some change and then rewrite it or output it to a printer.

From this analysis a number of recurring patterns can be detected. What the designers of most 4GL products have done is to provide pre-written templates for these operations. Templates have gaps into which specific pieces of information, such as the name of the file to be processed can be inserted. The emphasis in a 4GL is, therefore, on what is to be done rather than how it is to be done, since the supplier has already made those decisions in creating his templates.

The 4GL is best suited to data-intensive applications where relatively simple operations are being carried out on large amounts of data rather than complex processing of small volumes of data. The 4GLs use implicit iteration to overcome the problems of file processing, by relieving programmers of the error-prone task of controlling the sequence of reads and writes during file merges and updates. Similarly many of the decisions about data definitions needed in a COBOL program are also made by the use of implicit typing mechanisms.

The consequence of the 4GL taking responsibility for many of these features of the program is that the range of programs that can be generated is necessarily limited by the facilities provided by the supplier in his templates. However, most suppliers overcome this limitation by provision of a procedural language interface. This allows the programmer to code in a conventional language any features not representable within the facilities of the 4GL.

One of the characteristics of 4GLs that users are most conscious of is the style of dialogue used to obtain the information needed to complete the templates. Most of the standard techniques used in designing computer dialogues are used by at least one 4GL. Among the most popular styles are form-filling, question and answer and menu selection. There are also a small group of 4GLs which have developed forms of Very High Level Procedural Language. These languages employ small numbers of powerful statements that each embody a number of assumptions about how that particular statement is to be executed. The result is a program of comparatively few statements which is claimed to be quick to write and easy to understand.

Applications created with a 4GL do not exist in isolation from other software and data in the system. Consequently, it is necessary to be able to interchange data. For example, with a 4GL it is very easy to retrieve sets of data concerning the operation of a business from a corporate database. However to carry out a fuller examination of the data it would be very useful to be able to transfer the data to a spreadsheet. This can achieved by using the 4GL to create a file in a suitable format for the spreadsheet to read. A similar approach can be taken to transferring a list of names, addresses and other data retrieved from a database to a word-processor to form part of a set of letters to be sent to customers.

Finally, one of the most important aspects of applications developed using 4GLs is that the 4GL package, in building an application in response to a user's needs, also builds the documentation at the same time. The 4GL application is effectively self-documenting. This ensures that subsequent maintenance should be easier and quicker to carry out.

4   COMPONENTS OF 4GLS

The packages available in the market today contain a number of components to provide the user with the facilities described in the previous section. The most common features are now briefly described.

4.1   Data dictionary system

The data dictionary is the heart of the system recording all the information about the application being built. As the dialogue with the application builder proceeds, more and more detail about the application can be stored. In addition, the 4GL supplier can build in many defaults, which saves the user much time and effort by reducing the amount of information that has to be supplied. When the dialogue is complete, the data dictionary holds a complete specification of the application.

The dictionary is also the source for the documentation of the system. The contents of the data dictionary contain all the information necessary to provide a complete set of documentation of the system.

One minor drawback is that the data dictionary is available only to the 4GL software and can only hold information relating to the 4GL applications. Software written in other languages has to be represented in a stand-alone product and cannot be integrated with the 4GL applications.

4.2   Application development tool

The application development tool uses the information held in the data dictionary to run the applications. There are two approaches to this. Firstly, it is possible to use a compiler. This can be achieved from the information in the data dictionary either by generating a program in a 3GL, such as COBOL, and using a conventional compiler or by creating some internal code and executed. The second alternative is to use an interpreter. This is a program that uses the values stored in the data dictionary to control its run-time behaviour. By accessing the data dictionary the interpreter causes the sequence of I/O and other functions to be carried out in the correct sequence.

The two approaches have different benefits. The compiler can produce efficient run-time code, while the interpreter can respond immediately to a change in the contents of the data dictionary, without the necessity of re-compilation. This latter feature is very valuable when prototyping a new system as described in section 5.

4.3 Database management system

The data used by an application have to be held in some file structure. Most 4GL packages utilize a database to hold their application data. Indeed, some 4GL packages have been developed as an add-on to an existing DBMS products.

In some systems the DBMS also holds the data dictionary information in a specially protected portion of the database.

4.4 Data communications interface

Many 4GL applications are created initially on single-user workstations, although they are frequently intended to run on mainframes. To achieve easy movement of the application from workstation to mainframe, it is essential to have a communications interface in the 4GL package.

The interface can also be used to exchange data between mainframes and workstations to support the growing use of desk-top micros for intensive analysis of small parts of the corporate database.

4.5 Screen painter

One of the key parts of any system is the screen presented to the user of the application. Most 4GLs have facilities by which the user can design screen layouts directly on the terminal or workstation. The details of the position and contents of each field created are recorded in data dictionary. The user is provided with a range of utilities to modify and refine the design of each screen primarily by use of the cursor keys.

In this way the designer can see each screen as it develops, which is particularly valuable when the process is shared with a representative of the eventual end-users of the system. The ability to effect rapid changes allows a collaborative design of the complete dialogue without the delays inherent in modifying conventional source code.

A similar technique is also used for the production of printed report layouts.

4.6   Query languages

While 4GLs offer a means of developing software rapidly, all organizations need the capability to make one-off queries to their data. Consequently, most 4GL systems contain some form of query language, in many cases the *de facto* standard SQL.

4.7   Business graphics

With the development of more sophisticated workstations and terminals the possibility has arisen of presenting data in forms other than tables of figures. An important new feature of many systems is graphical output. The old saying that "a picture is worth a thousand words" is justified when users can receive histograms, graphs and pie charts in addition to conventional tabular data.

5   CONTRIBUTION OF 4GLS TO SOFTWARE DEVELOPMENT

4GLs have revolutionized the approach to software production in a number of ways. Some of the more important are now briefly discussed.

One of the key changes is by making possible user participation in systems design. The ability to specify an application very rapidly at a workstation and subsequently to amend it has enabled the end-user to become a real partner in the software design process. Formerly, users described, as best they could, their systems requirement to the analyst and, often many months later, received a completed software system. Inevitably, the results often reflected failures of communication between all the various parties. Users were disappointed by systems that failed to match their expectations.

The 4GL has radically changed this. The ability to prototype software in the presence of end-users eliminates many of the problems of understanding which dogged earlier approaches. User suggestions can be assessed quickly and where appropriate implemented directly. This significantly reduces costs by largely eliminating one class of error, usually uncovered only on delivery of the finished software.

Another key area of change is in the reduction of errors in writing code to access files and handle screens. This is a major source of errors in conventional code. However, with a 4GL, this code is no longer the responsibility of the programmer. The benefits here derive from substantially reducing the number of these very common errors.

Some user experience does show that although total effort can be substantially reduced, the project elapse time is sometimes unchanged. This appears to be a consequence of flattening the manpower peaks without materially speeding up the basic activities which form the software development process.

Overall, the use of 4GLs appears to lead to more reliable code, with less manpower. The 4GL provides good documentation in a uniform style which helps to ensure that as the applications evolve the overall reliability of the code is maintained.

Chapter 5
BUILDING BLOCKS OF A FOURTH-GENERATION SYSTEM

James Sharkey
RCMS Computing Services

1   INTRODUCTION

Business today, whether it likes it or not, needs to work with information. It is probably the most valuable asset any company owns. Whether one is in finance, sales, manufacturing, marketing, administration, or any other business discipline, one's ability to consolidate data, analyse it, and produce meaningful reports and analyses from one's own perspective is essential.

Capturing data is no longer a problem. There are mountains of it available in every business organization. On the other hand, managing information and continuously reshaping it into meaningful, useful forms are the kinds of activities where the right software can make all the difference. For information to be of any use to you, and to help your organization be more productive, you must be able to view the information in a way which reflects that organization's ever changing nature and role. This demands considerable flexibility on the part of any software used for the task and highlights the prerequisite that it must be capable of being made to respond quickly to any change which occurs in the company's mode of business. It is this very task which today's 4GSs attempt to address.

2   GENERAL SELECTION CRITERIA

How do you define a fourth-generation system?

The first problem which any organization will encounter when setting out to select a 4GS is what definition to use. Read any literature on the subject, whether it be in the computing press or in a software vendor's brochure, and you will find a definition of some sort. The chances are that these definitions will all sound somewhat similar However, some will emphasize the end-user requirements above all else; others will place the emphasis on professional application development requirements. Whatever the slant, it is likely to explain a 4GL in relation to its predecessor generations: machine language, assembly language and third-generation languages such as COBOL, FORTRAN and PL/I.

The main thing which sets a 4GS apart from its predecessors is its ability to handle tasks non-procedurally. Unlike earlier generations of computer languages, a 4GS does not require its users to specify how the task is to be performed. All it needs are simple English-like commands which tell it what is required; the 4GS will then determine how to carry out the required task.

This "what, not how" feature is the main reason for another major benefit of the 4GS: the productivity improvements which stem from being able to specify a task more concisely. In his book *Application Development Without Programmers* (Prentice Hall), James Martin states that "A language should not be called fourth generation unless its users can obtain results in one-tenth of the time with COBOL, or less."

If the ability to handle data in a non-procedural way is the major criterion a company has for deciding whether or not a particular 4GS should be purchased, it is not difficult to appreciate how potential purchasers can become very confused. Fortunately for buyers this criterion is only one of many to be brought into play when deciding on the right product.

As with many buzz-words in the computing field, the terms 4GL and 4GS can be abused. For example, some software vendors might market a simple report writer under the banner of 4GL because it fits the "non-procedural" description. As a consequence, some 4GSs are more complete than others and the unsuspecting

58

would-be purchaser needs to be extremely careful when evaluating the various alternatives available. A simple checklist approach to product evaluation, whilst being a reasonable method for weeding out the "also-rans", often fails to uncover the true nature of the product's features and capabilities. This can only be done with any degree of effectiveness by trying out the software on a real application.

Who are the users?

It is important to consider the user base and to ask the question "will the product meet the needs of the range of users in the organization?" Flexibility is just as important as functionality and it is critical to ensure that the identified user base is provided with a product that not only fits its immediate needs, but also has the potential for future growth as the user base becomes more sophisticated.

What are the users' requirements?

One method of classifying the users is to group them into non-DP and DP categories. The non-DP user will require a product that offers ease-of-use and flexibility. They will look for such facilities as: easy reporting, graphics, statistics, etc. The DP user, on the other hand, wants sophisticated applications-development facilities which permit rapid application building via prototyping.

What is the organization's information life style?

An important criterion for evaluating a 4GS is whether it can compliment the information lifestyle of the organization. Does the company favour an information centre approach or does it prefer to operate a development centre, or possibly a combination of the two? The type of environment which the organization operates will significantly influence the choice of product.

Is the product easy to use?

Terms often associated with the 4GS are "easy-to-use" and "user-friendly". These phrases have become synonymous with 4GLs because users needed to have very little knowledge of syntax or experience of using the system in order to make effective use of the facilities. In contrast, third-generation languages, such as COBOL, could not be regarded as "user-friendly" because of their fundamentally procedural nature and their demand for a detailed knowledge of syntax.

However, these bland phrases have, like many others, been abused over the years and tend to be somewhat meaningless. If "ease-of-use" is one of the criteria being used by a purchaser of a 4GS it is important that the term be qualified and defined more accurately in order to make any evaluation meaningful. For instance, does the buyer really mean "easy-to-use", or is "easy-to-learn" a more accurate reflection of what is meant?

When evaluating a 4GS all of these criteria need to be carefully addressed. Only when this has been accomplished can the detailed analysis of product features and capabilities begin. Unfortunately, all too often, buyers start by looking at features and then wonder why they are disappointed after purchase.

3   FRAMEWORK FOR DISCUSSION

The remainder of this paper examines three aspects of the 4GS: the data dictionary, the data-manipulation language or 4GL, and the man machine interface. These three aspects are analysed and discussed in terms of the various building blocks which are in turn classified into three levels:

1. The basics:

    These are 4GS features which most systems are likely to have.

2. The desirables:

    Some useful work would be achievable without these features but any 4GS without them will quickly run out of steam.

3. The power tools:

    These features provide the power, flexibility and productivity for the user and characterize the richness and fullness of the 4GS in comparison to lesser-qualified systems.

4 DATA DICTIONARY FEATURES

The data dictionary elements of any 4GS form the foundation of the system. The effectiveness of the product as a whole depends to a very large extent on how comprehensive these features are and how well they have been integrated into the system.

4.1 The basics

A relational-like file structure

The majority of systems available in today's 4GS market provide at least a rudimentary file structure based on the relational model. That does not necessarily mean, however, that they support the majority of the relational model rules. One can expect a basic 4GS to support a tabular data structure with rows and columns, where rows represent records and columns represent data items.

A minimal range of data types

Practically every 4GS will support a minimum of alphanumeric and numeric data types. Numeric data types are likely to be integer, decimal (packed), and possibly floating point. Most systems offer some kind of data type for handling dates although many offer no more than the ability to store a date as a six-digit integer or six-character alpha string with in-built functions for displaying dates in various formats.

Data item attributes

Most 4GSs provide an ALIAS facility whereby a data item can be given an alternative name. Typically this is used as a short hand version of the item name.

Some systems provide a column-heading facility which allows a data item to be given a meaningful heading for reporting purposes. Systems which do not provide this feature at the database definition level expect the user to provide customized headings at reporting time, otherwise the column name becomes the heading.

4.2   The Desirables

A relational database

A desirable attribute of any serious 4GS is a full relational data model, permitting any number of physically separate files to be dynamically joined at the time of reporting, based on the matching of one or more data-item values in the different files. This permits a great deal of flexibility, as databases that are designed and maintained independently can be brought together when required, even if that need was not foreseen when the application(s) were first designed.

An hierarchical option

The suggestion of a hierarchical structure might sound like heresy to the relational purists; nevertheless, in addition to those applications which are best handled by a relational approach there are others which fit naturally into a hierarchical treatment. Having both a relational model and a hierarchical model in the same 4GS offers the best of both worlds, especially if the two structures can be combined together in the same application. This provides the user with the ability to model the data in whatever manner best matches the way the data appears in real life.

Intelligent data types

For a 4GS to be effective it must provide intelligent data types. For example, if a data item represents a date the 4GS should be capable of recognizing dates which are invalid and rejecting them. It should also be capable of performing date arithmetic without the user having to build customized code to handle it. For example, the following code:

```
DATE1 = "10 December 1987";
DATE2 = DATE1 + 30;
PRINT DATE2;
```

will give a new date of 9 January 1988.

An extension of the DATE data type which very few systems provide is a data type which allows a point in time to be recorded. The ability to do time-based arithmetic is clearly an important requirement with this form of data type.

Database integrity

If a 4GS supports its own database management system, it should be able to guarantee database integrity of any database it manages. A technique used by some 4GSs for maintaining database integrity is called "shadow writing". With this approach, changes are *NEVER* made to the existing physical record, but are instead written to a separate area on disk. Thus, if a system failure occurs, only the pending changes are lost, and the database is automatically restored to its condition prior to the failure.

Data integrity

The ability to apply data integrity constraints to data items is an extremely important aspect of any 4GS because it allows the system designer to guarantee that data will always be accurate and consistent. Essential types of data integrity are:

(i)   LIMITS — data must be within certain value limits, either a discrete list of values or a range of values.

(ii) MASK — data is checked for a specific character pattern (such as dashes in a phone number).

(iii) REFERENTIAL — data is cross-checked against another related table to ensure its validity.

Data security

Data security goes hand in hand with data integrity and is an equally important aspect of any 4GS's infrastructure. It is vital to have the option if necessary to apply security measures at all levels of an application's data structure ranging from the database level right down to the individual field level. Furthermore, it should be no problem for the 4GS to perform "horizontal" security by restricting which table rows the user is allowed to see, based on some form of logical test.

Another useful facility in the area of data security is the concept of a "dynamic user view" which can provide the database administrator with the ability to alter each individual user's "view" of the database, including specification of which items can be accessed, updated, or created.

Virtual or defined fields

Some 4GSs support the concept of the virtual field. This is a facility which allows the user to specify a computation to be performed at the time the database is accessed. Each time the field is requested from the database, the computation, which is normally based on other fields in the database, is automatically performed and the virtual field takes on the result of the computation. This type of facility is especially valuable if it permits the virtual fields to be incorporated in the database description because, by doing so, it establishes a central definition of all computations and therefore guarantees a consistent view of the database for all users.

Alternate indexing

If rapid and efficient access to individual records in a table is a critical issue then it is important for the 4GS to provide a secondary indexing mechanism. This feature allows the application developer to provide rapid and direct access to any row in a table based on a given value of a field which is not defined as the primary index. This feature also offers substantial efficiency improvements when reporting on a subset of the data.

4.3   The power tools

Interfaces to foreign database management systems

A 4GS which operates on its own native file system can be an extremely effective tool for providing information systems. However, it will not be nearly as effective as the 4GS which is also capable of interfacing to homegrown file systems and other established DBMS, such as SQL/DS and DB2. A 4GS with this type of capability can more readily be adopted as a strategic product in line with the company's long-term information-processing objectives since it can provide a common language and methodology across all the DBMS used within the organization.

Dynamic database reorganisation

A popular approach to the development of information systems with a 4GS is the use of prototyping. However, a prime requisite for this type of activity is a means of carrying out dynamic reorganization of the database structure of the application being prototyped. The 4GS should provide the developer with a simple method for doing this without the need to use utility programs to dump and reload the database contents. Using such a facility, the application developer may then add or delete fields and tables, change their attributes, add or delete security and integrity constraints in a way which makes prototyping a practical proposition.

Integrity and security in database definition

Most 4GSs incorporate some form of data integrity and security facilities. Few, however, successfully integrate these facilities directly in an active data dictionary. The benefits of this approach are not difficult to appreciate:

- There is only one definition of the integrity and security rules.

- All users of the database are subject to the same set of rules.

- Application developers do not have to waste time writing similar code into all of the application programs to check for integrity and security violations. They need only be concerned with defining what to do should a violation occur during the running of a program.

Arrays and time series

A 4GS which provides array handling offers an alternative data structure for expressing a "one-to-many" relationship. Unfortunately, this is another issue which tends to ruffle the feathers of the relational purists, nevertheless, arrays can often make databases much easier to use, offer improved analytical capabilities, and, in many cases, significantly reduce storage requirements.

A special type of array found in at least one 4GS is the time-series array. In addition to the regular array attributes it carries a start date and a frequency or periodicity. These additional attributes allow complex time-based analyses to be carried out in a very straightforward manner.

Arrays provide a simple and understandable structure for multivalued fields, especially time-related data. A single time-series array can turn a two-level hierarchy into a single table; similarly it can turn a single table with 120,000 rows into a table with 10,000 rows.

5   THE DATA- MANIPULATION LANGUAGE (4GL)

The power and versatility of the 4GS is provided by the manipulative language or 4GL. The richness of the language, in terms of both procedural and non-procedural facilities, will indicate the overall effectiveness of the product and the scope of its potential usage.

5.1   The basics

Bulk data load facility

Most 4GSs provide some form of bulk-data-loading facility which allows data from external files to be loaded into the native file structure of the 4GS. With most systems this facility is of a non-procedural nature and not only covers straightforward insertions of new table rows but also permits updates and deletions to be performed.

Ad-hoc table maintenance

In addition to bulk data maintenance, most 4GSs provide a simple method for interactive, *ad-hoc*, row-by-row maintenance either through the use of simple commands or via user-defined formatted screens which map the database description field by field.

Simple report writer

A report-writing facility is an essential prerequisite of any 4GS. The report writer should, at a minimum, be able to:

- retrieve data from the database;

- report on a subset of the database based on certain screening criteria;

- sort the data into ascending or descending order of any field on the database;

- summarize the data to produce sums, averages, subtotals etc.;

- format the report in a readable and presentable form.

5.2 The Desirables

A comprehensive procedural language

If a 4GS is to have a major impact in an organization it must possess a comprehensive procedural language. It should provide all the functionality expected of a fully developed programming language, such as mathematical and boolean operators, looping, branching, error-handling and general I/O functions. It should not simply be a means of scheduling the sequence of non-procedural commands. Ideally, it should allow the application developer to use the 4GS as a complete programming language and eliminate the need to resort to the use of third-generation languages like COBOL and PL/I.

Procedural maintenance capability

The task of building a generalized maintenance facility for maintaining complex data structures is a particularly difficult one with some 4GSs because of their weak procedural features. This problem is most apparent when the data driving the maintenance process is not available in a simple, normalized form. If the 4GS possesses extensive procedural capabilities, then this type of problem becomes a relatively trivial one because it is capable of reading any type of record from an external file and unravelling its contents in a general way.

Metadata driven code generation

A typical requirement for any application developed with a 4GS is the need to write code which handles the on-line transactions. Application code for this type of activity tends to follow a set pattern regardless of the database table being addressed. Consequently, this aspect of an application development is an ideal candidate for a code-generator approach.

Development times can be cut back dramatically if the developer has code generators to draw on. If the code generators actually produce code which is capable of being customized then the developer has the added advantage of being able to incorporate additional functionality not offered by the standard generator.

A powerful and flexible report writer

For a 4GS to be worthy of its classification it should offer a comprehensive, non-procedural report-writing facility that can be learnt in a matter of minutes by end-users but is flexible enough to handle any format requirement such as special forms, letters and memos, mailing labels, etc.

Support for graphics

Another desirable feature is support for high-resolution, full-colour graphics. Most 4GSs which offer graphics typically provide facilities for line charts, bar charts, pie charts, and scatter diagrams.

Support for statistics

A statistical facility provides the user with a convenient and efficient way to apply established statistical techniques to the analysis of data. For the majority of statistical analyses such as multiple and polynomial regression, t-test and chi-square, results can be obtained quickly without the need for interfacing to an external statistical package.

5.3   The power tools

An extensive list of built-in functions

For the applications developer, probably the most time-consuming aspect of building an application is the coding of highly complex logic processes. This task can be made much easier for the developer if he has a wide range of functions and operators at his disposal. In-built functions such as SUM, AVERAGE, MINIMUM, MAXIMUM, COUNT substantially reduce the amount of code needed to describe the required process. Similarly, operators like AMONG greatly simplify the coding of complex conditional logic. For example, the following two statements are functionally equivalent:

> IF CODE AMONG(10,20,30,40) THEN DO;

> IF CODE EQ 10 OR CODE EQ 20
> OR CODE EQ 30 OR CODE EQ 40 THEN DO;

The benefits provided by in-built functions and operators are:

- development time is reduced;

- resulting code is more precise and compact;

- resulting code is easier to maintain.

An integrated decision support system

For the end-user who wishes to examine various alternative business scenarios it is necessary to provide a full decision-support capability including: "what-if" analysis, goal seeking, consolidation, forecasting, financial reporting and, most importantly, the ability to resolve simultaneous equations. To support these facilities the 4GS needs to provide further built-in functions for calculating such things as net present value, return on investment, weighted moving averages, etc. Support for time series arrays is also a valuable asset for this type of analysis.

Facilities for handling complex reports

As the end-user becomes more experienced at using the 4GS, more and more of the advanced features of the product are likely to be brought into play to resolve complex reporting requirements. Therefore, if the 4GS is not to run out of steam, it must be capable of accommodating the user's increasingly sophisticated demands which could include:

- the need to embed textual data in the report; (e.g. a letter or memo)

- the need to perform nested relational joins;

- the need to produce a report which incorporates spreadsheet style calculations;

Advanced application development features

Not only should the 4GS provide a procedural language which allows the full range of programming constructs for the developer, it should also be capable of providing a highly productive development environment. A 4GS can create this environment by providing such features as:

- A single, consistent working environment from which all features of the 4GS can be accessed without the need to flip from sub-environment to sub-environment. An environment which provides a common command syntax for both interactive and procedural modes.

- A comprehensive interactive debugging facility which allows the developer to identify problem areas in the procedural code.

- A range of system-defined global variables which hold such information as: today's date, the time of day, the active database name, the number of lines on a report page, etc. These variables can then be referenced wherever appropriate within the procedural language or queried interactively.

- A facility which allows procedures to be stored in compiled form. When such a procedure is invoked, the initial translation process is bypassed offering an improvement in processing efficiency.

6   THE MAN MACHINE INTERFACE

For a 4GS to be desirable not only does it have to offer improvements in productivity, it also needs to present an attractive face to the user. The man machine interface of a 4GS will have a big impact on the product's usability and will influence the attitude of the end-user as well as the application developer.

6.1   The basics

A command driven interface

Almost all 4GSs provide a command mode of operating with the system. With this style of operation the user is in complete control of the session by issuing a series of commands which tell the 4GS exactly what is to be done. To a brand-new user of the 4GS this style of working may not feel particularly "user-friendly" because the user is forced to take control rather than being led, step by step, through the desired activities. Consequently, a command-driven approach is more likely to be prefered by an experienced user of the system.

A menu driven interface

Many 4GSs provide an alternative man machine interface based on the concept of menus. Using this approach the user is able to direct the flow of activity by selecting options from a series of menu screens which display all the possible options available at that stage in the process. End-users with little or no previous DP experience find this style of working extremely attractive because they are not obliged to remember product syntax and this is especially relevant when the user of the 4GS is an infrequent user. On the other hand, experienced users quickly become frustrated with a menu driven approach because:

1.   they are forced to operate within the confines of the choices provided in the menus;

2.   they often have to step through several menus in order to effect a simple change.

An integrated help facility

Every 4GS should offer an integrated HELP facility which can be used by both end-users and application developers to provide assistance with syntax problems and general methodology questions. In addition to this it should also provide a means of obtaining an explanation of any error messages produced by the 4GS. All of these facilities should be easily accessible on-line.

6.2   The desirables

Customized formatted screen facility

A highly desirable feature of any 4GS is a complete screen-formatting capability which can be used to build customized interfaces between the user and the database. Such a facility not only provides for easy and efficient data entry and maintenance, it can also be used to provide a means for querying and reporting. To permit the rapid development of screen-based applications, the 4GS should provide a comprehensive "screen-painter".

A database editor

A powerful productivity tool in any 4GS is a fully integrated, screen-orientated database editor which allows the end-user to browse and maintain a database through the use of function keys and cursor positioning.

Efficient use of function keys

The 4GS should be able to interact with all the function keys available on a terminal's keyboard. It should be an easy task not only to customize the meaning of each function key used in an application, but also to reprogram that meaning as many times as is necessary within the same program procedure.

6.3   The power tools

Environmental windows

A 4GS which provides a window-driven operating environment gives both end-users and application developers a more convenient, more productive and more natural way of working. Windows permit similar types of data such as commands, history, general output, report output, and error messages to be grouped into individual display areas, thus allowing the user to view all the windows concurrently, or to select only those needed at the time. The user therefore has the flexibility to define the style of his working environment which best fits the task being performed. These customized environments can easily be created by opening, closing, scrolling, sizing, repositioning and modifying the attributes of any of the windows available.

Procedural windows

Procedural windows extend the concept of general environment windows into the area of custom-built applications. Using this facility, the developer is able to build applications which convey a common and consistent "feel" and appearance regardless of whether the applications run on a PC or a mainframe. Consequently, it provides the organization with a means of standardizing application style and also gives end-users who are experienced with working in a window-driven PC environment the added comfort that mainframe applications will not feel alien to them.

7　CONCLUSIONS

This paper has attempted to highlight those features of a 4GS which distinguish it from its competitors by analysing the various building blocks one finds in the typical system. It has also attempted to identify the attributes which practically every product has; the attributes which one expects to see in a product (but often doesn't); and the attributes one should strive for when selecting the 4GS for their organization.

Many organizations make their choice for a 4GS based on a detailed checklist of product features but they often fail to "look under the bonnet" and check out exactly how particular features are implemented and how effective they will be in practice. One message of this chapter is that if the right product is to be chosen, the selection process needs to go deeper than a simple checklist approach; it must involve some "kicking of the tyres" and "checking under the bonnet".

Chapter 6
WHEN APPLICATION GENERATORS ARE BETTER THAN FOURTH-GENERATION LANGUAGES

Terry Wilcox
Pansophic Systems (UK) Ltd

1   THE SOFTWARE TOOL MARKET

1.1   Three -centre concept

IBM has defined a number of interrelated architectures that assist in understanding where and how different productivity tools can assist in software engineering. The first concept is that of the three centres:

- Development Centre as the new DP department;

- Production Centre like the old data centre;

- Information Centre as the end-user computing area.

1.2   Three-tier model

We have an SAA technical architecture known as the three-tier model that helps us to fit in three types of computer machines and the two types of network that link them. It includes:

- mainframe operational and information systems: Wide Area Network (WAN);

- department (mini) machines with local systems: Local Area Network (LAN);

- workstation (PC) machines with personal systems.

1.3 Three acquisition methods

When we consider the software tool market, the critical application system driving force is based on the acquisition options available:

- Buy standard application package, if one can be found that is suitable, if it will provide a market advantage.

- Commission a firm to build your application, if you can get a reasonable firm to build it, if you can organize for maintenance.

- Create the application yourself, if your development people can do the job, if the development delays are acceptable.

This paper will look at the three centres, the three tiers and the three acquisition methods. The most cost-effective product should address more of the issues in more of the areas than any other product.

1.4 The nature of a 4GL

We can generalize to make a point:

A. Observation:

As a 4GL becomes more powerful it develops new statements that are the equivalent of many tens of COBOL statements.

Consequence:

When a 4GL statement has the power of tens of COBOL statements, then it is both powerful and inflexible.

B. Observation:

To retain flexibility, the 4GL must retain its low productivity (3GL) statements, while providing new powerful statements.

Consequence:

As the number of new statements increase, the training time will also increase.

C.   Observation:

A 4GL can be designed to offer either flexibility or ease-of-use.

Consequence:

Easy-to-use products that have a restricted set of statements tend to provide a lower level of productivity. Comprehensive products tend to be more difficult to learn and use.

D.   Observation:

4GL products tend to be either on-line or batch, and tend to be oriented about a single database environment. A 4GL language is unlikely to become an international standard like COBOL.

Consequence:

Whichever 4GL language you select is unlikely to be the most effective language next year.

E.   Observation:

4GL products tend to have no alternate vendors that support the same language.

Consequence:

Each product purchased requires a strategic decision that the life of the 4GL will exceed the life of the constructed application systems.

F.   Observation:

4GL products tend to have run-time monitors that interpret the high-level language statements.

Consequence:

Performance problems are a continual result of using such products. A 10% overhead on application systems can cost more than the development savings.

1.5   The nature of an application generator

Generalizations are not true of all AG products.

A.   Observation:

One hundred per cent generated source-code application systems can be compiled to match the most exacting performance requirements.

Consequence:

Compiled application systems have no run-time monitor, can run on any target computer and have good predictable performance characteristics.

B.   Observation:

Fill-in-the-blank frames are easy to use, while providing considerable productivity advantages.

Consequence:

AGs tend to be very easy to use, they avoid new programming languages and can be very productive.

C.   Observation:

AG products can generate different source-code application systems for a number of different target environments. AG products tend to be able to support both on-line and batch requirements for a number of different database environments.

Consequence:

An AG can become an installation standard for all application systems without having to select the most appropriate language for each development project.

D.   Observation:

In the long term we can expect AGs to include expert system generators that will ensure that all procedural programming activities are avoided.

Consequence:

AGs have a longer potential life than 4GL and even James Martin has stated that "4GLs are dead". AGs are positioned to evolve in a number of complementary directions. Plans include being able to migrate towards capturing business requirements, to generate efficient three-tier application systems, and to enable the most junior people to become cost effective in a short timescale.

2 WHAT ARE THE DEVELOPMENT-CENTRE OBJECTIVES?

System development managers have consistently reported that the following key issues (reference Price Waterhouse /Computing) are the critical objectives by which they are measured and the day-by-day problems that they are paid to solve:

- 48% project deadlines;

- 22% recruiting and retaining staff;

- 13% maintaining programs.

What are your objectives?

2.1 How can we reduce project timescales?

- Can we automate the development tasks?

- How do we produce accurate project timescales?

- What tools operate over the complete lifecycle?

- Will the system be easy to modify and change?

How would you reduce timescales?

2.2 How can we reduce skilled staff levels?

- Are the tools easy to use?

- Is it easy to learn and will it reduce training?

- Can we reduce the development resources?

- We do not want to learn new programming languages.

- Will new tools help to motivate our staff?

How do you recruit and retain staff?

2.3 How can we improve application maintenance?

- Can we make it identical to new development?

- Will we have high-quality source-code programs?

- Can we integrate with existing programs?

- Do we need a cross-reference of the design objects?

- How do we get effective documentation?

- But is it efficient in operation?

How do you reduce maintenance work?

3 WHAT ARE THE DEVELOPMENT AND MAINTENANCE TASKS?

- 1000 Business strategy planning.

  1100 Organizational architecture.

  1200 Data architecture.

  1300 Application architecture.

  1400 Technical architecture.

  1500 Migration planning.

- 2000 Business system analysis.

  2100 Data modelling.

  2200 Functional modelling.

  2300 Data flow diagrams.

  2400 Completeness and correctness matrix.

- 3000 Business system design.

  3100 Screen and report painting.

  3200 Field validation and flow specification.

  3300 Define logical data access and validation.

  3400 Define detailed business functions.

- 4000 Technical design.

  4100 Physical database design.

  4200 Performance definition.

  4300 Physical data access definition.

  4400 Define detailed technical functions.

  4500 Define environment detail.

- 5000 Construction and testing.

  5100 Create programs, screen macros and control blocks.

  5200 Create documentation and cross-references.

  5300 Create test plan and data.

  5400 Test modules, programs, systems and application.

- 6000 Implementation.

  6100 Migrate to production libraries.

  6200 End-user training.

  6300 Parallel running.

- 7000 Maintenance.

  7100 Change to technical design (4000).

  7200 Change to business design (3000).

  7300 Change to business analysis (2000).

  7400 Change to strategy plan (1000).

These tasks can be decomposed into lower-level tasks that cover in detail the entire development and maintenance lifecycle. A key conclusion is that maintenance is the application of new development tasks and it can be shown that new development is the application of maintenance tasks.

4 PRODUCTIVITY IN THE SYSTEM DEVELOPMENT LIFECYCLE

4.1 Business strategy planning (BSP)

- Use an analyst workbench tool.
- AG and 4GL products are not applicable.

Computer-aided software engineering (CASE) and analyst workbench (AW) products can assist in the drawing and verification of the complementary architectures that make up a BSP. Neither AG nor 4GL products can aid productivity in this area today, however the information captured by an AW can be migrated foreward into an AG.

4.2 Business system analysis (BSA)

- Use an analyst workbench tool.
- Consolidate into a central repository.
- AG and 4GL products are not applicable.

CASE and AW products are aimed at this market requirement and can greatly assist in the creation and modification of the diagrams that model the business requirements. Data modelling, functional decomposition and data-flow diagramming are the prime areas where productivity can be improved with a such a product. AG and 4GL products tend not to include graphical representations at the current time. The storage and consolidation of the analysis information in a central repository (dictionary) is of practical use.

4.3   Business system design (BSD)

- AGs can avoid program specifications.

- Prototyping provides end-user acceptance.

- Consolidate into a central repository.

- 4GL products are not applicable.

Traditional system and program specifications can be automated with application generators that are designed to capture the high-level human − machine interface information. AG and 4GL products may be used to create prototype models, but the people using such tools must be trained and motivated to take advantage of these techniques. AG products that use fill-in-the-blank frames and avoid any programming language are more likely to be appropriate to the business designers who are undertaking this work. Most users of 4GL products tend to need outline program specifications as paper documents at this stage with no productivity gains. Most users of AG products tend to create their specifications using the AG facilities, providing significant productivity gains. Again the storage and consolidation of the design information in a central repository is very important. If the same repository is used to consolidate the analysis and design information, then productive cross-references will assist with maintenance impact analysis.

4.4   Technical design (TD)

- AGs can avoid program specifications.

- Consolidate into a central repository

- 4GL products are not applicable.

Traditional program specifications can be completed so that a 4GL product can be used in the next construction phase dramatically to reduce the programming work. AG products tend to have many performance-tuning frames that can specify the most effective application design from a technical point of view. Data-access definitions to many different products may be specified, while a 4GL may imply a single DBMS implementation. Alternate technical designs can be evaluated with minimum cost, when an AG is used to generate sample systems.

4.5 Construction and testing

- AGs will create complied programs for testing.

- 4GLs will interpret without compiling.

- AGs can assist in system testing.

- 4GLs can interrupt the natural testing cycle.

A 4GL can offer very high levels of productivity in the area of programming. Testing productivity may also be improved, but the run-time monitor of the 4GL can cause some difficulty in knowing what data access actually takes place. An AG is able to generate 100% of all the application programs with any additional screen macros and control blocks. As normal source-code programs are compiled and tested, then the actual data flows can be traced with confidence. The better AG products would also include a testing monitor to relate the run-time diagnostics to the original design frames. It can be shown that certain 4GL products that employ an interface to a relational database are very difficult to test. The execution of the simple query program may display different results each time it is executed. As the database reacts to each query, the order of data may be changed and without unique keyed objects, then different executions may create results that are different.

4.6 Maintenance

We can generalize and say that maintenance costs are typically four to five times the cost of new development. Most established development centres are reporting that over 60% of their resources are spent on maintenance. We have also measured that 30% of all new development expenditure is spent on projects that never complete.

Significant productivity gains can be made with the best AG maintenance tools. Maintenance is initiated with a change in:

- Technical design

  ie database structural change.

- Business design

  ie additional field on a screen.

- Business analysis

  ie new dialogue function key options.

- Strategic planning

  ie change to another environment.

4GL products tend to demand traditional system and program specifications to be changed, then the actual programming work is greatly reduced. No productivity is found in determining the scope or impact of the maintenance change.

AG products tend to capture technical and business design changes, so that the impact and regeneration of all the affected programs is automated. Strategic changes can be the simple regeneration of the entire system to another target environment. Business-analysis changes should first be reflected in the models made by a CASE or AW product and then passed for business and technical design-change specification.

The role of a central repository has been shown to maximize the productivity in the maintenance cycle. As most new development is the application of maintenance and enhancement techniques, then the repository is a major source of productivity in new development projects.

5   WHAT ARE THE CONCLUSIONS?

5.1   Application generators provide

Application generators are aimed at the analysis and design of existing and new computer systems, not just at the programming of new programs. When coupled with an interactive testing facility, then the analysis, design, construction and testing of both on-line and batch application systems can be undertaken with a single approach. Source-code application generators suffer the overhead of having to go through a compiler. This is a development cost that avoids an execution penalty. If the transaction profile is so low that the operational costs tend to approach the development costs, then a query language (4GL) will be more applicable.

The benefits raised by customers include:

- prototyping and rapid development;

- minimum training;

- joint application development (JAD);

- very complex application design;

- relational and hierarchical database support;

- high-quality, bug free software;

- maintenance of existing systems;

- generated documentation.

5.2   4GL products provide

Rapid low-usage solutions to end-user requirements, with a tendency towards query-only applications. 4GL products are unlikely to be effective in the high transaction-throughput application requirements as created by professional development staff. The life of 4GL products is suspect as they are unable to evolve into higher levels of productivity without sacrificing flexibility. The most productive products are too difficult to learn, while the easy-to-use products are not as productive.

James Martin has said that "4GL's are dead", the implications are:

- that future graphic-based products will not employ yet another programming language;

- that a universal 4GL will not evolve as a world standard; and

- that current 4GL products have a limited strategic life.

Chapter 7

CONSTRAINTS IN PERFORMANCE AND FUNCTIONALITY CAUSED BY DESIGN AND MARKETING CONSIDERATIONS

Peter Bondar,
Honeywell Bull

PREFACE

Over the 1970–1980 time frame the use of 4GLs has become increasingly popular. With the arrival of 4GLs a whole number of subsidiary issues have been brought into question. Given the lack of maturity of the marketplace and its rapid growth this has led to a number of key areas not being satisfactorily addressed or being ignored completely. This paper serves to outline some of the variations that can be seen in the design and marketing of 4GLs in comparison to other technical and consumer products. It attempts this by comparing the theoretical views of marketing and also the design of products and contrasts this with the development of products by most companies today. If we look at the products so far today we see that there is large growth in the overall market well in excess of 50% compound growth per annum. Also in the UK marketplace there are a large number of players claiming to have some form of 4GL capability: at the last count over 300 different products were claimed to be available. One of the salient points which comes out, however, is that there is a large difference in functionality between all these so-called 4GLs, when they are all claiming very similar benefits.

1   THE BACKGROUND

If we look first of all at the large growth in the market we see that whereas the market itself has achieved rapid growth consistent year on year, we find that different sectors are performing differently. In the 1970s the information centre products that are end-user oriented were the most rapidly growing area. Today, we see that the products that were most commonly used within the context of an information centre were the most rapidly growing area. Today, we see that the products appertaining to the development cycle are enjoying the most rapid progression, and the forecast for the shipments of computer-aided systems-engineering products indicate these too will enjoy remarkably high levels of growth in the not too distant future. Within the database management arenas undoubtedly the move to relational and pseudo-relational database management is a "fait accompli". Most manufacturers are rapidly developing relational database managers, even though potentially much of the market is still addressed most suitably by codisil or network-based managers. If we look at the integrated projects supporting environments, (IPSE and the computer-aided systems engineering) case environments, we see today a tremendous amount of initial interest; this has to be contrasted against a relatively small number of buyers for these products.

One of the key points when looking at 4GLs, is the very large variation in functionality that exists. We can see two distinct groups: the information centre products and the development centre products. There are a number of additional ones such as the add-on type products, designed to enhance the existing environment: typically products such as screenpainters and COBOL program generators fall into this particular area.

In addition there are total environment products where the software developer is asking the user to abandon all of his existing database and code structures and replace them with a totally new system. Most of the relational database products such as ORACLE and DB2 are of this type.

One of the other things that comes out of a detailed analysis of the functionality of 4GLs is the degree of sophistication. For example in the area of screenpainting a very significant variation in the level of sophistication of products is immediately apparent. Some products have a glass teletype limited-display-attribute, limited-protection-mode of screenpainting, whereas others use both protected and non-protected field, extensive use of attributes such as blinking and reverse video and extensive use of colour. Some screenpainters only allow one screen per logical application, other screenpainters allow multiple screens per logical application. Each of these things is not necessarily apparent at the first pass through the product.

One of the things that tends to be similar is the benefit claims of most vendors. Typically productivity improvements in overall development of code over the design cycle, documentation, an ability by end-users to use the product and the ability to improve the quality of systems are all key examples. Some products clearly in the development centre area make no attempt at claiming capability at end-use computing environment; similarly some products that are clearly positioned in the information centre environment clearly do not make claims to their capabilities in the development centre.

However, with each product now attempting to widen its potential audience by enhancing its functionality in areas where it perceives itself as deficient compared to the competition, the benefit claims are starting to become much more generalized to all the 4GLs.

2   MARKETING THEORY OF PRODUCTS

If we now move on and look at the theory of marketing, in a simplistic case we are looking at five basic concepts: initial market research, leading to a concept of design that fulfils the requirements of the market research; a test marketing of the product to see that it actually does achieve these objectives; market feedback, resulting in modification if necessary; and then a full launch of the product on a national or international basis. Marketing is then performed by large organizations both in the consumer and technical world, do tend to follow these types of models to a lesser or greater extent, especially if the analogy is drawn to such concepts as cars very detailed marketing is developed very early on to allow the engineers the maximum time to develop a product in line with the market requirements.

If we look at market research first, we can break it down into several discrete groups. First of all detailed analysis is done of the market: this often takes into account major trends, cultural changes, political and socio-economic changes. At this initial research there is a requirement that is perceived with an embryonic stage for a particular type of product. At this stage a degree of hypothesis testing takes place which is usually a variation on attempting to refine the theoretical requirement.

After the hypothesis-testing takes place this is corellated to a demographic analysis which allows people to position the product in terms of socio-economic grouping and geographical locations. Further analysis is done on buying trends in terms of how the product is bought (whether it is bought directly from the manufacturer through retail outlets, through distributors, through franchises). In addition to this, market-trend analysis is performed to analyse the overall market for the product and what the key trends are. For example, in the case of cars, increasing levels of sophistication in terms of central door-locking, electric mirrors, windows etc, are overall trends and expectations, and a product that does not offer these facilities these days would be out of line with general market trends. Finally, within this area, competition is obviously a keen component: products that are as good as the competition are rarely good enough for a company to establish a lead over its rivals. The products must be innovative or exploitable in a dimension that the competition has not perceived.

As a result of the market research a concept or design is produced, often in computer parlance. This is a conceptual design review and this means it is a high-level overall chalk-on-blackboard approach. A prototype is a result of this initial concept of design in built in line with the perceived market requirement, and in an organization it is validated against those market requirements. In addition the organization often then checks that the product conforms with its internal and external quality procedures in terms of compliance with legislation, perceived consumer reaction etc.

The next stage is for a test marketing of the product: usually specific geographical or otherwise definable areas for the test are identified. Usually within the organization for test marketing a small task force of sales and promotional people are prepared and trained to take the initial product to the test market. Within the defined test market area — which is usually for purposes of analysis very well defined — the product is agressively marketed (probably more so than in comparison with its subsequent marketing on a general basis). As a result a number of incentives and variations are usually tried to see the sensitivity of the product to those particular subjects. Subsequent to the test market, a process known as market feedback takes place: the analysis of the performance of the product. It attempts to criticize any failures and also analyse any specific successes. Part of a ruthless market feedback analysis is the search for distorting factors that may have somehow influenced the performance of the product in the test market, relative to the perceived normal market. Inevitably some degree of mis-match between the customer expectation in practice and the theoretical model takes place. Often these can be relatively minor issues from an engineering viewpoint and may be easily resolved either from a packaging or engineering approach. A rectification programme is then applied to the product to bring it in line with the revised market expectations. As a result of going through this, if the product has not failed a stage resulting in a termination of the programme — and it is important to bear in mind that several products do fail en route and only one out of twenty initial concepts ever reaches any great measure of success — we then move on to the full launch.

At the full launch time the product has already been modified, the staff have been re-trained and, especially in a technical-product marketing area, a whole raft of product-marketing literature is produced from the initial test marketing, pricing is finalized and support levels for the product in the field are agreed. A sales programme is then prepared which communicates all of these things through the sales channels — be they direct, in the form of as sales force, or indirect in the form of distributors. The final point, often missed, is that the only way a product finally achieves success is by the commitment of the organization. Again in car-type analogies we have seen the development of elegance and sophisticated, well-priced products where, because the distributor or sales network was not behind it, the product flopped.

3   PRODUCT DESIGN

We now move on to the theory of design. In broad concept the idea of design is that we take the marketing input, build a product of prototype four, test the prototype as a result of achieving that, and then finally build a commercial product. Obviously, in the software development arena the anology to design and engineering is very pertinent.

If we expand this in a little bit more detail and take the marketing input the first requirement is for the product engineering people to understand the basic philosophy of what is trying to be achieved. The subtleties of the implementation that are not covered by documentation can be picked up by the product engineering people who then produce a functional specification.

The key point here is that the functional specification is a document that demarcates the revisions required from enhancement from the initial product and this forms the basis of the overall strategy that the marketing division will use to market the product to its sales organization. So the agreement of the functional specification with product marketing is a key milestone.

The next section is to build a prototype. The functional specification is the document that converts the theoretical model into the first prototype. The key point about a prototype is that the use of technology materials and techniques do not necessarily bear any resemblance to the technologies that will be used to build the final product.

Other important factors in prototypes are that the cosmetics and presentation of the product − unless this has been defined at an early stage as critical to the success of the product − are not usually well presented. The key emphasis in the prototype is to make sure that the prototype follows the physical structures expected to exist in the product. Cosmetics and presentation of the product are usually refined at a later stage with input from test marketing. This, to use the analogy in the car war, is why the initial prototype of a car is very bland: to allow the stylists and marketing people to produce different variations without driving the product down one particular direction to the expense of future options.

When it comes to testing the prototype the objectives are first of all, to make sure that the functionality required in the initial marketing specification is there and functions in a way that is to be expected. During the development and testing of a prototype at this time, the viability of improvements both in the fundamental design and the options for future volume production are considered.

The next stage is to build the commercial product. At this stage the prototype is taken and the production design is based upon the volume and maintenance requirements. Often this means that the product is simplified because large investments in up-front development can be written off against cheaper volume production costs. As a result of the test marketing the feedback can be applied to improve the functionality and change the presentation of the product to react to criticism that was established during test marketing. As part of the product plan we usually anticipate, that there will be significant changes to meet either legislative or marketing pressures. One of the major issues that is involved in the product plan is to make sure that these revisions do not require from the mental engineering changes can be accommodated within the existing bill structure.

Moving on from this, the first versions of the commercial release are usually based on a hand-built philosophy, instead of high-volume production from day one there is an initial small-volume walkthrough based very much on a hand-built philosophy to make sure there are no problems in the design or the actual production line. If all goes well, then volume production goes ahead.

4   MARKETING AND DESIGN IN PRACTICE

If we now look at marketing in practice we see that life is often very different in the software world. From a global perspective we find that most products are built then marketed: little market research is done in anticipation of a product being built. Most research that is done is done in an attempt to reposition the product having failed to achieve its original objectives; little, if any, test marketing is formally done. One scenario that emerges repeatedly is that somebody, somewhere has a bright idea and then, having had this product sitting on the shelf, they then decide to sell it to a variety of people. Because of this philosophy it is highly unusual to find that market research has achieved some volume of sales then research is then done in an attempt to find how the product is competing and what is required to maintain rapid sales growth. Also within the marketing concept, as we have already said, test marketing informally is highly unusual. Any test marketing is only done in the form of initial low volume of sales.

If we move on to design and build in practice, we find that the concept of marketing providing the initial conceptual design is very unusual. This is due to the fact that the products are invariably conceived and designed by technical staff with little view of what the marketing consequences are. Moving on from this, because of the mentality of the people involved in the initial design, prototypes customer physically implements as a production system and the feedback. The key thing that comes out of this is that the first product that is shipped is the commercial product. Bug detection is very much in the hands of the customers, not in the hands of the product engineering people. In marked contrast to hardware and other products the amount of bug fixing in early releases of the software product is very large.

If we look at the reasons behind this we can see that the very volatile nature of the market, the customers are very sensitive to market pressures and we can look to the rapid rise of relational database technology and as a key example of this, if a large proportion of the users are polled on why they are choosing relational database products it is based on a series of perceptions which may have very little to do with their business objectives, but just as in other markets perceptions of products are far more important than their actual physical realities. Because of intense competition technical changes happen at a very rapid rate and again this tends to outdate products very rapidly. There is therefore little regard to maintaining rigorous change control and retrofit programs. The general view is: "it will all be fixed in the next release".

Finally in the market place changes in perspective are fundamental in defining the rate of change required by the product and again the relational database aspect is probably one of the key ones in this perspective change.

Many of the products are devised in-house, with the people responsible for the development of the product working for a company usually producing some other product. As a result of their labours for the other company they come up with a base idea which they believe is marketable. As a result of this the intellectual knowledge gained in the production of the product is taken with them to produce the commercial product.

Because of the intrinsic nature of the software companies they are often very small and under-funded. This results in a rapid requirement to achieve some levels of sales and again this places great pressure on releasing a product before it has been fully tested. One of the other problems is that the products, because they are attempting to address the widest possible market, tend to be generalized rather than specific. Again, looking at the current UK market the number of products that have a significant amount of overlap is very large.

Finally, the culture of the companies: because of their evolution they tend to be highly entrepreneurial. This means that they are willing to take risks to achieve sales as the market demands they move very rapidly. This tends to mean that they have scant regard for historical commitments and also that the price book tends to be somewhat elastic. They tend to have an extremely paranoid reaction to one or two of their competitors and in situations like that the interplay between two competing companies can result in a rapid dropping of the price to the customer.

Because of the culture and the way these products have evolved it can be generally said that products escape rather than launch. It is only the very large software companies with turnovers in excess of $100,000,000 that tend to launch a product, the smaller companies tend simply to march out a series of requirements at a rapid rate of knots. As I have already said the customers do the test marketing, quality assurance and prototyping by virtue of their complaints. Because of this evolutionary type of development many products that have been in existence for several years tend to be very clumsy in their overall structure with a large amount of duplication of function in a variety of ways Therefore it is not unusual to find in some products that, for example, there are both screenpainters and screen painting languages which do not actually communicate with each other. Also, because software developers come and go within the organization, the user interfaces and command syntax tend to be inconsistent between early and late parts of the code. In comparison products that are relatively new to the market tend to be much more elegant and neat and avoid unnecessary duplication. One of the key points that comes out is that, over time, the products try and expand their potential audience:

95

we find information-centre products moving into the development-centre environment and vica-versa.

In larger companies a more formalized marketing and engineering approach tends to be prevalent, as it is in some smaller companies who have been unsuccessful in the past and have reached hard decisions. In these sort of companies products do tend to be better focused in terms of what they are attempting to do and who they are attempting to sell to. They tend to be more specialized and offer certain specific functionality and to excel in those areas. They also tend to be neater and elegant and less cumbersome than many of their competitors. On the down side of this, however, one of the major problems is that if this well-focused product does not meet the expectation level of the customers this may well result in failure despite the fact that the customer was not actually requiring some of the facilities that were not present in the product.

5   CONCLUSIONS

Several conclusions can be drawn. As far as the supplier is concerned, we often see functionality features provided because someone thought it was a good idea. Products often evolve in a piecemeal fashion with consequent disadvantages in terms of performance and cumbersomeness. Beware of products that attempt to move in and as far as the supplier is concerned, given the technological rat-race they are in do they have the staying power economically and from an R-D view point to be able to stand the heat in the features war.

From the biased perspective, one of the points that needs to be analysed is "Do you need all the features that you have in you tick list?" Often you will find that a product that has a relatively small amount of features will be far better with its functionality in its specific areas. This is often missed in evaluation. Remember also that the performance of the product, its portability, its flexibility, its price and its integration with existing systems are all mutually exclusive to a great extent. The key questions that a buyer must ask are "Which are the most important?": he can then rank his decisions. Clearly, buying a product that has no integration when a traditional mainframe environment is the anticipating target — with large amounts of traditional file structures — is not a good decision. Similarly, products that work well in one or two environments but are escpected to be imported to a variety of environments where these facilities are not available may not be a good decision. Other questions that need to be asked by the buyer are "Do they tend to be end-user oriented or DP oriented community?" Clearly they would be then biased towards information-centre or development-centre-type technologies. Again, centralized and decentralized is a major question: centralized organizations may only be buying one or two products and therefore the range of functionality and its level of integration may be key whereas in a decentralized environment, communications capabilities and ability to support relational technology may be more important.

As I have already said, existing investments in database are very significant. How much is it going to cost the organization to throw away these existing investments? What are the integration overheads of integrating 4GLs with existing database structures? Once these questions have all been addressed then the answers will be readily apparent to most people.

EVALUATION TECHNIQUES
AND
SELECTION CRITERIA

Chapter 8
MAJOR FACTORS IN THE SELECTION AND EVALUATION OF FOURTH-GENERATION SYSTEM PRODUCTS

David Martland
Brunel University

1   INTRODUCTION

There are many factors which affect the selection of 4GS products for any application. Some of the more important are:

- suitability for application;

- speed;

- size;

- cost;

- data portability;

- code portability;

- vendor reputation;

- ease of learning;

- ease of use;

- ease of maintenance;

- completeness.

These factors will be considered in the sections which follow.

2   APPLICATIONS

It is important to consider which applications can benefit from the use of 4GLs. Current 4GSs are really just tools which enhance productivity in certain application areas, and are not capable of solving arbitrary applications problems. In fact, lest the unwary should become overconfident, there is a mathematical theorem which shows that it is impossible to construct a general-purpose applications generator for arbitrary problems. However, many important applications fall in to well-defined categories, and solutions using modern equipment and design methods are possible. Rather than considering the design of individual computer-based systems, each needing individual attention, it is possible to consider broad classes of application, and to treat specific applications as particular cases.

I shall consider several applications types in order to identify any common features, and also to define classes which might usefully benefit from a general approach.

Examples of applications for systems development are:-

- directory enquiries;

- business accounts systems;

- share-dealings systems;

- point-of-sale systems;

- personnel systems;

- automated bank tellers;

- plant control;

- draughting packages for architects;

- electronic circuit design packages;

- electronic circuit layout packages;

- office communications systems;

- medical diagnosis systems;

- in-flight management system for aircraft;

- air traffic control systems;

- automatic railway control systems;

- publishing systems;

- computerized encyclopaedia systems;

- missile guidance systems;

- missile management systems;

- criminal records system;

- photographic records.

These applications have been selected simply to show the variety of applications types which are currently important within our society. Many of us work within restricted application areas, and do not realize that different aspects of computer technology may be very important within applications areas with which we are unfamiliar. It should also be noted that recording the list of applications does not have any moral purpose. Thus, if society deems that missiles are to be provided for a country's defence, it is not the role of the applications designer to query that decision, but to produce the system most appropriate for the requirements.

3   APPLICATION TYPES

In this section, brief descriptions will be given of a selection of these applications, together with the characteristics of each application.

3.1   Directory enquiries

Here the requirement is for a telephone directory enquiry system. Using current hardware, it may be assumed that users will make verbal requests to a human operator. In France enquirers may make enquiries by the use of a keyboard and

Minitel screen, and Bell laboratories have demonstrated the use of verbal requests to a voice-recognition system. Assuming that a suitable form of input to the system is adopted, the primary requirement is for a fast data-retrieval system based on a keyword search. It is desirable that pattern-matching search techniques should be used.

The system should be capable of storing a very large number of names, addresses and telephone numbers. Each individual query should be handled within a very short period (say one or two seconds). At any one time there may be several simultaneous queries from different enquirers. The database will change as people move, or change their telephone requirements, but a large part of the database will be static, so updates could be carried out in batch mode, or as a low-priority interactive task. Future requirements could be for automatic accessing of foreign directory systems.

Characteristics

Very large database. Very fast access time. Pattern-matching search. Multiple simultaneous queries.

3.2   Business accounts system

This type of application is for day-to-day commercial operation within a small, medium or large-scale business. Businesses have varied requirements, depending on the nature of business conducted, but many computer operations are similar for each business application. Usual requirements are for database files for regular clients, orders, stock, invoices, delivery notes, etc. The computer-based management of a business will be more or less complex depending on the size of the business and the importance of activities within the business operation. Thus a small business may handle complaints, returned goods, occasional clients by manual, or semi-manual methods, since these may be of low volume, whereas a large enterprise will have standard methods for each likely eventuality. Business use of computers normally requires operations on a set of database files which keep track with real world actions and events. For example, new clients can be registered on the clients file, client order requests can be satisfied by examining the stock file then allocating stock to the client and arranging delivery. In some cases orders may be passed on automatically to another supplier, who may then arrange delivery to the client directly.

Characteristics

Database size depends on business. Access time to items depends on business requirements. Most operations on database files are standard, and determined by nature of the business. There are few *ad-hoc* procedures.

Interactive use is desirable. Data-entry should be interactive, but some operations can be performed in batch-mode.

3.3   Point-of-sale system

In this example, a POS system makes use of laser checkout equipment to read bar codes on products. Each bar code is associated with an item description and the current product price. The system must be capable of rapidly associating the bar code with the description and price, and displaying them for the benefit of the operator and customer. Additionally the system must be capable of interacting with the laser reading device, and producing totals for display on an LED screen, and also itemized bills in printed form. Provision for price updating should also be provided, and an additional requirement is for all transactions to be recorded for later analysis.

Characteristics

Interfaces to special hardware devices needed (laser readers and LED displays). Comprehensive bar-code database needed. Very fast code association needed (at least two per second). Security for price changes needed, (to avoid employees changing prices). Communications with accounts systems needed — either networked communications or data uploaded to system via intermediate storage device.

3.4   Personnel system

Companies need to keep details of all their personnel. Skills of individual employees are noted, and can be used for resource management. Personal details can be recorded, and used for employee welfare. Additionally, performance measures can be adopted which may determine promotion, or which can be used to identify training needs, or safety problems. Information about employees is usually confidential, requiring careful observance of legal constraints on computer data storage, and changes slowly. Access to the data should be controlled, but may be required from several different company locations.

Characteristics

Possibly large database. Data changes slowly. Short access times to data are not necessary. Confidentiality requires security and integrity measures to be adopted. Each employee record may require large text fields.

Future systems

It should be possible to store photographs of each employee (for security). Facsimile documents may need to be associated with employee records.

3.5   Automated bank tellers

Here the requirement is for a network of automatic bank tellers, operating continuously (or almost continuously), offering a range of services, including cash dispensing, account queries, cash and cheque deposits, and automatic bill paying. Each automatic teller must communicate with one or more central systems to authenticate clients using the system.

Characteristics

Communications. Security. Special hardware requirements. Very large databases. Well defined transactions (Special transactions still handled by discussion with human teller or bank manager). Acceptable user response time (should be significantly less than using a human bank teller).

Central computer resource will be handling a large number of transactions concurrently.

3.6   Plant control

Controlling the equipment in a factory or plant is likely to involve a large number of different software components. There is likely to be a wide diversity of hardware, which to be fully automated will need interconnection by communications links. Individual hardware units, such as machine tools or industrial robots will need programming, and there will be a need for programs to monitor and control the overall state of the plant. Some of the procedures used within the plant will need to be fast acting, although if the plant is a fairly stable system, changes can be gradual.

Characteristics

Possibly very large number of software components. Communications essential. Some operations need real-time response. Database requirements depend on application.

3.7   Design and draughting packages

These packages typically require the use of special hardware, for example one or more high-resolution graphics-display terminals, together with pointing devices such as mice, or graphics tablets. Performing graphics operations with adequate interaction speed generally requires very fast processors. Software requirements tend also to be quite specialized. It is likely that a database of graphics components will be needed.

Characteristics

High-performance hardware and software needed. CAD is often treated as a high-performance application area. Graphics component database

3.8   Electronic circuit design packages

There are several stages in the production of modern microchip circuits. It is normal to perform electrical and logical-level simulation of large chip designs before producing a circuit layout. Additionally, modern circuits often include a large number of sub-circuit modules, which may be held in a module database. Simulation of the circuits requires high-speed processors (mainframe), and for testing, special-purpose debugging software will be desirable.

Characteristics

Database of circuit components. Simulation models require high-performance computers.

3.9 Electronic circuit layout design

Packages for electronic circuit layout may form part of a circuit-design package. These packages may have some features in common with architects, drafting packages, yet will also make use of software to perform routing of connections between components.

Characteristics

Highly interactive. Database of modules needed. Layout software.

3.10 Office communications system

The paperless office has not yet arrived in every organization. However, it seems likely that many organizations will use electronic data storage, and electronic communication methods in order to provide useful administrative functions automatically. Clearly the hardware requirements are for networked personal computers, of modest power, with text-editing tools. Database tools can be useful for keeping track of documents, and memos. Document distribution within organisations can be handled simply, with a mailing system to allow recipients to add their comments to a document as it is "passed round". It is desirable if users can operate their computers in a multitasking mode, as this will allow them to receive and respond to messages from elsewhere, whilst being able to carry on working after any interruption.

Characteristics

Interactive. Multitasking software desirable. Communications software and hardware needed.

3.11 Medical-diagnosis system

There have been several medical-diagnosis systems produced. Some of the better systems can effectively diagnose illnesses which even medical experts would find difficult. Often these systems are rule-based expert systems. It is not essential that all diagnosis systems should be interactive, as they need not be used routinely. However, if automated diagnosis is to be widely used in general practice, interactive use with a short response time will be very desirable. In some practices, the patients themselves interact with the system before seeing a doctor for consultation. This implies that questions asked must not be too technical, and that the computer system must be very easy to use. Additional information can be supplied by the doctor, in response to more detailed medical questions. The distribution of specialist software to a large number of practices is likely to cause some problems, although the commercial development of optical disc media is likely to help with the task of keeping software up to date.

Characteristics

Expert-system based. Must be easy to use interactively if patient interaction required. May require high-performance processors. Software distribution and updating required.

3.12 In-flight management system for aircraft

There are a great many sub-systems in a modern aircraft, and a system which can control and monitor most of these sub-systems will be very useful. Such systems are built into the very latest aeroplanes, and can provide the crew with status information about important units such as instruments, and also useful facts such as the occupancy of the toilets, lighting, or in-flight entertainment systems.

Characteristics

System is an integral part of modern aircraft. Many sub-systems may be involved. Communications between sub-systems essential. Systems are normally considered to be specialist.

3.13 Air traffic control systems

In order to manage the flow of large numbers of aircraft into and out of airports, automated air traffic control systems are needed. These pick up details of aircraft entering controlled airspace by the use of special-purpose hardware, such as radar, or transponders within the aircraft. If necessary, radio communication with the pilot can be used to identify aircraft, and to issue instructions. It is also possible that future systems controlling modern aircraft will also be able to perform some control functions from the ground control system without the need for pilot action. The system must be capable of tracking a large number of aircraft simultaneously, and predicting any undesirable events, such as collisions or near-misses. A comprehensive system should try to prevent any such event occurring, and should be capable of providing appropriate advice if such an event seems likely.

3.14 Criminal records system

Here the requirement may be for a combination of textual and pictorial information. Details of known criminals will be stored, together with several photographs of each person held on the system. Additionally, fingerprint data may also need to be stored. Currently police forces almost certainly use photographic storage for the images of each individual, and for the fingerprint data, but in future it is likely that such images will be stored electronically. This will allow matching processes to be applied to the images, in order to identify or eliminate suspects for new crime. The storage requirements for pictorial images are much greater than for text data.

Characteristics

Very large database for text and images. Input from many different points. Data query from many different locations. Security on queries.

4   PROPERTIES OF APPLICATIONS

From the examples given, it can be seen that there is considerable diversity in the characteristics for many different types of application. The following questions at least should be asked when considering the development of an application:

- Does the application require a large database?

- Does the application require fast access?

- Does the application require data input from many locations?

- Does the application require data retrieval from many locations?

- Does the application require images to be stored?

- Does the application require input from special hardware?

- Does the application need to control special hardware?

- Does the application need real-time response?

- Does the application need interactive response?

- Does the application have security problems?

- Does the application have unusual integrity problems?

- Does the application need to operate continuously?

The answers given to the questions above will enable the development of the application to be viewed more objectively, and appropriate systems developed.

5   SPEED

Many of today's 4GS products are fast enough for straightforward commercial applications, yet they are unlikely to be able to handle applications requiring very high-speed operation. However, this should not be seen as a major disadvantage to using 4GS products for a wide range of applications. There are always trade-offs to be made in the selection of any development tools, and in the case of current 4GS products these trade-offs are made in favour of ease of development and maintenance, quality and ease of use of the developed system, and against speed and size constraints. In the context of an organization requiring the development of a large number of applications modules, whilst any one application could be implemented for very fast operation using high-level, (or even low-level) languages, a great many developers would be required to design and implement all of the modules to the required performance standards.

There are however some things that can be done to speed up systems developed using 4GS systems.

First, the modules to be speeded up need to be identified. There is normally little point in speeding up a module that gets called once a month and runs for ten minutes. Frequently used operations should be optimized first.

Where database operations are concerned, it is useful to know which entities are frequently used as keys within queries on each database. These entities can be declared to be primary keys, or indices for the database, with the possibility of considerable improvement in speed.

Some systems allow the access mechanism to be specified for accessing records via specific keys. Many systems use B-tree storage, which is fast, but it may be possible to perform access operations more rapidly if hashing methods are used. As always with hashing, it is likely that the storage requirements will increase if this access method is used, as hashing only works effectively with storage occupancy less than 70%.

It is also useful to know if the query language system performs any optimizations, and how it operates. In a compound selection, one selection criteria may reduce the size of the selected data a great deal, whereas another may have little effect on the size of the data. Thus the ordering of selection criteria within a compound condition may have a significant effect on performance. To see this, consider the set of brown-haired, one-legged men within a town of modest size (say 30,000 inhabitants). A selection of all the brown-haired men in a town from the set of all people in the town, will reduce the size of the set by a small factor, say 4 or 4. However, there may be fewer than 100 one-legged people in the town, so selecting the one-legged people first reduces the size of the selected set by a factor of 300, which means that the second selection criterion can be performed much more rapidly. Some systems may function more effectively if compound selections are replaced by a sequence of simple selections.

There are some systems though, often based on special-purpose hardware, which can perform compound selections with several components very effectively. If such a system is used, then compound selection criteria may be more effective than sequentially applied single criteria.

Where relational database operations select and join are used, it is probably better to perform select operations before join operations, although some systems may optimize select and join operations appropriately.

Lastly, the procedural language used to develop applications using a 4GS may be interpreted for ease of development. Many 4GS systems allow applications to be developed using an interpreter, but a compiler is available for producing fast code for the developed application.

6 SIZE

Nowadays many hardware systems are large enough to support quite sophisticated applications. Even personal microcomputer systems now have enough main memory (typically 0.5 to 4 Mbyte) and backing storage (typically 1 Mbyte to 100 Mbytes) to be able to run useful systems. Small businesses can easily benefit from the use of one or more of the easy-to-use applications development systems which are available to run on microcomputer systems. It is always possible to develop new and larger applications, so that it may be a simple matter to produce a salaries system for a small company using off-the-shelf software running on a small machine, yet producing a similar system for a large international company may require the use of much more powerful hardware systems.

Very ambitious projects may require the use of numerous large computer systems networked together, with very large mass-storage devices, such as optical storage discs. Such systems have additional problems arising from the nature of the distributed databases.

Applications development systems often trade-off system-size constraints for ease-of-use requirements. Thus, there is often an assumption made in the use of a 4GS system that a sufficiently large hardware system will be available. The system may have to be significantly larger than would be needed to support optimized software, yet the ease with which a system may be constructed is considered to be of more importance than the size of the developed system.

If a system does turn out to be too large, various methods can be used to reduce the size effectively. One method is simply to use a compression/expansion algorithm on the data which is stored. This approach can be adopted to achieve significant data compression, but will normally slow down data processing as data will need to be expanded for use, and if any data is modified, the modified data will need to be compressed. If special-purpose hardware is used, such compression/expansion can be achieved with little effect on the processes using the data, but in a single processor system the compression/expansion processes will slow down the performance.

Another method of reducing data size is to perform a detailed analysis of the application, and to use a coding scheme to reduce data size. For example, an estate agent might use codes such as "4D" to mean "four bedroomed-detached" in the context of property descriptions, and particulars of persons wishing to buy or sell property. The input and output interfaces to the developed system could refer to property as "four bedroomed-detached" — input by menu selection, and output by code expansion — yet internally the system would make use of a compact code. Note that use of codes may have a beneficial effect on the speed of data access (but is not guaranteed to do so).

7   COST

The cost of developing systems using 4GS has dropped considerably during the last few years, as many suppliers now supply microcomputer-based, or minicomputer-based versions of mainframe products. This means that early stages of development can be carried out using cheaper versions of the software running on cheaper hardware. Many of today's 4GS systems run on similar hardware, so the cost of evaluating 4GS software may be relatively low. Thus, a user with IBM PC hardware may be able to purchase several copies of different 4GS products at prices per copy ranging from £500 to £5000, and if any software proves to be unsuitable for an application, the loss is limited to the cost of the software, and the (hopefully) short period of time spent evaluating it. It is assumed that the total value of systems being developed will have a value considerably greater than that of the 4GS tools, either with a large volume of low-cost products, or a small volume of high-cost products.

When a suitable 4GS product has been found for an application, if it is required to run the application (for reasons of speed or size) on mainframes, the PC-based evaluation copy can be used to develop the system which will subsequently run on the mainframe systems. Once a decision to purchase has been made, some suppliers will give favourable prices for mainframe development systems, and the much greater power available on some modern mainframes may provide a better environment for applications development.

8   PORTABILITY

It is important to be able to move applications from one machine to another. This is just as true within one manufacturer's range, as it is across manufacturers' ranges. Effort spent in developing applications for hardware/software environments which change will be wasted unless means can be found of moving the application from one environment to another. Many current 4GS products make use of a standard query language, such as SQL or INGRES, and some products allow code to be developed in standard languages such as C, PL1, FORTRAN, COBOL. The use of standard query languages clearly means that in the worst case, where a vendor withdraws support, it will be possible to transfer an application based upon a query language to another 4GS system. Similar remarks should be made about the used of standard procedural language as the "glue" to hold the queries together, although the use of standard procedural languages may not be the easiest way of developing an application within a 4GS environment.

Much of the onus for ensuring portability for applications is going to fall upon 4GS suppliers, who will wish to ensure that applications developed now will still function in five or even ten years' time. Some systems produce code in a standard language, such as C or COBOL, so the problem of moving an application could be resolved by porting the generated code to the new environment. This would freeze the application in its current state, and so should only be looked upon as a last resort. In any case, the problems of porting high-level programs are often not trivial. Assuming that working 4GS systems running on the target machine are available, the simplest approach would seem to be to move the specification of the applications system to the new environment, and use the 4GS to generate a new system. 4GS vendors will have some responsibility for ensuring backwards compatibility with earlier versions of their software.

It should be pointed out that, if the claims of the 4GS suppliers are to be believed, it should be possible to implement quite sizeable systems within a very short timescale, even using prototyping methods to establish the system requirements. Assuming these claims to be correct, there seems little excuse for any application developer failing to provide an adequate system specification when developing the first version of any system, although it is certainly possible that short-cuts will be taken when documenting the application system precisely because 4GS systems are so easy to use. Where applications are developed with satisfactory documentation, should it be necessary to reimplement them using a different 4GS system at a later date, the system-independent documentation should enable the recoding task to be undertaken quickly and correctly.

Besides being able to move whole applications, there are many situations where it is desirable to transfer data between applications, or from older systems. Many 4GS systems have numerous data-exchange protocols allowing import and export of data in standard formats. These facilities will be very useful if a new system is being constructed which uses existing databases or file systems. It often happens that an organization will implement new systems facilities using 4GS techniques, yet retain its original programs until they need to be reimplemented. There are also occasions when it may be desirable to use more than one 4GS system in order to produce an application, and the use of data-interchange protocols can be very helpful in that situation.

9   VENDOR REPUTATION

Many, though not all, of today's 4GS products are marketed by large, well-established organizations. Purchase of a 4GS product from a vendor who subsequently ceases to support the product for any reason can cause many problems to the purchasers of that product. There is no guarantee that large organizations are going to be more satisfactory in this respect than small ones, so the purchaser should be aware that precautions need to be taken to ensure that any applications developed cannot be hampered through non-support by the vendor.

10   EASE OF LEARNING

It should be pointed out that there are two classes of user for any 4GS product. Some users develop applications using the 4GS system, whilst others use the developed applications. Some users both develop applications and use the developed applications. There may be a considerable difference between the computer expertise of these two types of user. Ideally a system should be easy to use for the applications developer, and for the end user. There are likely to be trade-offs between end-user requirements and developer's requirements.

For typical applications most naive end-users will need to learn to use keyboard layout, simple menus and form filling.

More sophisticated end-users may need to know how to use query language for *ad-hoc* queries, text editing, document preparation, spreadsheet software, simple procedural language.

Application developers using 4GS products should have a knowledge of:

- relational database concepts, such as entities, attributes, relations, and operations such as select, join, project;

- the concept of views within a database;

- for some applications, knowledge of distributed database features could be an advantage;

- data dictionary systems;

- procedural languages, such as C, Pascal or COBOL;

- multi-tasking software;

- modern hardware, including knowledge of pointing devices;

- window management systems.

To say that every application developer must have a particular set of skills is clearly not true, as many application developers do satisfactorily develop applications without all the experience listed above. In the context of 4GS systems, some knowledge of relational database systems concepts, and some knowledge of data dictionary systems will undoubtedly make understanding and evaluating 4 GS systems a much simpler task.

11   EASE OF USE

Naive end-users like user-friendly interface, for example menu displays, help screens, meaningful commands. They normally prefer a fairly slow presentation.

Systems developers like fast systems, with quick turnaround times. If a developer is kept waiting for the system to display the next menu, he or she is likely to feel frustrated. Developers often do not care about commands being meaningful, as long as they can be typed with one or two fingers.

Additionally, if a systems developer has to develop a large system to be user friendly, there will be a greater need for more help screens, dialog, and menu screens, which the developer might find tedious to produce.

A system should not necessarily be judged harshly because developers find it hard to use, as it may produce applications which are liked by end-users. If the market for the developed applications is very large, difficulties experienced by developers will be relatively unimportant in the development process. It may be necessary to motivate developers by other means, in order to compensate for difficulties which they experience in the use of such systems.

There should be no need to select a tool which is hard for developers to use, and often developers will respond well to tools which they like. Note that few developers seem to enjoy producing adequate documentation or help screens for naive end-users, and it may be useful to employ people who are not computer specialists to carry out these tasks.

12   EASE OF MAINTENANCE

Large 4GS systems, and systems developed with them, will need maintaining. Maintenance arises for a number of reasons, but major reasons are undetected errors in the current system and unanticipated needs by the end-user. A simple example of a maintenance operation which is frequently required is that of adding a field to a record within a database. Some systems will require that the whole of the existing database be restructured, perhaps by copying to a new database, whilst others will be able to modify the existing structure quickly and effectively.

Also, it may not be possible to perform certain maintenance operations with a system while it is being used by others, so continuous operation of applications which require maintenance attention will be difficult.

Choice of 4GS systems for applications development should carefully take into account the maintenance requirements.

13   COMPLETENESS

Some 4GS systems provide a user-friendly environment in which a large number of tasks can be carried out, yet may prove impossibly difficult to use for some applications. For example, if it is required to perform certain complex mathematical calculations in an application, a system which has a limited function library and lacks the ability to define new procedures or functions will prove hard to use. Such systems do exist, and may nevertheless be suitable for a wide range of applications. Indeed, they may be easier to use for applications within their capability than systems which are more general. If a 4GS product is required to have wide-ranging applicability, then it will be necessary to ensure that general computing operations can be carried out. Systems which make use of high-level languages such as C, Pascal, COBOL, or Fortran can usually be used to generate solutions to arbitrary problems, although they will require expertise on the part of those who have to program them. Systems which use simple, easy-to-use and understandable commands for implementing applications may turn out to be innapropriate for particular applications.

14   CONCLUSIONS

A number of important factors in evaluating 4GS systems have been considered. It has been shown that there are a large number of applications which today's 4GS systems are not capable of developing, yet at the same time there are a significant number of applications which can be developed very satisfactorily using 4GS software.

Chapter 9
CRITERIA FOR THE EVALUATION OF FOURTH-GENERATION SYSTEMS

Jim Toller
CCTA

1   INTRODUCTION

1.1   Purpose

4GSs are becoming increasingly important because of their ability to produce good-quality, maintainable computer systems faster and with less technically skilled staff. In this context, there is an increasing need for DP installations and projects to consider 4GS software as part of an overall software solution.

However, the assessment, evaluation or comparison of software involves acquiring an understanding of a product's capabilities and functionality and then organizing this information into a coherent framework. Most software vendors supply product advertising material which lacks technical detail and avoids those areas where the product is deficient. Product manuals, if provided, contain a wealth of detail but are often impractical to use if the time for the evaluation is limited.

This paper describes an approach to the evaluation of 4GS that has been developed by CCTA for use in government and which is thought to be of wider interest.

1.2   Background

The material on which this approach is based has been used in practice by CCTA staff on a variety of projects for some years.

The approach is documented in full in a report published by CCTA in July 1986, entitled "Application Generator Assessment, Evaluation and Selection" [1].

The report has been updated recently and the revised version is available, from HMSO.

1.3 Outline of the evaluation method

The method involves the following steps:

- customization: identification of project specific requirements and the weighting of the standard criteria;

- product identification getting a list of all the relevant products;

- familiarization with those products and shortlisting down to about three;

- scoring the shortlisted products;

- aggregating the detailed scores up to one number for each product.

These steps are described in more detail in paragraphs 7 to 13 below. The greater part of the paper, paragraphs 14 to 23, is given over to setting out, in summary, the criteria for scoring.

It is not intended that the method should be followed mechanically. It is presented procedurally in order to show what has to be done. How it is applied in practice depends on circumstance.

2 SCOPE

2.1 What is a fourth-generation system?

A number of labels are used: fourth-generation systems, fourth-generation languages, fourth-generation environments and application generators. While such labels are useful for discussing the various different types of product that are available there is no consensus about their definition and the differences are not relevant in this paper. In what follows, therefore, the term "application generator" or "AG" is used to cover all the products in this class without distinction.

The prime requirement an application generator is to be able to develop applications in significantly less time and with significantly less comprehensive skill levels than when using conventional programming. However, an AG must be capable of constructing a variety of applications; in order to be able to do this, AGs need to exhibit the functional capabilities identified in the next two paragraphs. While for most applications these will be mandatory requirements, there are a number of smaller products around, described in promotional material as application generators, which may be useful in particular circumstances. Generally speaking such products are easy to use and are very productive within their intended, but limited, range.

There are more AG products capable of developing on-line applications than are capable of developing batch applications.

- Reacting to user demands, there is a general trend within the computer industry to develop new systems to operate primarily in an on-line rather than a batch mode. On-line systems are usually simpler and more efficient for the user and tend to move control of data away from the computer departments into the user departments.

- While individual on-line application systems vary widely, they all exhibit a degree of commonality in their structure. They all consist of conversations, dialogues and exchange. In general, the exchanges are relatively small and have a simple structure.

- The development of on-line applications using conventional programming techniques requires programmers to possess skills and experience in sophisticated software such as TP monitors and database management systems. Such programmers are currently in short supply and are expensive to hire or train and difficult to keep.

For these reasons, it is useful to consider the required batch and on-line capabilities separately.

2.2   Functional capabilities of AGs for implementing on-line systems

To implement an on-line TP system the AG must be capable of exhibiting the architectural characteristics of a TP system. This implies the ability to construct conversions, dialogues and exchanges. To define an exchange requires the ability to:

- define a non-trivial pre-map process (processing to be undertaken prior to the display of an input screen of an exchange, to the application user): here, non-trivial implies the ability optionally to access multiple record types or record occurrences within the process in addition to normal processing such as arithmetic and conditional logic;

- define the application screen format to be displayed and the data fields to be entered (there should be few or no restrictions);

- define a non-trivial post-map process (processing to be undertaken after results have been received from an input screen);

- update or access multiple record types or multiple record occurrences as a result of the exchange;

- determine by algorithm, directly or indirectly from the data input, the next exchange to be processed;

- pass information between exchanges in a temporary area in order to allow the construction of multi-exchange transactions.

Implicit within this definition is the concept of an on-line transaction success unit and the associated scope of the success unit.

In addition to building conversations it is also necessary to build some kind of login and some kind of menu structure. In some products there is specific support for this part of the system, in others it is necessary to use the general-purpose conversation-building machinery.

2.3   Functional capabilities of AGs for implementing batch systems

It is much more difficult to encapsulate the essential requirements for batch systems. In general, they should:

- be driven from a sequential input file containing "business transactions", possibly containing a single "transaction" which initiates the production of a report referred to as a control file;

- define batch business transaction boundaries (for recovery, integrity and performance purposes): the entire process may constitute a single "transaction";

- perform non-trivial user-defined arithmetic, conditional or control operation sequences;

- process (ie be able to read, optionally update, or create) multiple record types and multiple record occurrences within a batch business transaction;

- produce printed output or reports in user-specified formats.

3   PROCEDURE

3.1   Rationale

Products have different backgrounds; because of this they have different strengths and weaknesses. Weaknesses in one area will not necessarily eliminate a product from consideration since project requirements are rarely absolute. The method is designed to assess the suitability of products for the total requirement of a given application.

In order to compare products it is necessary to reduce the information collected during evaluation to a single number and in order to do this it is necessary to sum impressions in some way across a wide range of criteria. In this method, a chained weighting technique is used, with scores being allocated at the lowest level of criteria, then weighted, aggregated and normalized up the heirarchy. The effect of this rather complicated procedure is that the final score is insensitive to the inevitable professional disagreements about detail.

3.2 Customization

Individual installations and projects will need to adapt the method to fit in with their own procedures, the context of the software selection and the type of application. This is likely to involve changes to the detail of the steps of the method and may involve simplification.

- Think about how much it is worth spending on software selection. Is getting "something that will do" more important than getting the best? What will be the penalty of getting it very wrong? Slightly wrong? A strategic purchase for an organization or a large purchase is worth more effort than a tactical purchase to meet some smaller, short-term requirement.

- Think about who should do the evaluation. Some consultants have lots of experience of this type of software and its selection; it may be that a few consultant days would save a lot of time and effort.

- Identify any mandatory requirements there may be. This is necessary because the weighting technique averages everything: it does not recognize the concept of the essential. Much of what is in paragraphs 5 and 6 will usually be mandatory requirements. Be careful not to make solutions into mandatory requirements.

- Assign weights to the evaluation criteria. Different applications and application mixes will attach different importance to different facets of the software. For example, the intended users of the AG may all be experienced programmers who do not need and may not want a very friendly interface.

- Identify any desirable requirements there may be that are not covered by the standard evaluation criteria. It may be desirable, for example, to be able to access libraries of scientific subroutines written in FORTRAN from within the AG.

123

3.3 Product identification

The first step is to draw up the list of products from which the selection is to be made. How long this list is and how long it will take to prepare it will depend on the experience of the staff doing the work and the size of the project. Typically the list will contain between 5 and 15 products.

With experienced staff it is often possible to eliminate a lot of products very quickly at this stage. For a small project running on a UNIX box there is no point in listing first-division IBM products.

The important thing is to make sure that nothing important is left out and it is often enough to talk to a few people with experience in the field. There are a number of publications available now which list and review large numbers of products. A recent example is the survey from INBUCON. Software directories are sometimes useful although their coverage is very uneven. For very large projects it may be worthwhile to advertise and to invite product suppliers to nominate themselves.

3.4 Familiarization and short listing

In this step, the objective is to get down to about three products, all of which could probably do the job. All the products on the shortlist should meet the mandatory requirements.

Again, how long this takes will depend on the experience of the staff involved and the size of the project. It may be enough to use product glossies. Technical overviews, in the 20 to 40 page range, are often useful and are increasingly available. It will not usually be necessary to attend demonstrations or to consult reference manuals.

3.5 Scoring

The shortlisted products are now looked at in more detail. At this stage demonstrations, reference manuals and reference site visits are usually required.

Hands-on practical work may be helpful, although experience suggests that such work is expensive and the results, particularly with regard to productivity, can be misleading. One good reference site with a similar application or application mix is worth a lot of evaluation. Practical work may, however, be justified by wider objectives, for example a requirement to train or involve programming staff or to promote the idea of using AGs.

In order to collect the information needed to score products it may be helpful to use the questionnaires set out in reference [1]. These are particularly helpful to staff with little experience of this type of product.

The result of this step is a score for each of the criteria in the evaluation model for each shortlisted product.

3.6 Aggregation and ranking

In this final step chained weighting is applied to individual criterion scores to produce a single score for each product.

The criteria are arranged in a hierarchy and each intermediate and terminal node is assigned a weight reflecting its importance. There are about 50 individual criteria in the standard method, although this may well be reduced by customization, and the depth of hierarchy varies between one and four. At the first level up, individual criterion scores are weighted, added and then normalized to give a score out of ten. These scores are then, in turn, weighted, added and normalized, rapidly reducing the number of scores as the procedure climbs the hierarchy, until, at the top, there is a single score. We can then rank the shortlisted products in terms of technical merit for the application.

3.7 Choice

The actual choice will be made on the basis of this ranking and on a number of additional factors, in particular price and other components of what may be a large procurement package. AG software may be a minor component of some larger whole. If, in this larger whole, application generation is not doing well, it may be appropriate to separate it out into a separate procurement.

It may be appropriate to take the selected product on trial, particularly if there was no practical work during the evaluation. Most suppliers will allow a free

30-day trial; if this is not enough, which it will not be for a substantial product, most will arrange for rental for a few months.

It is often useful, after a product has been selected and installed for a period, typically one or two years, to review the use that is being made of the product and the claims that were made at the time of purchase. This may the time to consider buying more products in the same range.

4   CRITERIA

4.1   Summary

This section identifies a hierarchy of assessment criteria against which AGs can be scored. The main headings are set out below and a more detailed presentation follows.

What it can do and how much it will cost to do it

- Generality — the types of applications which can be developed.

- Usability — reflects overall productivity anticipated from the product and the skill levels required to use it.

- Integration with other system components — degree of integration with major data management products which run in the same environment, eg a data dictionary.

- Capability of system components — total data-management capability available to the user, from the AG or elsewhere.

- Efficiency — machine resource usage for the development and production running of the applications.

Environmental factors

- SSADM. Virtually all government projects use SSADM for analysis and design; a good fit with clear, easily documented transition from design to implementation is desirable.

- Control capability — of increasing importance for large projects.

- Environment independence — important if systems need to be moved to other environments. Conformance to relevant standards.

- Product credibility — support, training, documentation and general credibility of the product and vendor.

- Other project — specific requirements — functionality required for specific projects or applications. Not always necessary.

4.2 Generality

The AG's generality is a measure of the extent to which the product meets the functional capabilities indicated in 3.2. The AG's generality determines the types of applications which can be developed.

On-line systems

Most AG products may be used to construct on-line applications, although, some products require a degree of imagination in their use to achieve this generality. The following areas should be looked at:

- File handling — what restrictions are there? Can it handle more than one record type on a screen?

- Screen handling — how good is the screen painter? How much of the application can be expressed in terms of screens and their properties?

- Communication areas — necessary for multi-exchange transactions.

- Complexity restrictions.

- Help facility.

- Multi-user capability.

127

Batch systems

Some AGs are not capable of constructing batch systems. This is because AGs are generally more cost effective when used to build on-line applications. In such circumstances, a purpose-built report-writer package can give some support to the batch application requirement.

- File handling.

- Reporting.

- Algorithm complexity.

- Multi-user capability.

4.3   Usability

The ease of use of the product when developing applications is a major factor in determining the overall potential productivity achievable from the product and the skill levels required to use it.

Specification language

- Suitability for programmers.

- Suitability for non-programmers.

- Style and quality.

- Batch on-line compatability: specification language should be more or less the same.

A potential advantage of the AG approach is that by reducing the skill requirements, it becomes possible to build systems with analyst-programmers, so avoiding the problems associated with the analyst producing program specifications for the programmer to code. However, while most AGs are to an extent usable by people with little formal programming training, DP skills are still necessary to understand the concepts of good system design etc. Few AGs are suitable for use by untrained end-users, although such people can often be turned into AG programmers in far less time than it takes to train a COBOL programmer.

Development tools

The tools available to the application developer significantly affect the developer's productivity.

- Specification editor sophistication.

- Screen painter.

Testing tools

- Incremental testing.

- Debugging facilities.

Development environment

It is desirable that the AG is usable effectively without a significant programmer learning overhead and that applications can be developed and tested with minimal delays. These objectives are achieved if the AG is well integrated. Ideally, the user of an AG should only be required to master a single environment, which has all the facilities he needs. In general, AGs which interpret their code provide better development environments than those which compile the code.

- Integration of editors and compiling facilities.

- Speed of compilation turnaround.

- Development environment help information.

- Batch and/or on-line application specification.

While applications usually will be developed on-line, it may on occasions be desirable to have the option of developing them (ie specifying and testing them) in a batch mode. Several products allow the specification, but not the testing of applications.

Definition of application data and program constructs

Most AGs make significant use of globally maintained data and file definitions; this avoids the need to respecify. However, restrictions on the use of these definitions affect the products usability.

- Flexibility of global definitions. How clever are the defaults and how easily can they be varied?

- Order of element specification. Do things have to be specified in a strict bottom-up way? Not being allowed to refer to things before they are created can be irritating.

4.4   Integration with other products

It may be necessary for an AG to interface to other data-management products. These products may have been installed as part of a strategy or standard. It may be that the AG is required to extend an existing application which uses other products.

The ability to interact with other products reduces the possibility of having to install software which duplicates existing capability, or requiring duplicate skills for different development environments. It is also likely to be less costly in terms of hardware and software than separate environments. Where products need to interact with other components, the interaction is particularly important with:

- data dictionary — it may be desirable to hold all dictionary data in one place where it can be properly managed;

- DBMS — hardware and people costs of big DBMSs are high. One may be quite enough;

- TP monitor — it may be desirable to have a single TP service satifying all applications and all users.

4.5   Cabilities of other system components

When assessing software for a project, it is not reasonable to assess the capabilities of an AG in isolation from the capabilities of other components of system software. This is equally true if the components are supplied as separate products, or are supplied as part of the AG. Other major system components are:

- data dictionary;

- DBMS;

- TP monitor;

- report writer;

- query language/processor.

There may in addition be a requirement for specialized application packages, such as a statistical tabulator. The method described in this paper does not attempt to undertake a detailed evaluation of these components although in the revised version it may be enlarged to cover DBMS. Instead, a single score is attributed to each. The derivation of this score is likely to involve an exercise similar to that described here for AGs.

4.6 Efficiency

Computer installations usually find that applications expand to fill available machine resources. In such cases, resource usage is important. However, the importance of machine efficiency depends on the number of times a transaction is initiated. If a transaction is run infrequently, then machine efficiency is less important than if the transaction is replicated on many machines or is the subject of very high transaction rates.

It is also important to be aware that the measurement of the efficiency of an AG may not be simply a matter of measuring CPU resources used. It may be necessary to think about memory usage and input − output activity.

When an organization acquires an AG, it frequently acquires other advanced software such as a DBMS. Such software is usually resource intensive in its own right.

When planning capacity consider the requirement for development and run-time capacity separately. There is often a trade off between the two: the price of good run-time performance may be expensive compilations.

4.7 Fit with SSADM

SSADM produces detailed data and process-design documentation. Typically the data design coming from SSADM can be implemented directly, without the need to modify the logical design to take account of physical constraints. The process design, however, is unlikely to be expressed in terms that can be implemented directly (although work is in hand to change this) and some care is usually necessary to ensure a smooth transition between design and implementation. It is clearly an advantage if a product vendor can show how this can best be done and if this interface is documented. The objectives of such an interface should include:

- eliminating duplication between the design and implementation activity;

- eliminating gaps;

- facilitating the creation of adequate documentation, covering both design and implementation.

4.8 Control

While unimportant for one-off or very small projects, the rapid development of code and data structures requires that, for significant developments, the AG provides good control and documentation of the resources (files, databases etc) used. This usually means that the AG must interface closely with the organization's data dictionary and that the dictionary has sufficient access control and "status" functionality.

- Usage documentation − what are the relationships between differant parts of the system. What programs use this file? Does the user have to maintain these links?

- Development control. Can completed programs be protected? Are multiple versions allowed?

- Audit control. Is there any logging of who does what and when?

- Quality-assurance monitoring. Is there any support for monitoring quality? Particularly important if inexperienced staff are to be used. An area addressed by few if any products.

- Performance monitoring and control. Can usage of potentially expensive constructs be identified?

- Effect on the organization.

The introduction of some products into a department is likely to have a much more significant impact on the way that department works than will other products. "Tactical" products are those which can easily be introduced to solve immediate one-off problems; they will involve a short educational and installation lead-time. "Strategic" products require a much greater commitment, in order to get the correct infrastructure into place, to use them effectively.

4.9 Environment independence

Environment independence is important if it is likely that the application will be moved to another hardware or system-software environment. An advantage of the AG approach is that the technical environment-dependent aspects of the application are separated from the specification, which should allow the specification to be implemented on other environments with minimal changes.

To what extent does the product conform to relevant standards? Does it conform to the recently published ISO standard for relational database, SQL? Does an application built with the product fit in the OSI or XOPEN framework?

4.10 Product credibility

Some products claiming to be AGs are produced by small or relatively unknown software houses or are written and supported in foreign countries and marketed here by agents. Other products are new to the market place and are therefore as yet untried. Such products are not necessarily of poor quality, that the systems need but it is necessary to assess the likelihood of the software and the marketing agency still being viable in the future before committing to using a product.

- Vendor assessment — is the vendor a large and extablished company with a track record?

- Product's field experience. New products usually have problems. Is the product good enough to make the risk worthwhile?

- Documentation.

- Training.

- Support. Often thin with new or newly successful products.

5   CONCLUSION

A method for evaluating 4GSs has been outlined and set in context . The core of this method is the scoring of products against a number of standard criteria. Customization is required to fit the method to particular circumstances but the requirement for detailed technical knowledge of data-management software is much reduced.

The method was developed in and for government but it is thought to be of general applicability.

6   REFERENCE

1 Application Generator Assessment, Evaluation and Selection, CCTA, Gildengate House, Upper Green Lane, Norwich, NR3 1DW, 1986.

Chapter 10
SELECTING A FOURTH-GENERATION LANGUAGE

Alfie Windsor
4GL Systems Ltd

1 INTRODUCTION

The title of this chapter may be "Selecting A Fourth-Generation Language" but I do not intend it to be another one of those painstakingly detailed reviews and comparisons of the technical facilities of tens or even hundreds of different products, or a complex description of a selection system involving markings, weightings factors and the like. I aim for a much more meaningful perspective. I will examine the problems and needs of DP managers and users now, and over the next five years, to determine what sorts of advanced programming tools they need so that we can be sure that selected tools match the demands to be placed upon them. This review will also encompass the wider issues raised by 4GLs such as establishing the right infrastructure for their effective introduction, efficient implementation, and of the organizational problems to be addressed. I will show that success in the 4GL environment is determined by a much wider set of criteria than a grading of technical facilities alone.

It is virtually impossible to tread the 4GL minefield without coming across the works of James Martin, so I would like to start by taking the bit between my teeth. James Martin has proclaimed: "4GLs are dead − I should know I invented them."

I think he is completely wrong. His views stem from his recent book *5th Generation Languages*, so you might reasonably expect a certain amount of publisher's hype to gain attention and sell copies.

My second point is more serious. Mr Martin is often called a computer guru, and whilst I have the greatest respect for him and what he has achieved, I do have some problems with gurus in general. Following them is rather like orienteering – you run

135

like mad to get to where you are sent, but when you arrive you are immediately given a new destination. Just as we are waking up to 4GLs our guru wants us to chase 5GLs.

To be fair he has the advantage over most of us: he has the high ground and therefore has a much broader perspective. If you adopt his long-term view he is right of course: 4GLs are doomed — but then so was COBOL. Let's accept that 5GLs are, perhaps, a panacea for the future but that we need efficient and effective solutions to today's problems now. We need demonstrably better facilities that will allow us to resolve these problems and to meet the demands for more and more systems, more and more quickly. We know that COBOL cannot cope and that it does not react quickly enough to market forces so the answer for the time being has got to be 4GLs.

2   WHAT IS A FOURTH-GENERATION LANGUAGE?

The words themselves tell us something but not much. Cast your minds back some years to the early days of COBOL. COBOL was originally conceived as a formal language to be used by systems analysts to define user requirements in an English-like way so that systems could be generated by the computer. Systems would be developed more quickly, more accurately and for less cost. In other words the perennial programmer was about to disappear even in the late 1960s and early 1970s.

I am sure that many people will have heard that little speech or something very like it from a number of 4GL salesmen. But what do we mean by a 4GL?

There are a lot of misconceptions around:

- Some take the view that with a 4GL you do not need a full and systematic analysis and design of user requirements.

- Others believe that with a 4GL you sit and prototype with users to produce a working system.

- There are those who see 4GLs as a panacea to all systems needs whether they are corporate mainframe systems or end-user needs on PCs.

- Another group think that 4GLs will solve all your problems to give:

  - quicker development;
  - better user relationships;
  - more flexible systems;
  - hardware independence;
  - database management system independence;
  - well-documented systems.

- 4GL denotes some form of standard advanced programming language. This is a serious problem. At present there is no agreed definition of what a 4GL is or what it should do. The end result is that almost anyone who sells any sort of software product can, through skilled sleight of hand, suddenly market it as a 4GL. There are any number of voluminous and expensive tomes around describing and comparing the various offerings. At the latest count there were at least 500 products claiming to be 4GLs and 100 products that are generally "accepted" as such. These diverse products can in the main be grouped into at least five types of product which offer very different facilities. The industry needs guidance and I would look to the BCS or IDPM or NCC to provide it. A CODASYL- or ANSI-style committee may be overkill but there needs to be a shake-out if 4GL suppliers are not to become the double-glazing companies of the DP industry.

Possibly the least professional view of all — and one which I have encountered on numerous occasions — is that the best (or is it easiest?) way to choose a 4GL is to just get one in and try it. If it does not work throw it away and try another one, or two or three. . . . In a recent Pergamon Infotech survey of 4GL users more than half the respondents claimed they did no research before purchase. I find this view baffling; you certainly would not adopt that approach to a mainframe purchase or to selecting key staff. No — in selecting these you would go through a very careful selection and screening assessment exercise before reaching a decision. The same should apply to a 4GL.

Individually these products may live up to one or two of the expectations just discussed — but none that I know of will meet all of them. In order to make a sensible selection we therefore need to have a clear view of what we are trying to do with the product we are buying. In other words we need first to determine our selection criteria and only then go through a selection exercise. As I warned earlier it is not sufficient to base selection on a simple list of technical features: a much wider set of considerations must be addressed. In 4GLSs we have a four-stage approach:

1. Define requirements: identify and quantify the various selection considerations.

2. Identify potential solutions: match these requirements with the functionality of products.

3. Shortlist: determine the one or group of products which most appropriately meets defined needs.

4. Selection: trial and test of the shortlisted product(s) in order to make a final objective selection.

In making our selection we are faced with a bewildering array of choice — a greater choice perhaps then we have ever had to cope with previously. Unfortunately the waters are likely to get more muddied as time progresses.

For the purposes of this chapter I will take the second stage first because a review of the features and "approach" of the various products will help to explain why the need to consider some of the selection criteria is so important.

3   SELECTION CONSIDERATIONS

What are we trying to select?

3.1 A programming language?

That seems fairly obvious, but let's just consider the offerings. There are at least five very different families of products on offer:

1. System builders, developed primarily to enable the production of on-line systems. These are now being extended with interfaces to lower-level / other languages or with add-on modules to allow the generation of batch routines. Examples include Oracle and Ingres.

2. Application system builders which facilitate the production of batch as well as on-line systems. Products include Focus, QuickBuild and Mantis.

3. End-user facilities which allow non DP staff to generate and run their own reports and enquiries. Products include Easytrieve, Filetab, CA-Earl and Datatrieve.

4. 3GL generators: the various products which generate COBOL code from a higher-level, English-style syntax. Products include Delta and Rapid Gen.

5. Decision support systems and expert systems which allow modelling and "what if" processing and "intelligent" systems. Products include FCS, System W, Crystal and Expertech.

3.2 A database management system (DBMS)?

There are different approaches to the way in which data is stored and retrieved.

*   Some systems such as Unify, Adabas and IDMS-SQL have their own integral database; indeed they are primarily database systems extended to include program and report generation facilities.

*   Others, like Powerhouse and Application Factory interface to other proprietary DBMSs such as Dec's RDB.

*   Another subset will allow both these options.

Consideration must also be given to the types of data structures supported: relational, hierarchical, CODASYL, inverted files, flat files or networked approaches all have their own strengths and weaknesses and are particularly well suited to specific processing problems. Some products support one or a number of these options.

3.3   A data dictionary system?

Whether they are called dictionaries, directories or libraries, this sort of facility is inevitably available but, as with DBMS, the facility can be built into the product or provided as an interface to other proprietary systems. The key question though is whether the dictionary is:

- Passive, in that information goes from the dictionary to the DBMS/4GL but at run time the dictionary is not needed and cannot be updated. These are not generally available to users, do not produce DML and often need to be compiled into program code. They tend to be simple validation and checking repositories for information and the source of basic documentation.

- Active, so that it is user driven, providing facilities for the effective control of information, and also generates DDL and DML. Examples would be Oracle's SDD and Concurrent Reliance.

- Proactive, which provides sophisticated facilities for generating complete systems from descriptions held in the dictionary and for user management and control of meta-data.

The most advanced of the latter are now acting as front-end systems generators — producing 4GL code with the minimum of human intervention. Interesting developments on this front are ICL's QuickBuild – DDS interfaces and the bridging of the LBMS analyst workbench, Automate, to Oracle's SDD.

3.4   An analysis and design method?

With 4GLs prototyping has come of age but two camps are developing. On one hand we have the totally committed who believe that it is now possible to produce systems using only a prototyping approach. I have seen examples of up to six different types of prototyping used in place of more conventional stages. The other camp are the structured-methods brigade who are firmly entrenched around

SSADM, LSDM, ISDM and all the other SDMs. The way ahead I believe lies in a compromise. Figure 10.1 shows the NCC systems lifecycle model and I believe that the arguments for this and structured methods remain valid even with 4GLs.

Figure 10.1 A system development life cycle.

In 4GLSs we have extended the structured method approach to encompass the whole of the lifecycle and we are exploring how prototyping can be used to the best effect within each stage to simplify and speed it up. We have evolved our own very intensive approach to feasibility studies and requirements definition called TIDS - the total immersion design system — which allows us to complete these tasks in one week rather than three to four months as previously.

3.5 A DP or a user tool?

The man machine interface is critical to the successful application of the product. A number of different approaches are adopted:

- Language-based: the user is required to provide often fairly complex keyword and parameter inputs with the minimum of prompting in order to be provided with a screen-based form to fill in. This approach is most favoured by experienced DP staff.

- Menu-based: provides lists of options that prompt the user down through a number of levels until the required screen is available. This simple approach is generally more favoured by non-technical staff.

- Parameter-driven: skeleton systems already exist and the user redefines individual headings and fields on prepared screens so that a tailored system can be generated.

The trend is towards an easy-to-use interface based around windows, menus and fill-in-the-blanks, with screen, and now, report painting. In this environment our traditional view of a language with narrative commands, verbs and conditions is becoming inadequate and outdated. A more appropriate concept is of a development environment. That is why within 4GLSs we generally refer to the 4G environment rather than the 4G language.

Selecting a 4GL therefore has wider implications than the simple technical viewpoint. With this background in mind we can return to the first stage of our selection process — determining requirements.

4   DETERMINING REQUIREMENTS

Most DP managers face at least one of the following problems:-

- A growing backlog of maintenance and development work that is (almost) unmanageable.

- Urgent business pressures for new and replacement systems which more accurately reflect users' needs, which are more reliable and more flexible. In many industries, financial services, the manufacturing and retail sectors and, increasingly, professional services, it is the quality, appropriateness and timeliness of DP systems that gives companies their competitive edge. Public utilities, central and local government all face the pressures of "commercial" operations through privatization and competition.

- Increasingly sophisticated and knowledgeable users who expect high-quality systems and greater autonomy from central DP control.

- Less skilled DP "indians" as experienced people become chiefs or join other tribes.

- The need for greater productivity from the same (or fewer) staff.

Many of you will feel that you face all of these problems. Despite this, in the survey I mentioned earlier, nearly a quarter of users could not say why they used a 4GL.

These problems can be rationalized down into four broad topics:

- business needs and priorities;

- people considerations;

- IT infrastructure;

- product functionality.

These are considered below.

4.1 Business needs and priorities

This means understanding what systems are required to support business operations and corporate priorities for their implementation. Figure 10.2 indicates that there are three broad levels of business activity which can be supported by DP: corporate management, management and "production" staff.

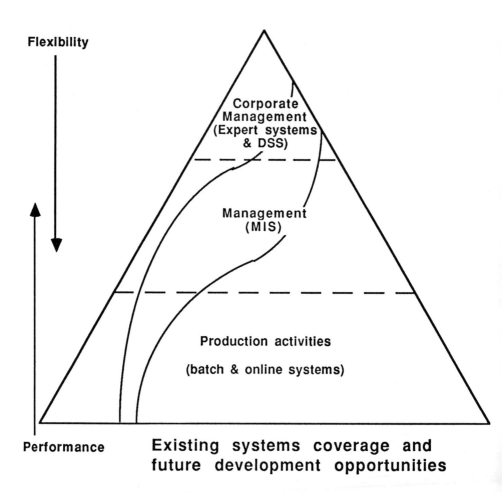

Figure 10.2 Nolan triangle showing business system needs.

At the lower end production work tends to be well defined, high volume and repetitive in nature. It needs high-performance computer systems. This work is well supported by batch and on-line systems. Management have less well defined activities although a number of their monitoring and reporting tasks are recurrent. They tend to be supported by management information systems and more recently by PCs. This level of management has relatively little effective DP support as MIS is generally late and/or inadequate.

At the corporate management level the picture is very bleak with hardly any penetration of DP services. This is perhaps a reflection of the nature of their real work which is highly individualistic and one-off. It needs highly flexible and responsive systems. The two curves on Figure 10.2 split the diagram into three slices. The right-hand slice indicates the extent of existing DP systems coverage: very extensive at the production level to virtually nil for corporate manag ement. All these existing systems need to be maintained and eventually replaced. The central slice shows the scope for new developments. These are made possible by improved price performance of equipment, by new products such as decision-support systems or new technology such as integrated desktop computers, phones, intercoms etc. The greatest scope exists at the middle-management level. The left-hand slice represents those areas of work which are not susceptible to computerization (at present) or which cannot yet be financially justified.

This general statement needs to be made specific to your business. This means the production of a corporate strategy plan with three components:

1. Business plans and priorities which set out the prioritized goals and targets for each aspect of corporate operations. It addresses business questions and options and is not a statement of DP systems needs.

2. IT systems needed to achieve and support the realization of business goals. This considers the "ideal" solutions to business needs, not what systems or problems may currently exist.

3. IT migration plans which compare future needs with current systems and environment and sets out how to achieve a smooth transition from one to the other.

It is only through this approach that a comprehensive, prioritized statement of existing system maintenance and new systems-development needs can be produced. This provides an unambiguous answer to the first two selection-considerations questions raised above about the type of programming language and database management systems that are needed. It may be that more than one product is needed at any one time or that different products will be needed as time passes.

4.2   People considerations

The first question to be answered is who will be using the 4GL to build systems — full time DP professionals, frequent, technically proficient users or occasional, novice users? The answer will come from an analysis of the corporate strategy plan. In general, key corporate-wide systems are likely to be developed by DP staff, specialized department or team systems may well be evolved by proficient users. The novice user would be limited to the production of *ad hoc* enquiries or one-off reports. The man—machine interface discussed above is the critical factor in this equation but other issues such as documentation, training and help facilities will all have an impact on the acceptability of a product.

There are a number of considerations, for example:

- Commitment of staff is very important. It is easy for DP staff to feel threatened by the introduction of 4GLs with their attendant productivity improvements. Staff may be concerned either that they must achieve more work in the same time or that numbers will be cut so that fewer people can do the same work. The reasons for the move to a 4GL need to be clearly spelt out.

- Experienced staff may feel that, with a highly effective 4GL, their technical edge will be lost or that the work will become less interesting.

- Staff organization may need to be reviewed. The previously clearly defined posts of programmer, designer or analyst can become very blurred, necessitating changes to responsibilities and tasking to perhaps only the group of DP staff using a 4GL.

4.3   IT infrastructure

We have already touched on the prototyping-versus-structured-methods debate and seen that whilst they support separate lifecycle activities the two cannot be considered in isolation. You will all be familiar with the graph in Figure 10.3 which shows that most system errors originate from an inadequate definition of user requirements.

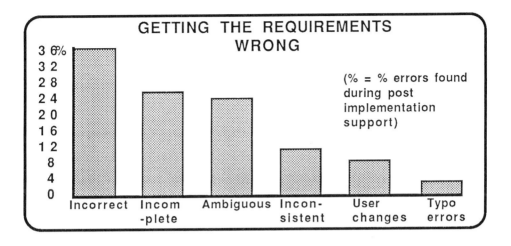

Figure 10.3 Getting the requirements wrong.

4GLs, even using prototyping, do not generally obviate the need for a full and systematic determination of user needs. We still require:

- effective lifecycle management;

- efficient structured methods;

- economic automated aids;

- vigorous quality assurance and audit services.

In fact with the growing demand for systems they become more not less important. These need to operate within a comprehensive software engineering approach which ensures that the principles of control and structure are applied to all aspects of our work. Within this framework it is possible to seek ways of improving performance, shortening timescales and enhancing communication. Prototyping is a valuable aid in this, as is TIDS. Change and compromise is not only possible but desirable.

Use of a 4GL inevitably brings productivity enhancements. This means that DP can respond more quickly to business needs or that more accurate and timely information can be provided to decision-makers. Effective project management and

147

change control are even more important in ensuring that systems are not changed or developed, or reports produced, simply because DP now has the ability so to do. The corporate strategy should remain the arbiter of priorities to ensure that development does not get out of hand.

The operations environment must also be examined to ensure that potential products will work within the current and planned operations environments. The interaction of the 4GL and existing applications must be considered.

Finally there are resource questions, particularly regarding machine utilization and overall systems performance. The means of implementing the system — compiled, semi-compiled, interpretive or table-driven — will have marked effects. Similarly products which are upwardly compatible and allow PC development of mainframe systems could be most attractive.

4.4   Product functionality

The last phase in defining requirements is to review the various technical facilities available and to assess their attractiveness and value. In 4GLSs we have identified 270 separate factors grouped into a number of categories:

- application development;

- data management;

- efficiency;

- interfaces;

- environmental independence;

- utilization management and control;

- user-defined facilities.

A number of other published works have their own lists of features and facilities.

5   PRODUCT SELECTION

In 4GLSs we have evolved an objective and methodical approach to the assessment, comparison and selection of products. It includes the above and a number of other factors such as:

- supplier's pedigree and credibility;

- product base, development plans and stability;

- documentation;

- training and support;

- costs;

- benchmarking and trails.

A number of organizations have evolved their own approaches, similarly based on points, weightings and factors, although a surprising number of these concentrate on the technical functionality of products rather than the key wider issues. However, the actual mechanics of selection are not the central issue. The main principle is to identify the products which most closely match needs and to do this in an objective and supportable way to ensure that the best value for money is obtained.

METHODOLOGY
FOR
FOURTH–GENERATION

Chapter 11
APPLICATION DEVELOPMENT VIA EVOLUTIONARY PROTOTYPING WITH COST AND TIME CONTROLS

Martyn Jeffreys
Jeffreys Systems plc

1   INTRODUCTION

The development of all but the simplest computer program is a complex and high-risk task. Several things can happen:

1. The program takes an inordinately long time to develop, or is grossly inefficient.

2. The program, when delivered, fails to meet its users' (perceived) needs.

3. The users regularly need the program to be changed after it is supposed to be "completed".

This third effect, often quaintly termed maintenance, can account for the major part of the software cost of a program.

For many years 2 and 3 have been seen as failures by computer professionals to discover their users' needs, and 1 as a failure to break the program specification down into small well-specified programming tasks that diligent (or well-managed) craft programmers could implement into efficient code.

No allowance ever seems to be made for the systems-implementation uncertainty principle — that the act of implementing a system changes a user's perception of his needs.

A comparison is often made with engineering (eg civil), where the design and implementation processes are quite separate. The systems analyst (consultant civil engineer or architect) designs the program (building) which the user (client) approves; and then the programmer (bricklayer) codes (builds) it from the specification (drawings). The emergence of the new structured analysis methods, such as SSADM (structured systems analysis and design method), has thrown even more emphasis on the separation of the design and construction processes.

However, in some situations, programmers have for many years started development before the users' requirements were fully appreciated, and with the recognition that development may well continue after the program is being seriously used. Variants of the structured analysis approach have been devised where program "mock-ups" are used to demonstrate more clearly how the program will behave. All these approaches have recently been called prototyping and all are characterized by the production of working programs before it has been finally decided exactly how the finished program is to work. A comprehensive review may be found in Rapid Software Prototyping (see Reference).

In this chapter I describe one such development approach which I and my colleagues have used for many years. It was once called interactive staged enhancement (since that is what it was!) − abbreviated ISE − but it is now more fashionably termed evolutionary prototyping or pseudo prototyping. If one key programmer is involved (and for all but the largest systems this is to be preferred) the attractive term virtuoso prototyping may be used.

Since our variant of evolutionary prototyping, ISE, evolved in a software house environment where there is a distinct danger that clients will ask for their money back if programs are not delivered within cost and time budgets, cost and time controls are crucial to the method.

The core of the method is to produce a first working skeleton of the program as soon as possible. This program is then steadily enhanced with more and more functionality over time, with the user or a representative approving and amending at every step.

2   THE METHOD

2.1   Selecting the team

The biggest weakness of most complex human endeavours — and evolutionary prototyping is no exception — is that highly competent people are needed to ensure success. In the case of ISE two key team leaders are needed. The most important is the user project leader (UPL) who will represent the users as a body and is responsible for monitoring time and cost progress. His commitment to making the project a success, either by ensuring that the user-needs are catered for in the program or that users are persuaded to accept a limited facility, together with regular and diligent examination of the evolving program, is absolutely essential to success.

Ideally the UPL should be an energetic, respected and ambitious member of the user organization who feels that the success of the project will constitute career development.

The other key leader is the analyst programmer (AP). He needs to be skilled in the chosen language (3rd or 4th generation) and chosen hardware environment. He needs to understand how to write highly modular programs and make significant changes during development. He also needs a very good relationship with the UPL and an ability to discuss the program in a relaxed and supportive way with other user personnel whom he will encounter during the project.

Significant commercial projects can be developed with just these two (the UPL and the AP). More typically the AP will be supported by a team of two or three and even the UPL can have one or two assistants.

2.2   The outline systems specification

The first step taken by the UPL and the AP (or often just by the UPL) is to produce an outline systems specification. The use of structured analysis techniques can be used if time and money are available. The purpose of this stage is to ensure that everyone understands what the system is to achieve and how it is to look in broad terms. If a very detailed specification is produced, it must not be allowed to inhibit

152

program changes seen as desirable during development. A detailed specification is just one way of solving the problem.

2.3   Planning the development

If the project contains a number of clearly separable elements, it is conceptually broken into those elements at this stage. For example, a comprehensive system for a manufacturer might consist of modules for:-

- order entry/finished goods stock control;
- financial ledgers;
- raw material purchasing;
- production monitoring.

Each one of these sub-systems might be given to a separate analyst programmer (or team) reporting to the AP project leader. Ideally, if time permits, one person does the lot, serially — it is invariably cheaper this way.

Each module is then broken down by the AP in consultation with the UPL into a series of target "showables" and "deliverables" with dates, on which each key functional entity will be first demonstrated (a showable) and by when it will be considered completed (a deliverable).

For example, an order entry/finished goods stock-control project might be broken down into major modules:

- Order entry completed by ...
- Picking slip and invoice production by ...
- Finished goods entry to stock by ...
- Inter-depot transfers by...

Each one of these modules would be further broken down to small function steps. For example order entry might comprise:

- Customer name and address verification by ...
- Credit checking ...
- Discount application ...

153

And so on. Each larger module would have a deliverable date and every module a showable as well as a deliverable date.

These target dates can then be converted into a budget for programmer time (and hence cost).

2.4   Cost and time budgets

The AP estimates how much time it will take to complete each deliverable. It is an almost impossible task since he knows that during development some things will prove much more difficult — or extensive changes will be demanded by the UPL — and others will be easier than he fears. He takes his pessimistic estimates and adds 30%. (Programmers always underestimate, some workers have suggested adding 75%.)

The UPL takes the AP's estimate and adds a further secret 30%. This is to allow the UPL to commission additional changes. Again others have suggested this figure should be 75%.

Notice that a budget is set for each step by the AP and is known and agreed to by the UPL.

It is agreed between the AP and the UPL that the system will be completed within 70% of the (AP's) target budgets for time and cost! This clearly has implications on the way the AP computes budgets. The remaining 30% will be reserved for final tuning, last-minute changes and close AP support of the live program (and its users) during the first period of live running.

3   THE MODUS OPERANDI

As soon as possible after the budgets have been agreed the AP produces a demonstrable skeleton system. This will typically consist of menu screens plus one or more data-entry screens. These days the skeleton can be produced in hours (or at most days).

Regular progress meetings — at least fortnightly — ensure progress will be demonstrated with working code, and the system will be critically examined by the UPL (and perhaps other users) and improvements or difficulties discussed. It is of course imperative that the program is designed to be changed easily. The examination of cost and time budgets is mandatory at these meetings.

The inevitable changes to the program suggested at these meetings have cost and time implications, and the lot now falls to the programmer to point out that certain changes will increase costs or extend time deadlines.

Some programmers find this the most difficult part of the method, because it runs against the whole ethos as seen by the programmer — satisfying the user. The UPL must balance the value of the enhancements against delay or costs. The great advantage of ISE is that since development can continue after the the system is useable, some desirable enhancements can be delayed until "phase 2" and next year's budget!

The UPL is again the key to the success of the progress meeting. It is the UPL who monitors progress and whether the program is fulfilling user needs. If progress is slow or the AP is finding things too difficult the UPL can detect this (the demonstrations are disappointing) and must report this to DP management before it is too late.

3.1 User involvement

The UPL is a user representative. It is his responsibility to ensure that the "users" ie the people in the organization who will praise or curse the finished system, are more likely to praise than curse. Attendance at progress meeting by other members of the user organization — including some quite junior ones — is often very sensible. It has been our experience that rules for data validation are often better understood by clerks than their manager. A clerical officer who has a hand in designing the data-entry screen, is more likely to defend the system when it goes live than someone who is handed a carefully thought-out screen designed by a genius.

The more the users can feel part of the development and the more they feel significant contributors to its success or failure, the more likely it is that they will make it succeed.

3.2 Live testing

The UPL and AP may agree on test data and perhaps even parallel running, though our experience is that programs fail on real data not test data, and true parallel running is almost impossible. Vast amounts of effort can be spent in tracking down discrepancies only to find that they are due not to a bug but to a failure to achieve true parallelism. A better approach is to have a series of spot checks on key paths through the program, coupled with involving all users in bug hunting. The key thing is that users must expect bugs — always. They must never become complacent.

In the early days of live running, users should feel part of the debugging team and should be praised for finding errors. It must be clearly explained that bugs are a natural — even healthy — part of computer programs. That users should find them, demonstrates the users' intellectual strengths and business efficiency. At all costs avoid the situation where the users are told "the program is now completed". It will only be followed by "Oh no, not another bug — don't those computer people ever get anything right?"

3.3 Disaster planning

A careful consideration of what will happen if a major disaster occurs, must be considered at every stage. Programs — particularly new programs — can corrupt files and render the system unuseable. All possible scenarios must be considered and a fallback position agreed. The user organization must continue to function at all costs. The UPL is responsible for this, fully supported by the AP. All user management must be aware that disasters may occur and of the proposed strategy in each case.

4   THE USER PROJECT LEADER'S ROLE

The UPL has such an important influence in making the project a success that it will be fruitful to set out below a summary of responsibilities. They include:

- Ensuring that the project is on time and to budget. It is made clear that if at any stage the UPL has worries about progress he must escalate his concern within the DP department (or software house). It is of course the responsibility of the DP (or software house) management to make sure the UPL understands this, and to impose their own checks as well.

- Controlling the project by:

    1. Insisting that cost and time budgets are examined at every progress meeting.

    2. Weighting the number of changes made to each aspect, to ensure that the project does not bog down in one area. Further changes will be inevitable, but saying, "Let's settle with what we've got for the moment and improve it next year in phase 2" will ensure that a useable sub-system is completed on time.

    3. Insisting that at every progress meeting, he sees the agreed enhancements from the previous meeting actually working. This is vital. This check on progress must consist of comparing what has been promised with what is working!

- Ensuring that the system will satisfy user needs by:

1. Expressing requests for changes at each progress meeting.

(ii) Encouraging contact between the development team and the ultimate users (especially data-entry staff) — perhaps by inviting them from time to time to progress meetings and involving them in debugging.

(iii) Training other users and "selling" the system in the organization. Getting one key system in and running to the delight of the relevant department is one way of making everyone else clamour jealously to be the next beneficiary of the wonderful software!

157

5   SUBSEQUENT DEVELOPMENTS

Everyone should expect further changes to be requested post-live running. The only system that no one wants to improve is the system no one uses! The users will want to change a good program because:

- They can see ways of making their jobs easier.

- They can see ways of making their jobs more effective.

- The business changes.

- They find irritating restrictions or clumsiness with minor aspects.

- The program is a fundamental part of their job. As their job develops they want the program to develop.

Provided the program has been developed by ISE further changes are just a matter of restarting the development process.

6   THE ADVANTAGES OF ISE

1. There is a higher probability of user acceptance of the finished product.

2. The AP is forced to design programs that are highly modular and hence capable of easy change. This imposes a strict programming discipline and makes for good programmers. The use of 4GLs is clearly a great benefit here, though efficiency may be sacrificed in some 4GLs for the sake of programming ease.

3. Inefficiencies in the program are likely to be discovered during progress meetings and remedial action taken (by writing the code differently) immediately.

4. The AP, forced to make programs work for every progress meeting, is at all times debugging changes just made. The AP not only has an easy time of debugging, but is far less likely to get lost in the programs. (Getting lost in a program is, we believe, a more frequent event than is generally realized. It is one of the causes of inordinate development times and lingering bugs.) The frequent

feedback the AP gets both from the user and from the computer (because the programs are almost always working) is highly motivating.

5. If the AP does get into difficulties, it is very apparent at progress meetings and remedial action can be taken at an early stage.

6. The AP is responsible for all aspects of the program's design and implementation. This can give great professional fulfilment and lead to becoming an even better programmer.

7. Further enhancements to a "finished" program are often no more than restarting the development process. Though programs can become obsolete when the original design or business purpose are inappropriate, the fact that high modularity is forced (or progress meetings become very painful) means that programs have a much longer life. It has been our experience that systems are more often than not rewritten for somewhat dubious reasons; a new fashionable language has become available or technology changes and no one wants to feel left behind. "We really ought to be using Modula 2 under UNIX with the THRUNGE relational paradigm (or what will my c.v. look like?)".

8. The process of program development is cheaper. The structured analysis approach can be very expensive in both time and money. It produces copious documents which describe the system to both the user and the programmer. It is nearly as cheap (it can be cheaper) to get an AP to describe the system in a programming language (3GL or 4GL) and show it to the user by demonstraton. Since each chapter is "read over to the user" as it is written (at each progress meeting) any mistakes are quickly noticed, easy improvements from the user are quickly incorporated and when the "analysis documentation" is completed the system is finished.

9. Cost and time control by the user (the ultimate funder with all techniques) is greatly improved. Since the program progresses by a series of staged enhancements to a working system, not only can the team get a good feel for progress towards the first really useable version, the user can also stop development at an adequate but not perfect subsystem or subsystem aspect. Remember that the program works at each stage. Stopping development leaves working code!

7 DOCUMENTATION

This chapter would be incomplete without a note on documentation. Documentation is thought to be essential because of the complexity of most systems and the apparent impenetrability of most programs (at least at a first glance). Comfort is felt by senior managers and auditors if there are several filing cabinets full of paper in English describing the programs. The structured analysis methods are very good at producing documentation. In ISE, documentation, if produced, must fulfil a specific purpose.

The outline system specification is produced to ensure that everyone agrees in broad terms what the system is to do.

As much user documentation (information to enable users to use the system) is built into the program's text-displaying "HELP" facilities as possible. As much program documentation (information to help the AP or a successor in remembering or discovering how the program works) is built into the code as comments. The best way to confirm whether or not the program documentation is adequate is to get a colleague of the AP to read the program (before the AP gets another job!). If the colleague cannot understand it, it is inadequate!

Certain other documents may need to be produced. For example a system-overview description so that users (and others) can understand how subsystems interrelate and what data is stored. A technical-system overview is also needed, to say where files are stored, where the source is, etc, etc. The responsibility for all this is down to the AP; however the UPL may be the best person to write user manuals if he feels the culture in the organization wants them.

Sometimes a simple introduction to novice users is prepared. Users often feel more comfortable with this. However it must never replace training, and "HELP" facilities should be sufficiently comprehensive that a complete novice could learn all about the system just by using it. Part of the design criteria should be that no user can do significant damage (by, for example, deleting all last year's data), without a clear warning – perhaps two – coupled with a simple and clear back-out procedure. This means that a novice need never feel capable of breaking the computer, and that a vandal would need to be deliberately malicious. We used to tell frightened novice users that if they broke the system it would be our fault and we would be pleased — they would have found a bug or a piece of sloppy code.

All the documentation should be on the machine together with the source. The closer the documentation is to the source, the more likely it is that the AP will keep it up to date.

8   CONCLUSION

Our method of evolutionary prototyping, ISE, outlined in this chapter, was once described by a detractor as "Write a program — any program — then modify it until it's right". We think he was almost correct!

9   REFERENCE

1 *Rapid Software Prototyping*, S. Hekmatpour and D.C. Ince, Mathematics Faculty, Open University, Walton Hall, Milton Keynes, MK7 6AA (1986).

Chapter 12

VALIDATING SOFTWARE SYSTEMS: SPECIAL REFERENCE TO FOURTH-GENERATION SYSTEMS AND DATABASE SYSTEMS

Mark Porter
Brunel University

1 INTRODUCTION

In so far as a 4GS or database system is an instance of a software system, it goes without saying that such a system should be validated. Validation is usually interpreted as a process of verification against a specification, hence this chapter concentrates on specification methods.

The area of specification is now being generally addressed by techniques based on mathematical notation, such as Z [6] and VDM [7]. However, 4G and database systems have certain characteristics which set them apart from other software systems, therefore this chapter focuses on this particular type of software activity.

2 ASPECTS OF SPECIFICATION

The specification of a 4GS must address a number of different aspects of the desired system. The following is not a comprehensive list, but it shows the size of the problem:

- data structures (especially integrity);
- data entry (ie the validation of input data);

- data retrieval (ie display and report formats, query formulation, menu structures, etc);

- data size (with respect to available capacity);

- data access control;

- system performance.

3 AN EXAMPLE

Obviously this chapter cannot adequately address all of the aspects listed above, but the intention is to show that proven methods of specification do exist, and can be used by practioners. To this end, a small example will be used as a vehicle for demonstrating the application of some of these methods.

This example is a variation of one often used in textbooks on database systems, involving suppliers, parts and orders.

- Each order is for one part from one supplier. In addition to the supplier number and the part number, the quoted delivery date is also recorded.

- Each supplier has the name and the address recorded.

- Each part has the description and the price recorded.

4 SPECIFYING DATA STRUCTURES

Although a number of database structures have been used for commercial systems, this paper only deals with the relational structure since the vast majority of 4GSs use this.

The first step is to define the overall data structure. This can be done using the idea of functional dependency, which is described in most database textbooks [3] . Figure 12.1 shows the functional dependency diagram for our example.

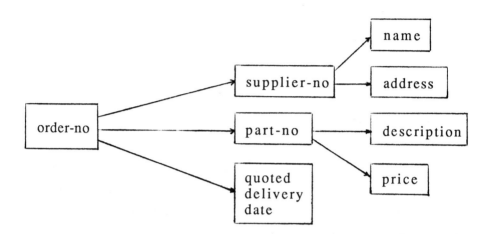

Figure 12.1 Functional diagram for the example.

This diagram can then be used in order to normalize the structure into a number of relations (tables), each relation having a required form. The set of third normal form relations for the example is shown in Figure 12.2.

Each of these relations has a primary (ie unique) key, and each non-key attribute is directly dependent on the primary key. Some systems can be arranged to enforce the uniqueness of the primary-key items, but with others it remains the responsibility of the user to do this.

A bigger problem is that of referential integrity. This addresses the case where one data item refers to another in some way; it is necessary to ensure that this is done in a consistent way.

An instance relating to the example is the desire to delete a supplier. If the supplier in question is referenced in one of the orders, this creates a problem: should the order also be deleted, or should the request to delete the supplier be rejected? A system with referential integrity would allow either option to be automatically enforced, but unfortunately this facility is rare in commercial systems. A number of methods have been devised to deal with the question of referential integrity, notably RM/T [4], [5], ERA [1], and Chen's entity/relationship approach [2].

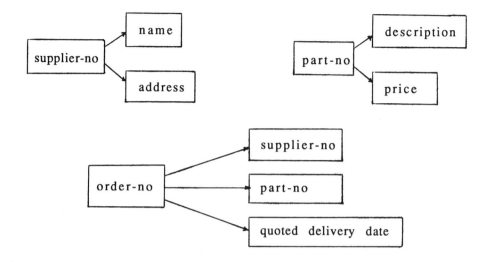

Figure 12.2   Set of third normal form relations for the example.

5   DATA ENTRY

The main area of specification in data entry is that of data validation. This can be split into two main sections: checking each item on its own terms, and checking each item against other items already in the database.

Firstly, consider checking each item on its own terms. One method is set-based: checking whether the item is a member of a defined set. This could be specified using a PDL approach:

> eg   IF colour is-a-member-of {red, green, blue} THEN accept ELSE print "error"
>
> or it could be done using Z, VDM, etc.

For numeric quantities, a valid range of values can be defined:

eg   IF quantity 0 THEN ...

Finally, a valid format can be used. For example, a recent car registration such as A777XYL can be defined as

<letter> <digit> <digit> <digit> <letter> <letter> <letter>

These methods can be combined. For example, a valid date can be defined as

<numeric-1> / <numeric-2> / <numeric-3>

AND

$1 < = $ numeric-1 $ < = 31, 1 < = $ numeric-2 $ < = 12, 1 < = $ numeric-3 $ < = 99$

Secondly, consider validating a data item against existing data. For example, when creating a new order the supplier number must be entered, and logically that supplier must exist. One way to represent this would be:

IF input is-a-member-of {set of supplier numbers} THEN

accept ELSE print "error"

This, of course, relates back to the specification of the integrity of data structures.

6   DATA RETRIEVAL

Firstly we consider query formulation. Is it intended to use a query language such as SQL [3], or to use a forms-based approach? Both of these support different ranges of queries, and it should be clear what the users will be able to do.

A standard query language is in effect self-defining, since there will normally be an existing specification of its capabilities. The forms-based approach is however less standard, and the capabilities should be specified. For example:

- Can queries be combined using AND and OR functions?

- Can overflow boxes be used to enter extended queries?

- Can a query refer to more than one table?

Secondly we consider display and report formats. Again, there are a number of questions to be answered.

- Form-based display: can boxes be in any position, be of different colours, be highlighted?

- Sorting: can tables be sorted on any field? On combinations of fields?

- Report generation: how flexible are titles and headings? Can free-format text be included? Can pie-charts and graphs be generated?

Finally, the specification of menu structures. In addition to defining the structure, the dynamic use of the menus should be made explicit. For example, can direct access be gained to any node of the structure, or are just UP and DOWN modes available?

A diagrammatic representation of a menu structure is particularly useful since it can convey the "feel" of the system quite well. A suitable structure for the example is shown in Figure 12.3.

7   DATA SIZE

A simplistic view of this area is to specify that the data shall fit into the storage system provided. Although this is indeed the essential requirement, it is useful to have a reasonable idea what the data size will be. The final data size will, of course, be dependent on the physical implementation details for the system to be used. However, the designer usually has a feel for this, and can incorporate this into the estimate.

The basic process is now as follows:

- estimate the number of bytes for each key/attribute;

- calculate the aggregate number of bytes for each record;

- multiply this aggregate by the estimated number of records in each table;

- calculate the aggregate number of bytes for the total set of tables;

- allow for system overheads.

The last procedure can be a detailed examination of the various overheads for a known system, through to multiplying by an "overhead factor" for an unknown target system.

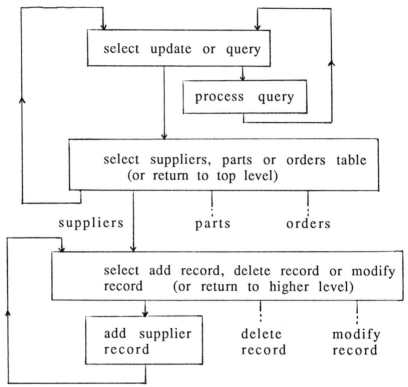

Figure 12.3 Menu structure diagram.

8   ACCESS CONTROL

Typically, this involves the use of user passwords, so that the system can check that the potential user is authorized to use the system. Once a user has gained access to the system, the system can use the user identity to allow (or disallow) particular operations.

User operations are normally modelled as user/process/object definitions, where the elements are defined as follows:

- the user is as identified by the log-on procedure;

- the process is one that acts on a data item: eg add, modify, delete, read;

- the object is a data item: eg field, record, table.

A basic set of these definitions for the example might be:

- all users may read all data items;

- all order-clerk users may add records to the orders table;

- the supervisor user may perform any operation to any table.

In addition to a controlled log-on procedure, it may be appropriate to specify some aspects of physical security. For instance, it may be desirable that end-users do not have access to the computer room.

9   SYSTEM PERFORMANCE

In common with most computer systems, the performance of a 4GS or database system is probably the most difficult aspect to specify, or even to measure. The performance is obviously very dependent on the physical system design and on the characteristics of the computer system hardware. However, the history of systems which are "correct" but just don't run fast enough teaches that specification and validation of performance is essential.

This topic, in particular, can only be touched on in a chapter of this type, but we hope to show that it is amenable to a range of techniques. The example illustrated here will, we hope, demonstrate the enormous range of performance which can be obtained in practice, and show that performance can in fact be modelled reasonably well.

In terms of combinations of a range of operations performed upon a range of data items, there are a huge number of possible operations each with an associated processing time. In practice, however, response times are often categorized as "fast" or "slow". Here, fast usually means less than one second, and slow means longer.

Since a 4GS can easily produce response times greater than ten minutes, we need to have an idea of how long "long" is.

Queries are often categorized as follows:

- Direct query.

- Search mode query.

- Join query.

A direct query, such as "Find the price of part number N" should be very quick to execute, and should certainly happen in less than one second.

A search-mode query, such as "Find all parts with price N" will normally take longer, and a join query, which involves more than one table, will normally take longer still. However, even a direct query can take a long time under adverse conditions.

Consider a system with disc block size of 1024 bytes, and disc block access time of 30ms. If the record size for a certain table is 512 bytes, then a table size of 100,000 records would require 50,000 blocks. The time to scan this table serially would be:

50,000 blocks @ 30ms = 1500 seconds (25 minutes)

Hence a direct query executed by serial scan could take up to 25 minutes.

Fortunately, this query can be answered much more quickly by the use of indexes. A typical index is built as a three-level tree (see Figure 12.4.). For 100,000 records a set of 50 records per node would suffice (50 cubed = 125,000).

If we assume that each index record takes 20 bytes, we have

For each node: 50 records @ 20 bytes = 1000 bytes (say 1 block)

A single record access takes four block reads (three-level index plus data), hence

Execution time = 4 block reads @ 30 ms = 120 ms

So the index method is over 10,000 times faster. This indicates the enormous range of execution times possible depending on the implementation details.

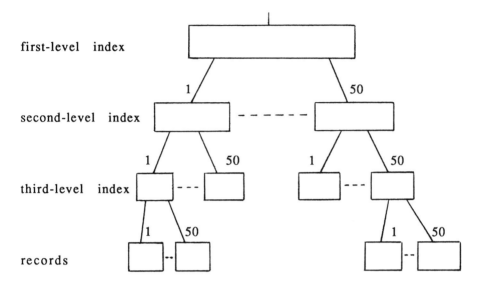

first-level index

second-level index

third-level index

records

Figure 12.4 Three-level tree structure for index.

10 RELEVENCE TO PROTOTYPING AND SYSTEM LIFECYCLE

The advent of the 4GS has brought with it a great interest in prototyping. This is not surprising, as it is now much quicker and easier to produce a prototype system.

However, there is a danger that a strategy of producing a series of prototypes evolving into a "final" system yields a poor system if this policy is not based on sound specification and verification. This problem can be overcome by the use of techniques such as those described in this chapter.

11 CONCLUSION

It may be that in the long-term, mathematically based specification and verification techniques such as Z and VDM become universal in software development, including the 4GS area. However, at present practioners in industry and commerce may find less mathematical methods more appropriate. The methods outlined in this paper should form the basis for the sound development of 4GS and database systems. In fact, the whole hearted adoption of these techniques should speed up the adoption of mathematically based techniques by acting in a transitional role.

12 REFERENCES

1 T.R. Addi. (1985) *Designing knowledge-based systems*, Kogan-Page, London.

2 P.P. Chen (Ed) (1983) *Entity-relationship approach to information modelling and analysis*, North-Holland.

3 C.J. Date (1986) *An introduction to database systems*, Vol. 1 (Fourth Edition) Addison-Wesley.

4 C.J. Date (1983) *An introduction to database systems*, Vol. 2, Addison-Wesley.

5 B.R. Dillistone et al. (1987) "Using databases to automate system development" in Proc. Conf. on Automating System Development, Leicester Polytechnic.

6 I. Hayes (Ed) (1986) *Specification case studies*, Prentice-Hall.

7 C.B. Jones (1986) *Systematic software development using VDM*, Prentice-Hall.

ORGANIZATIONAL IMPACTS

Chapter 13

FOURTH-GENERATION SYSTEMS AND THE ORGANIZATION — PLANNING FOR SUCCESS

Steve Scott
P-E Consulting Services

1   INTRODUCTION

4GSs have advantages such as speed of development and disadvantages such as lack of flexibility. Some organizations and projects manage to gain significantly from them, others fail miserably. What are the key pointers to success? Is the size of the project or the organization of importance? Where do structured methodologies and prototyping fit in? What about the future? This review attempts to answer some of these questions and to relate these tools to a more general information technology context.

There is a significant difference between a system to maintain 30 simple data items for a person and a system with one thousand items, interrelated in complex ways and used for different purposes by a number of people. This difference is reflected in the power of the tools used to create the system as well as the scale of the organization needed to develop and maintain it. The confusing variety of 4GSs simply reflects the fact that people have begun to give up the struggle to make one language cover the full spectrum of requirements. Whether or not this is right I will leave for another occasion. Whatever the reasons, we now have a large number of new-generation languages, application generators that develop run-time code, application generators that develop third-generation source, workbenches that connect into one of the previous three, and workbenches that simply develop dictionary prototypes, all vying for a place alongside more traditional development methods.

2   OBJECTIVES

Before we can look at the way these products can be used succesfully we must first establish what their objectives should be :

- Fast effective development.

- Reduction and ease of maintenance.

- Help with staffing problems.

- Justification development.

It is important that we keep these objectives in mind when looking at which products to use and in setting out the organizational plan aimed at making a success of the purchase.

Throughout the chapter I will be concerned primarily with the needs of larger organizations. Most of the successes with 4GSs have been in smaller businesses and on smaller systems. I hope to point the way to methods aimed at giving the traditional DP manager the benefits of the small organization together with the rigour of the really large. Such people will then be able to reap the benefits the 4GS pundits are promising.

3   PREREQUISITES

It was a wise system developer who said that if you get a system right manually then some form of automation will work successfully. Put another way, a new technique is bound to fail if it is brought in to solve the wrong problem.

To apply this to the computer world we need look no further than the development ethos of a company. If the reason that systems are not developed effectively is that the dialogue with users is unhelpful or that management are not controlling that or any other aspect of the business effectively, then the best of tools cannot solve the problem.

These then are the prerequisites for success :

- User confidence and cooperation. Although this may not be present when you start, it must be worked on at all times. An uneasy exchange of shots over the trenches is not the right basis for a successful development partnership in any circumstances; least of all when a new development tool is coming into play.

- Positive, flexible, structured approach. This phrase sums up the amalgamation of the well-ordered techniques absolutely necessary in the largest of projects and the small-team atmosphere that has been shown time and again to yield the most astounding productivity results.

- Realistic development plan. Neither users nor staff will be properly motivated by a plan that expects either too little or too much. The plan must have both short- and long-term objectives and should yield early and useful results for the users.

- Correct organizational atmosphere. 4GSs tend to require a positive attitude to the promulgation of information because errors are usually not as clear cut. Together with the need within structured techniques for peer review this tends to imply an organization with a carefully controlled mixture of formality and helpful cooperation.

If your organization does not work that way, then you should be heading in that direction before the tools and techniques have arrived. When they do arrive you must use them to enhance the atmosphere even more.

4   STRATEGY

In the section above I have talked of the need to start work before the tools arrive. One of the jobs that needs to be done is to evaluate in a rational way the 4GSs that are right for your purposes: this chapter should help you do that. All I will say on the subject is that you must first be fairly clear what those purposes are and should not enter the evaluation phase with preconceived ideas on the nature of the solution.

Deciding on the nature of your real purpose should be part of a clearly developed strategy, in the building of which you should :

- Plan before. Which is tautological, but expresses the need to avoid trying to work out tactics when the development is already well under way.

- Plan for business benefits. It is very easy to lose sight of the end product that is really required, and both users and managers often need to be reminded that the aim is to develop something that does the job both quickly and at reasonable expense.

- Spread expertise from the start. Organizations where people do not pass on information or where initiative is not recognized and made public, do not fit in well with the 4GS way of development. Methods are not always as straightforward with these products and it is often important to be aware of other people's ingenious solutions.

- Involve users early. Obviously if the 4GS is one for the users to build with, then they will be involved at that point. It is well worth getting them involved at the evaluation stage in such a case. A user-friendly tool that is seen as a getout for the computer section or as a central imposition will not achieve the same success, especially with computer-literate users. Equally if it is a professional 4GS, it will not work if the users insist on doing what cannot be done, and this is best avoided by bringing them in on what you are trying to do and how you plan to go about doing it.

- Remember the old systems. I might also add, remember the people supporting and using them. Virtually all the talk of 4GSs is concerned with their efficacy for new systems development. However, most organizations have a vast investment in existing systems and these cannot be replaced overnight. It is worthwhile deciding whether the 4GS must have some use on the old systems (for enhancement etc), whether a separate one should be used for them or whether simply to get your heads down and redevelop all those systems as fast as possible. Once again the effect of these decisions on users and user confidence should be taken into consideration.

5   WHAT TO PLAN FOR

I said above that you should clarify objectives and plan, but what should you plan for in terms of development?

Over the years many analyses have been done showing where time is spent during the development cycle and most come up with a figure of around 20% to 30% for coding and unit testing. The simplest mathematics will tell you that even a 50% reduction in coding time will therefore only reduce the development effort by 10% to 15%. Many 4GSs when honestly analysed do not offer even 50% savings. This is illustrated in Figures 13.1 and 13.2

What is required is some way of reducing other parts of the process by similar dimensions. There is a place here for some of the newer tools (IPSEs) designed for just that purpose. However, I think that before we rush into automation we ought first to look at the process more carefully to ensure that we are improving what is correct and as fast as possible in the first place. Figure 13.3 shows what we should be aiming at.

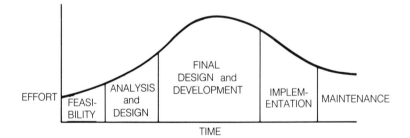

Figure 13.1   Normal development effort through time.

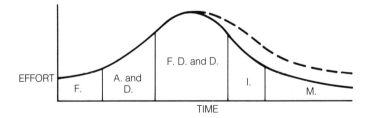

Figure 13.2   With reduced coding effort.

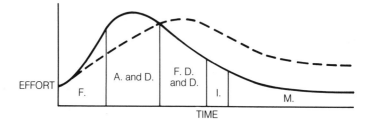

Figure 13.3 Correct development pattern.

Several key points need to be made about this new pattern:

- Research has shown that careful analysis in the initial stages can significantly reduce later effort and ensure better results.

- Well-structured and stylized techniques with good checklists tend to ensure that each stage of the process is reached in an orderly and timely fashion.

- Prototyping can be combined with structured techniques to ensure early analysis is as deep as possible.

- The graph pattern in Figure 13.3 can be achieved without a 4GS, but the actual timescales can be reduced using such a product.

6   THE PLACE OF PROTOTYPING

As mentioned above, prototyping can be used to improve the quality of the analysis work and thus of the end product. Up to now it has been used most frequently and apparently with most effect on smaller systems. However my own experience has shown that even within a structured environment it can be used as a presentation technique when talking to users and that it can:

- Show them what is coming in a way that they can relate to their working practices and requirements.

- Break down their fear, both of terminals and of the tasks the system will require them to do.

- Continue to formalize their view of their own job and of the developing computer system. This formalization process is started by structured techniques and helps them to help you in building for success.

- Make them communicate. Again experience has shown that most users can use a prototype discussion session much better to bounce ideas off and to get through to the analyst what their real needs are.

- Ensure they give time and thought. Most of us have been asked to develop systems without the user dedicating sufficient time to the study work. Prototyping tends to intrigue them more and is about the most effective way of getting them together and discussing things relevant to the matter in hand.

- Tighten your thoughts. As with all presentation techniques prototyping makes you think beforehand about what is being presented and I have found that the extra concentration during the actual event is also very useful for clear thinking.

- Confirm that you can produce. Though this is the last on the list it is often one of the most important aspects of prototyping. However, it is also one that needs handling carefully because too good a prototype can lead them to expect results too quickly. The key point here as elsewhere is the quality of the relationship with the user, which must be nurtured at all times.

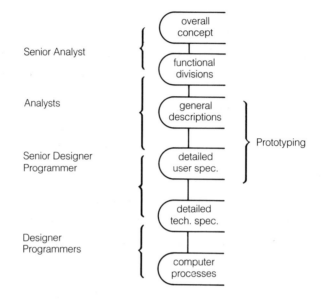

Senior Analyst

Analysts

Senior Designer
Programmer

Designer
Programmers

overall
concept

functional
divisions

general
descriptions

detailed
user spec.

detailed
tech. spec.

computer
processes

Prototyping

Figure 13.4   The place of prototyping.

7   WHO DOES THE PROTOTYPING?

The style, titles and number of people involved on a project obviously depend on the organization and system. The current massive Inland Revenue or DHSS projects cannot be run in quite the same way as a cornershop inventory system. However, in any project the aim of prototyping is to get a better view of the end product as near the beginning as possible. Figure 13.4 also shows some of the levels of analysis involved in a typical development and the point at which I think it is most appropriate to start prototyping.

In such an analysis of the development task I have acknowledged the real need to do some elementary design work all through the project and this is where prototyping can prove useful.

Because programmers are being called in earlier, before many of the more detailed procedural problems have been resolved they must do the following:

- Translate business terms to machine. These people will now have to take a specification talked through with users and convert it direct to code. If well controlled this can mean the elimination of an entire process of design — the program specification, and can thus create further savings.

- Design screen dialogues and report structures. Programmers are thus being brought in at a level of decision that is often denied them in traditional organizations.

- Evaluate detailed security and recovery. These matters are under emphasized in most organizations. However, if attended to they should be set as policies at the senior level and dealt with in detail by the programmers.

- Talk to users. All the above tasks will necessitate discussions with users and where possible this should be done directly. This is good for the enhancement of employee skills.

Given this range of new tasks for the coders, I have chosen to call them Designer/Programmers.

The training for such people will tend to be different as it may be shallower on specific technical aspects but on a wider front covering many traditional analyst and designer skills. To be most effective higher-calibre individuals are also called for, but this is probably the situation even in traditional developments.

8   TESTING TECHNIQUES

Most 4GSs are at least successful enough to ensure that testing is reached more quickly; thus the importance of this aspect becomes more apparent. In addition more responsibility has been given to the new designer programmers and thus system testing must receive even higher emphasis because it must now be used to check their design decisions as well as the accuracy of the code.

While testing becomes more important a 4GS has an ironic tendency to encourage lack of care because of the simple fact that code tends to fall over less easily. I do not think that our techniques or the technology are quite ready to bring in the rigorous testing techniques of systems engineering. At present commercial DP systems are still really beyond the scope of the quasi-mathematical methods of that discipline. What is needed is a step in that direction:

- Test by checklist. Standard lists can be drawn up reminding us of such things as background text on screens. In addition basic checklists encourage us to add our own and thus plan testing more effectively.

- Lay more emphasis on the system test. It is nearly always beneficial to talk through plans with someone else.

- Ensure that part of the documentation is a test guide rather than a completely unuseable set of ancient test data.

- Split the work into two phases, the first to ensure that basic screen traversals work and the second to refine both detail validation and the elegance of the code itself.

- Minimize database changes. In most larger computer systems such changes usually have ramifications beyond the immediate unit and if not controlled can cause problems. Emphasis should therefore be given to early design work aimed at getting the database design right and ensuring that changes are thus foreseen where possible.

Overall the emphasis should be on controlled and well thought out testing.

9 PROJECT CONTROL

In anything but the smallest sytems, project control is of great importance and in the largest projects involves great skill and many dedicated specialist staff. The main techniques used are drawing up a network of neccessary jobs and identifying milestones, usually associated with points in the critical path. Unfortunately many installations do not do this or do so in such a crude way that prototyping and different methodologies cannot be dealt with.

My personal opinion is that having to look again at the methods used is a useful exercise that should be undertaken more often. In general the milestones that are set up should be of the sort :

> "develop receipting function prototype" or
> "reach agreement on archive definition"

rather than the more typical :

> "sign off statement of requirements".

At each point the overall timescales can be reviewed and a decision to proceed taken or a changed strategy adopted as necessary. This does not mean that there cannot possibly be a point at which the user agrees to proceed. What we are recognizing here is the fact that within each major checkpoint there are a number of minor ones and that good control lies in the careful management of the iterations within those checkpoints. As in all other processes , an honest helpful relationship with the user will ease this process.

Specifically when dealing with prototyping you should define the minimum state to be reached within a given period and keep track of the iterations necessary to achieve that state. When monitoring progress it is then possible to gauge it against the objective and propose alternative actions should any be required.

In summary then on project management I would like to express it in the following terms:

- Define your objectives carefully.

- Monitor and ensure those objectives are met.

- Watch out for and highlight potential changes to objectives and requirements.

- Control the application of change very carefully.

10   CONCLUSION

During the course of this paper I have been concerned to raise a variety of do's and don'ts concerning the way you should organize yourselves for a 4GS. I would be very concerned if anybody should take the need for these changes as a reason for not using a 4GS. The message I want to pass on is that great success can be achieved with these products if they are used well and in the right context.

What is important in setting yourself up for results is to adopt a positive and flexible approach. It is also important not to be myopic about the kind of objectives to be met. This lack of myopia must be passed on in one way or other to the clients you deal with.

To return to the objectives mentioned at the beginning:

- Fast effective development can certainly be achieved by the combination of a 4GS with good methods.

- Maintenance will be both eased and reduced on systems developed in this way. Further, many 4GSs can have a useful role in maintenance of old systems for report production and add-on amendments.

- Staffing problems can be eased by attracting people to newer technologies and giving them more interesting work to do. Fewer staff can also do the same work, but this is normally offset by a rise in requirements.

- If you follow these guidelines and exercise care in selection you will almost certainly also have justified the investment made.

As the final statement of this chapter can I reaffirm my belief in 4GSs by stating the following business benefits to be gained :

- More chance of completing a viable solution.

- More comprehensive systems from the start.

- Because less is left out maintenance is lessened.

- And because the products are easier to use, maintenance is also easier.

To paraphrase some famous words : "go forth and develop".

Chapter 14
ORGANIZATIONAL IMPLICATIONS CAUSED BY THE FOURTH-GENERATION ENVIRONMENT

Simon Holloway
DCE Information Management Consultancy Limited

1   INTRODUCTION

Every person involved in the system development lifecycle will be affected by the increasing level of automation and support. Some traditional DP roles will be radically altered, while some will become obsolete. With the adoption of automated methods, the concentration of human effort will be in the planning, analysis and design stages. New skills will need to be acquired by the programmers of today if they are to adapt to the changing environment. Although the development of an organization's major data and processing architectures may still involve large teams, much of the subsequent application systems development will be achieved by small teams or by individuals.

At the end of 1985, two of the UK's leading independent consultants looked at what were the possible areas of impact of 4G tools on an organization.

David Gradwell [1] felt that there were three major areas of impact on organizational requirements due to new application development tools, be they 4GSs or CASE tools or whatever. The organizational structure would need to evolve to meet these new needs. He stated that the three were as follows:

- The distinction between programmers and analysts will weaken and then disappear.

- The importance of strategic analysis is increased. Data administration will become essential. Cross-project planning and cross-user department planning will become essential.

- End-users will need support in their use of decision support software. This will further emphasize the need for a data administration function.

Roger Tagg [2] delineated three areas of change needed for an organization successfully to use 4GSs:

- The demarcation lines between programmers and analysts become less valid.

- The position of DP within the organization will change, with the necessary change in the sort of person who is manager of the area — more a business manager.

- The involvement of end-users in actually developing solutions to their own problems.

As can be seen, they agreed on only two aspects, namely the distinction between programmers and analysts, and the involvement of end-users. Since that time, the Institute of Data Processing Management have issued a report [3] suggesting that organizations who have purchased 4G tools have not been as successful as they expected. It is perhaps unfortunate that no real reasons for this situation were discussed in the report. My own feelings are that this situation is due to two main factors:

- Firstly, the size of the sample involved in the survey was not representative of all the products.

- Secondly, and of far greater importance, the organizations had not thought about changing their methodology for developing systems, the new software and its associated new techniques, as well as catering for the new problems that the software causes.

In this chapter, I shall put forward my ideas for changes to the organization that need to be considered to take full advantage of 4G tools and to prepare for the coming 5G products. The areas I shall cover are as follows :

- Application developers.

- Data administration.

- Database administration.

- Project management.

- Security administration.

- End-user involvement.

2 APPLICATION DEVELOPERS – NOT ANALYST OR PROGRAMMER

4G products have been designed to shield developers from some of the major time-consuming environmental elements they have had to deal with in the past, such as operation system, JCL, TP monitor etc. This liberates time which the developer can use in concentrating upon the organization – the actual business problem being addressed – and improves communication between DP and users. Figure 14.1 illustrates this point.

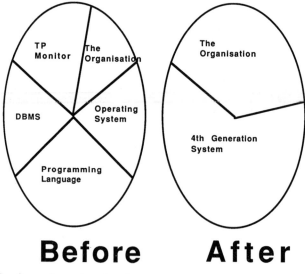

Figure 14.1   4G software impact on developers.

4G products also enable developers and end-users to develop applications much faster than with conventional languages. The developer can often create programs that have a tenth of the number of instructions that COBOL would require, and in a tenth of the time. The end-user is helped by 4GLs by being able to specify what he or she wants the computer to do, and not how to do it. This has led to a new problem, that of the overworked analyst.

David Gradwell at VLDB in Brighton [4] felt that 4G products in the main did help in the following areas :

- Productivity gains in program coding and testing.

- Reduction in the need to understand TP monitors and database management systems.

- Easier end-user access to data.

On the other hand, he saw that 4G tools had led to overloaded development machines as well as giving no real support to the analysis phase of the development of a system. In addition the majority of 4G products had two major failings :

- No support for word processing and text management

- Little or no version control

He went on to talk about the arrival of CASE tools, and stated his belief that there was a collision between these two sets of products. It is my belief that we need both sets of tools to be able fully to develop and maintain applications. The current way in which certain CASE tools have reverted to generate COBOL, and their rigidity in making changes, I feel, is a backward step. When working for Applied Data Research, in 1987, I found they held that you needed both sets of tools to co-exist, not only for ease of maintenance, but also to evolve rather than revolutionize application development.

Analyst's workbench ADTs

Figure 14.2 4G products – CASE tools clash?

As far as system development careers are concerned, the demand for DP expertise will continue. End-users will not want to manage large-scale "production" applications themselves, and information centres will not be used for this purpose. However, there will be a trend for DP professionals to specialize in a certain industry. The background of an individual in banking, insurance or manufacturing will become more and more important as compared to experience with this or that operating system or programming language. Also, personal communication skills will become a major factor in job placement and advancement. The DP community must learn to speak the language of the user, not expect the user to learn DP jargon. Again, 4GLs have the goal of expressing a program in business terms rather than DP terms. Using a common language will improve communication skills, and we will see the ascendancy of information centre specialists. These are individuals with high communication skills who are well trained in the usage of information center products. They serve as a resource to assist end-users in developing their own applications in the information centre.

In a combination of CASE and 4G tools, DP will have a two-edged sword that will speed the phases of an application lifecycle. At the same time, they will radically effect the working practice, not only of developers and analysts, but also the end-user, who must contribute more to the analysis and design process.

3   PROJECT MANAGEMENT

Without a project manager, bad systems are implemented late and over budget. Sometimes there is no doubt that this happens with a project manager, but the single most overriding characteristic of a project manager is that he or she achieves goals, reaches targets and delivers on time. Expected to manage technology, people and the change process, the project manager can face the following potential difficulties even before the development process for a new system has begun:

- dissatisfaction of users with previously developed computer-based systems;

- project management methods and organization structures inappropriate for new systems development;

- inadequately skilled systems development staff;

- poorly developed systems planning mechanisms.

The project manager will need to be technically competent so as to choose the technical computing strategies most appropriate for the application development. He or she will need to be an effective planner, a good controller of a team and sensitive to the problems of implementing change. He or she will need to be a good manager and capable of training members to discharge their duties efficiently. Part of the success will depend on the organizational relationships between the manager and the rest of the organization. It is important for the project manager to establish a firm base in the organizational hierarchy and, in particular, to be sure of an own upward reporting mechanism.

The role of the project manager can be divided into five components, as shown in Figure 14.3. It is likely that the project manager will need to review and constantly modify the business justification for the project.

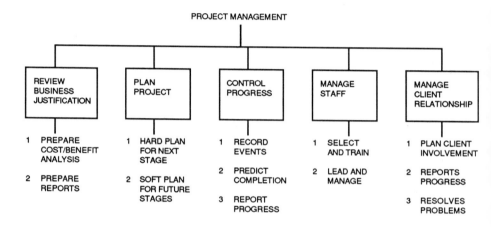

Figure 14.3 Five components of project management.

During the project development cycle, there is a constant need for everyone in the team to reinforce the benefits of the work being done. Short- and long-term plans will need to be prepared in detail, justified and costed out; and the preparation of hard plans for the next stage and soft plans for future stages will be an important part of the project manager's job. This is because there are always deviations from the plan which, when identified, will cause re-planning to be done. Controlling progress means monitoring the work of others and hence there is a need to manage staff. The project manager is also responsible for managing the relationships between the team and the client. This means many things:

192

- influencing the attitudes of the client staff;

- controlling and motivating team members to present a positive and helpful attitude towards the client;

- selling new ideas;

- reporting progress.

In a modern 4G environment, the notion of creating or establishing an application system and application programs is an activity distinct from writing the application program. While in some organizations the same person might do both tasks, in other organizations the task of establishing applications and their assigned resources may be accomplished by an "application administrator", who may be a project leader, data administrator, chief programmer or developer. This person determines the specific application programs which are going to be built and assigns the specific dataviews, panels, reports and other programs. This role is distinct from writing the application program.

4   ORGANIZATIONAL IMPLICATIONS OF DATA ADMINISTRATION

The positions of the data administrator and the database administrator are relatively new to DP environments. Traditionally, their functions and responsibilities are handled by various people participating in individual projects or departments within the DP environment. However, the database environment makes it necessary to centralize control and management under one administrative group.

Data administration, according to the British Computer Society Data Administration Working Party (DAWP) [5], will primarily have a co-ordinating role, and will otherwise play a controlling role, related to the use of data. A more active role than this should only by adopted when necessary to advise, train, or co-ordinate to achieve specific longer-term goals. There are areas where guidelines need to be drawn. Outside these areas, data administration will rarely have authority or responsibility, but as a general rule, inside them data administration will be involved at a level that reflects existing or potential data-related problems. Data administration is not responsible for actual values of the data of the organization, but will be concerned with the meaning of the data. A definition derived by DAWP [6] for data administration is as follows :

> Data Administration is the corporate service which assists the provision of information systems by controlling and/or co-ordinating the definitions [format and characteristics] and the usage of reliable and relevant data. Data that is internal to an organization can be controlled, whilst data from external sources [eg tax rates, independent marketing surveys] that is used by an organization can only be co-ordinated.

Data administration is primarily concerned with problems that cross company organizational boundaries. It follows that the relationship between data administration and the organizational structure is the crux of data administration.

Data administration is as concerned with the way the company is organized as it it with data — someone with a mathematical bent might define data administration as the intersection of data and the organizational structure.

In order to have successful data administration — that is to have good data — a company must be prepared to pay the price. This price is not so much in terms of money and resources, but in terms of organizational willingness to adapt, co-operate and spend time and effort helping to set up and carry out successful data administration. There are companies where the different parts and functions are not prepared to co-operate with each other, where any issue crossing organizational boundaries is seized on purely as an opportunity for political in-fighting. There is virtually no chance of making data administration work in such companies. Attempts to set up data administration will fail, and can be of value solely in showing up this intrinsic weakness within the company.

The scope of the data administration function must be as wide as is needed by a particular organization, in order to achieve the aims of cost-effective use of the organization's data. A data administration function will always perform a service role, and will be involved in the identification and solution of the data aspects of the problems of the organization. Data administration does not directly control data, except data about the data of the organization and data about its own function.

4.1 Responsibilities of data administration

There are a number of areas in which the data administrator should have responsibilities. These break down into roughly 14 major task areas :

- Data administration policy — the establishment of the principles of data management which in their turn determine the responsibilities of data administration.

- Identification of corporate information requirements — the determination and the obtaining of acceptance of the policies for the identification of corporate requirements.

- Generating a corporate awareness of data — educating the company about the importance of data. An awareness of the value of data as a company asset has to be created. In addition, the knowledge of what data exist and for what purpose the data are used must be communicated.

- Data analysis — the selection of the data analysis methods in conjunction with the development of procedures for its use. Assistance with the production of business data models and the monitoring of the consistency of the results.

- Data definition — the establishment of standards for the definition of data and the medium for the recording and communication of the definitions.

- Data dictionary control — the establishment of the requirements for procedures for data dictionary control.

- Problems related to data.

- Physical data models — in that database administration [5], provides technical support for data administration: performing database design and development, being responsible for organizing and defining the logical view of data, providing education on database technology, and providing support to users in operational database-related activities.

- Impact assessment — assessing the impact of data changes.

- Data access — the design and acceptance of access authorization rules for an organization. The arbitration of disputes that arise from requests for access to data.

- Privacy, security and integrity — the implementation and the ensuring of compliance within the company of aspects of the Data Protection Act. The establishment of the strategy for specifying the requirements for privacy of data. The determination of the strategy ensures that the requirements for data integrity, data security and privacy are addressed during physical systems design.

- Data duplication — the promotion of a policy for a single source of data and the encouraging of the sharing of data across applications.

- Data achieving — the establishment of a strategy for achieving data.

- Monitoring usage of data — monitoring live running to ensure that the strategies for data integrity, data security and privacy are being followed. Monitoring the use and the content of the data dictionary to ensure compliance with the established rules.

The responsibilities of the data administrator will vary from company to company. The responsibilities will vary both in areas covered and the degree of responsibilities involved. Thus the data administrator may control, manage, advise, audit, plan, set standards — or any combination. It would be wrong and dangerous to try to specify a set of exact responsibilities that will suit all companies. The right set of responsibilities for the individual company will depend on the particular nature, business and history of the company. There are however, certain factors that will strongly affect the responsibilities of the data administrator :

- homogeneity or complexity of company structure;

- company policy on centralization and decentralization;

- use of database management system;

- system inconsistencies;

- data-protection legislation;

- corporate business plan.

5   THE CHANGING ROLE OF THE DATABASE ADMINISTRATOR

The database administrator is primarily responsible for the technical implementation of the database environment, the day-to-day operations of the database, and the policies governing its everyday use. The database administrator's responsibilities include :

- Establishing technical standards and guidelines : making sure that all the data are defined, organized and represented in such a way that multiple uses and applications are allowed, and that end-users, programmers, and analysts have specific, standard guidelines by which data may be input, updated or accessed.

- Supporting policies and conventions of management : making sure that the users maintain the policies and conventions determined by management, including the data administrator, governing the use and evolution of the database.

- Reviewing application system candidates : determining whether to conform to the design requirements of the database or whether they need to be modified before they are converted to the database system.

- Database design : analysing the needs of the users on a priority basis and employing the most cost-effective techniques for the design for the database to ensure that the immediate and future requirements of the users are met effectively.

- Control of the database environment : continuing monitoring and control of the database environment after the system is in full operation, including data dictionary maintenance, system additions or extensions, and documentation.

- Technical implementation of data integrity requirements : implementing the necessary data locks and restriction, conducting periodic security audits, supervising the authorization of access to specific data, and investigating all known security breaches to protect the integrity of the data in the database.

- Training for the database environment : holding responsibility for the education and training of the users in the principles and policies of database use — which includes making current documentation available to the users.

The database administrator is a clearing house, a central agency for the collection, classification, and distribution of the information and skills necessary to the success and maximum benefit of the database system.

The database administrator's primary functions lie in the areas of design, control, and evolution.

5.1 Design

The database administrator designs the database to reflect the immediate needs of the users and accommodate their future needs. Some of the general responsibilities of the database administrator in the design of the database include the definition of the access to the database (including the logical and physical reference paths and methods), and the allocation of physical storage in the database(s). The database design should not only reflect the users' needs at the time of the design, it should also provide the means for incremental growth throughout its lifecycle to meet the future needs of the users. Therefore, the design effort is extremely important to the overall success of the database system.

There are two major impacts on the way in which this role has to evolve, namely 4G tools and CASE tools. With the former, there is need to be able to adapt current physical design techniques to work with prototyping systems. To gain the maximum benefits, the underlying database management systems must, I believe, be relational, so as to take advantage of flexibility and of ease of use. Both Applied Data Research [7] and Cincom [8] have done something in this area of prototyping. The second impact from 4GSs on design is the ability to exploit tuning possibilities effectively.

This normally seems possible only within a fully integrated environment, ie the database management system and 4G product are supplied by the same supplier. In the case of CASE tools, as they progress further down the line of first generation of physical model from conceptual model, the black art of design for a particular database management system disappears. This is the area where expert systems are really starting to get a hold, for the vast majority of design techniques can be implemented a sets of rules. The role of the database administrator will therefore lessen in this area of design.

5.2   Control

After the database system is in full operation, the Database Administrator initiates control techniques to ensure the consistent and effective performance of the system.

Through testing and acceptance procedures, the database administrator is satisfied that the design of the database is fulfilling the immediate requirements of the system, and that it is evolving properly to conform to the future requirements of the system. By monitoring the inputs and outputs of data through edit and validation rules, data checking, and access controls, the database administrator identifies any inconsistencies in data integrity.

The database administrator also reviews all existing application systems for their consistency with the data definition and usage standards, so the systems can be effectively converted to the database environment without major revisions. The database administrator makes sure that the development of new application systems effectively meet the users' requirements as well. The database administrator monitors the use of the database through access statistics and request/response statistics to assure the maximum efficiency of the system.

In this area, once again database management system suppliers are working to automate the tuning process, through the use of expert system technology.

5.3   Evolution

The database administrator determines the specifications and design of the extensions, services, and utilities for the database environment. They also document the evolution of the environment via the data dictionary. The database administrator maintains the system development lifecycle and the procedures for security, privacy, integrity, and recovery. This helps to ensure that the system remains effective in meeting both the current and future needs of the users.

This role is still needed. It is very difficult to envisage there being no human involvement in the sort of tasks described.

6   SECURITY ADMINISTRATION

The issues of privacy, security and integrity within the database environment are important in database design, performance and maintenance. Privacy, security and integrity are all closely related concepts, but, in fact, the differences among the three are substantial. The specific definition of each of the concepts is as follows:

Privacy	the right of individuals or institutions to control the collection and dissemination of personal information.
Security	the protection of the computer resources from accidental or intentional destruction, modification, or disclosure.
Integrity	the correctness, accuracy, and timeliness of data within a certain level of appropriateness.

The data administrator and the database administrator are responsible for the privacy, security, and integrity within the database environment including all data and processing. Security of the database includes the protection of data from deliberate or inadvertent disclosure, modification or destruction. System integrity is the consistency, completeness, adherence to specifications, freedom from intrusion, and predictability of a system.

6.1   Computer security issues

One might ask at this point, "Why do we need security ?" The answer is not a simple one. One of the primary reasons is the growing realization that data are assets of a company. Because computer professionals have done such a good job of establishing computer resources in the business environment, many businesses today would not survive beyond a week to ten days if they could not process their data. For example, imagine how long a bank or department store would stay in business without its computerized data or the ability to process it.

Many years ago when DP was a purely "batch" process, security and control were implemented through external, physical measures. The exposure was low because much of a company's vital information was not stored on the computer. As DP has matured, almost all of a company's data have moved to the computer. Storage of all records on computers means that highly sensitive information about company planning strategies or personnel is now stored electronically rather than in someone's locked filing cabinet.

As we make advances in computing technology, the exposures associated with potential loss of integrity in our computing environment also increase. The development of large shared databases, increased ability to access data on-line, and the proliferation of remote terminals are no longer restricted to computing professionals. For instance, consider the growth of automated teller machines, point-of-sale terminals, grocery checkout scanners and the increased use of electronic transfer of funds, all of which have directly affected the general public.

Of course, this increased impact of computers on the general public has also enhanced awareness of security issues. The public is rapidly becoming aware that the data are now owned by the bank or the credit service bureau, but that the data are really theirs. So the need for accuracy and integrity of data is coming closer to home for the general public. Anyone who has ever had a personal loan request refused because of information supplied by one of the many credit agencies has certainly felt the impact of the need for data accuracy.

Another item of increased public awareness is the publication from time to time of incidents of the use of computers to perpetrate fraud or embezzle money. While only the largest cases received widespread notoriety, each insurance funding scandal or misappropriation of funds through the misuse of computers plants yet another seed of doubt in the mind of the public.

The last and perhaps most important incentive for the establishment of computing security is the increased interest by legislative bodies in accounting controls and individual privacy. Legislation is now in force in the following countries: USA, France, West Germany, Sweden, Canada, and the UK.

6.2 What to secure?

We have to ask ourselves what we should be protecting :

- Is it the data?

- Is it access to the data ?

- Is it access to the physical storage devices on which the data are stored?

- Or is it some combination of the above ?

To answer this question we must look at the objectives of security administration, which are as follows :

- To implement the security policy of your organization, using the security facilities that are available and cost effective.

- To maintain the security details appertaining to your organization.

Therefore security in my view, should be based on data and data content, and not on storage device and terminal access. What sort of facilities have you available in your 4G environment? Beside OEM access-control packages, such as RACF and ACF II, certain 4GE products have facilities built in to protect data and access to it. This is normally implemented by the use of facilities in the underlying dictionary and/or database management system.

7   END-USER INVOLVEMENT AND SUPPORT

The watchword of the 1980s and the 1990s is user involvement. The end-user will be involved in every aspect of DP, including design, development and testing. Singer [9] states that the demand for this involvement has come from factors which operated in the late 1960s and the 1970s :

- A strong feeling that DP technology was so complicated that accountants, managers, etc. could not possibly understand it. As a result, organizations consistently found that computer systems did not meet the basic needs of the users.

- The rising cost of complicated systems was another factor. The time taken to develop systems is longer, and in addition requires more people to work on it. The hardware cost per CPU cycle may have dropped, but the cost in development time has risen dramatically.

- The consideration of purchased software packages as being a valid alternative to in-house development is a third factor. The selection of a good package requires experts not only from DP but also from the end-user groups.

- The growing awareness of end-users that the data they need to perform their jobs can be obtained from the computer.

If the trend towards direct user involvement is to be successful, DP managers should take the lead in developing a planned, realistic approach to working with end-users. Too often a combined team of DP personnel and end-users will sit round a table with all the co-operation of two nine-year-old boys fighting over a cricket bat! In the 1980s and 1990s, such unbusinesslike behaviour cannot be tolerated. The stakes of economical survival and profitability are now too high to allow individuals or groups to play ego games inside an organization. DP managers are in perfect position to break the cycle of disagreement and mistrust which seems to developed whenever their staff and the end-users get together. Several very simple steps have been suggested by Singer [9] to help ensure that such a team approach can be achieved :

- Non-technical users must be educated in basic DP concepts, such as disk versus tape operations, database as opposed to conventional files, and in-house development versus purchased packages. The nature of the educational process will depend on the situation and circumstances of the organization and the specific project.

- Verify that all DP staff involved in a design project with users have a basic understanding of the application in question. Just as many DP managers are surprised by the breakdown of basic computer knowledge of users, user management are equally surprised at the lack of communication caused by DP staff who have absolutely no idea what users are talking about.

- Once both DP and users have been cross-trained to some degree, DP managers can then take the lead by planning the entire task around a formalized project management approach. The degree of formalization will depend on the length, the complexity, and the importance of the task or project in question.

Besides user involvement in the development of their own systems, there is another significant trend in recent years, namely the information centre. The function of an information centre is to encourage, train, and support end-users to develop applications themselves. With help, end-users can generate a wide variety of applications including data query, data input and editing, report generation, decision-support systems, and many classes of application programs. The traditional DP systems lifecycle is thus bypassed, which gives users results much faster, but at a cost of their own time. In theory, developers are then free to concentrate on systems without having to shift priorities to accommodate an end-user's *ad hoc* requests.

Information centres utilize a wide variety of languages and tools, usually including general-purpose tools such as query languages, report generators, graphic generators, decision-support systems, and application generators. Additional specialized tools may also be used for financial planning, statistical analysis, project management, text processing, desk-top publishing, and computer-aided design. It is important to note in regard to this area that although the software tools get most of the spotlight, they still need to operate upon data. The data must be stored and managed somehow, usually by limits upon what end-users can and cannot do with those friendly software tools. Two distinct schools of thought on this subject have evolved, namely the "truth database approach" and the "dual database approach". The dual database approach mandates that redundancy between operational systems and decision-support systems is a valid approach. Examples of database management systems that support this are IBM's DB2 and IMS, FOCUS, and ICL's IDMS with INGRES. The truth database approach dictates that there will be one and only one copy of the database for all users. Examples of database management systems that support this approach are CA's DATACOM/DB, Cincom's TIS/XA and Cullinet's IDMS/R.

The Information centre has not only had to tackle this software problem of which approach to adopt, but also has fallen into the mistake of "empire building" in a number of instances. The information centre should provide assistance to the end-users to develop their own solution and not do the work itself. The one main exception to this rule would be in the case of board-level management. Here the best way was described by David Owen of ICL Asia Pacific PTY at MNCC'85 [10]. Each senior executive had a computer expert as an assistant. This person provided the technical knowledge and wisdom to be able to extract the required information using the best possible software tool in the quickest possible manner. In the paper he described how these consultants were used to help the executives put together the organization's yearly plan: whereas it used to take some three months to do this, it was now possible to do it in three weeks. Here we have a fine example of effective and efficient service to the end-users.

Perhaps the greatest danger of information centre operation, or of the spread of small computers and user-friendly software, is that multiple, uncoordinated data structures will be used. The answer to this is well-controlled data administration.

8   CONCLUSIONS

If we are to use 4G tools effectively, we must be prepared to see our organization structures evolve. The role of DP is changing rapidly and the needs of our end-users are changing even more and even faster. With the realization amongst senior user management that to survive in business in the 1980s and the 1990s, they will need to be able to tap the information resource more effectively and to control it, we in DP have to be able to respond quickly and effectively. This is not possible with :

- the use of 3GLs ;

- the use of 3G methodologies, such as SSADM and information engineering in their current form ;

- the rigidity of the current DP organization, as shown in Figure 14.4;

- the demarcation line and in-fighting between end-users and DP.

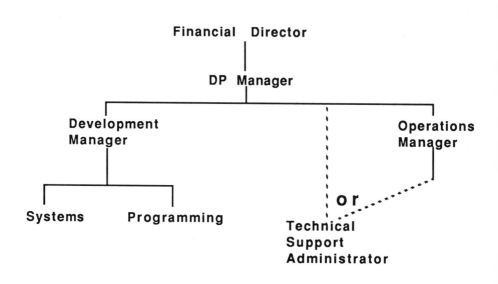

Figure 14.4 Traditional DP department structure.

How can we tackle this? What is it we must do?

4GLs in themselves are not the answer. A new language will only help in the coding and testing phases of an application's lifecycle. We need to be able to assist the analysis and design phases much more to produce the goods for our end-users. The adoption of prototyping techniques, has certainly, when done in a controlled way, proved to be of assistance in the design phase. The CCTA have already started to adapt SSADM to use prototyping and to work more effectively with certain 4G tools [11]. LBMS and CACI have also started to adapt their methodologies to use prototyping.

The currently available methodologies are very paper oriented. David Gradwell [4] has spoken of them building not only paper mountains but paper mountain ranges!

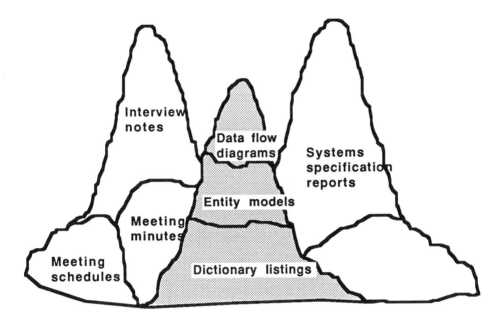

Figure 14.5 Paper mountain ranges.

It is here that CASE tools will assist with the automation of documentation and graphics. They will also provide the means of tackling the "analyst overload". We must be prepared to adopt a methodology that suits our organization, as well as being able to work with our current software and hardware. To take advantage of 4G technology the methodology we choose must support not only prototyping but also structured analysis and design. The methodology must be flexible, so that new techniques can replace old ones without a complete reworking of the methodology. This is only possible if the methodology is based on a framework approach, as advocated by the British Computer Society Database Specialist Group's Information Systems Analysis and Design (ISAD) working party in their *Journal of Development* [12].

DP structure must evolve to take account of the changes in demand upon its services, and the changes in technology. Too often I have seen as a consultant organizations, whose structure is based upon technology of the late Sixties, with the power base in the wrong hands. In addition DP managers are themselves to blame for their lack of knowledge of new software and techniques. They have to spend time on keeping abreast of our changing work. We must understand the importance of data as a resource to our organizations, and give power within DP, if not within the organization, to the administration of this resource. I have in a forthcoming book looked at ways that data administration can evolve in an organization to get to the right level [13]. But it is not just data administration that is important. Development of systems has changed dramatically, thanks in the main to 4G technology and to adoption of methodologies. The use of teams of coders, designers, analysts and end-users has proved effective when all the right planning has been done up front.

What sort of organization should we be aiming for then? In Figure 14.6, I show what I believe should be our goal.

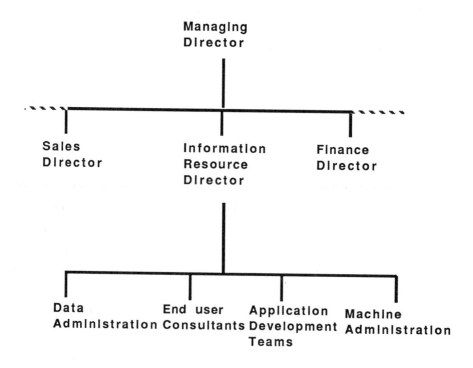

Figure 14.6   DP – the future structure?

The probable outcome of the latest 5G work will be to strengthen communications between users and developers. This communication will not be confined as at present to the specification document, but will use computer-graphics facilities, as seen in current CASE tools and prototyping techniques. If the prototype is to be easily converted to the final system then 4G tools technology will be used as a basis for the software needed.

The use of 4GSs and CASE tools will remove the current bottleneck of systems development, but only if DP itself recognizes that it must reorganize itself. In addition we must realize that software tools on their own will not help. Neither will methodologies on their own solve the problem. It is the combination of the tools and the techniques with the right organization.

The potential for new methods and machines and software within an intelligent workbench falls under the heading of "knowledge transfer". This includes not only the initial capture of knowledge during analysis, but also all mapping activities, such as physical database design. In each case, the rules governing the activity will be defined and used in a rule-based expert system, to support and automate a given function in the application lifecycle. These principles of knowledge engineering and artificial intelligence, combined with the use of models of business prototyping will allow the users of computer systems to become more completely involved in their creation. Computer systems will become an extension of the business, with the creation of new systems and maintenance of existing system being triggered solely by changes in the business environment.

9 REFERENCES

1   "Application Generators For Improved Productivity", D.J.L.Gradwell, in *How to Manage The Information Resource*, edited by S.Holloway, British Computer Society Database Specialist Group, 1985.

2   "Organizational Environment Of Successful Use Of 4gls And AGS", R.Tagg, in *Fourth Generation Languages and Application Generators*, edited by D.Martland, S.Holloway and L.Bhabuta, The Technical Press — Unicom Applied Information Technology Report Series, 1986.

3   *4gl Report, Volume 1 A Survey Of Best Practice,* Institute of Data Processing Managers, 1986.

4   *Analyst/Designer Workbenches,* D.J.L.Gradwell, 13th VLDB Conference, Brighton, September 1987.

5   *Data Administration : A Manager's Guide,* British Computer Society Data Administration Working Party, 1987.

6   *Internal Paper Of British Computer Society Data Administration Working Party* 1982.

7   *Methodology Sales Pack*, Applied Data Research UK Ltd., 1987.

8   TIS/XA Manits Sales Brochure, Man-003-25m-8604-TH&W, Cincom.

9   *The Data Processing Manager's Survival Manual* [a Guide For Managing People And Resources], L.M.Singer, John Wiley and Sons, 1982.

10 *Practical Benefits Of Executive Decision Support Systems,* David Owen and Mark C. Volpato, Proceedings of the Malaysian National Computer Conference, Kuala Lumper, Malaysia, November 1985.

11 *SSADM Implementation (QuickBuild)*, Information Systems Engineering Report, Information Technology in the Civil Service, CCTA, Draft for Development, January 1987.

12 "Information Systems Development: a Flexible Framework", *Journal of Development,* Information Systems Analysis and Design Working Party, British Computer Society Database Specialist Group, editor R.Maddison, 1983-84.

13 *Data Administration,* Simon Holloway, Gower Technical Press, 1988.

USER
EXPERIENCES

Chapter 15
A USER'S VIEW OF THREE DIFFERENT FOURTH-GENERATION DEVELOPMENT ENVIRONMENTS

Gerard Lennox
Consensus Information Technololy Limited

1   INTRODUCTION

For some considerable time I have read the technical and computer press, scoured the libraries, even spoken to academics, attempting to gain a real perspective on how effective the different 4GLs are in practice.

At best I received glowing recommendations from highly satisfied users (carefully picked by the marketing arms of the 4GL companies). At worst I acquired, at vast expense, lengthy documents of technical checklists with weighting factors.

None, however, actually attempted to contrast different languages based on their use within one organization.

Let me explain what I mean. Very few organizations have deliberately tried more than one 4GL environment. Those that have, have done so more out of pique or unwillingness to persevere with just one system when the latest craze or fashion had finished. Indeed, a number of companies that have tried more than one system don't talk about the "failures", wishing rather to blame the 4GL for the inability to produce working applications on time and to specification.

I also suspect that one of the reasons I have not been able to find a real contrast is that many organizations wish to maintain their competitive edge, be they in commerce or the public sector, by keeping such information to themselves.

More importantly where I have found successful installations it has been a particular type of work directed towards a 4GL. In this way, it was difficult to compare systems under differing conditions using the same people and the same company environment as a bedrock on which to base the comparisons.

This chapter is an attempt to redress the balance and yet as I write it I realize that some of the comparisons will be out of date even before you read it. In the field of 4GLs improvement, innovation and change are the only real constants. What is perceived as a problem in one product today will be addressed in such a way as to turn it into a positive virtue in just a few short months.

As an example of this consider the ORACLE relational database system: it is considered by many to be slow (as are all RDBMs). Yet Version 6 will incorporate techniques borrowed from large mainframes on hierarchical database systems to give transaction processing loads equal to if not better than IBM mainframes running the CICS IMS systems.

2   THE   ENVIRONMENTS COVERED

I write this as a practical user of many 4GL environments. For many years I have been involved with organizations designing and developing application software using a variety of 4GLs.

In designing applications my teams have deliberately used software engineering techniques where appropriate to allow us to divorce the logical design from the environment on which we were going to run it.

We have also spent some considerable time developing applications for other organizations again using 4G environments of different types. As a consequence I now feel we have a solid base of experience using essentially the same people and development methods so that we can sensibly contrast the performance, usability and constraints of different languages.

For the purposes of this exercise I have chosen to compare three very different systems. They are the PICK operating system and development environments, the ORACLE relational database management system and finally the ICL QuickBuild development set.

Each has been compared under the following headings:

- application development;
- data management;
- efficiency;
- interfaces;
- environmental independence;
- management and control;
- man machine interface;
- analysis and design.

At this point I must make it clear that there are many other systems which could have been chosen but the author has personal experience of these three. They each represent well-established types of systems used by many organizations especially in the UK.

I am indebted to the help and training provided by all of the organizations concerned and of course my colleagues at Consensus.

3 CONCLUSION

At first sight it might appear a little strange for the conclusion to a paper to appear in the middle rather than the end. However, I would like to put forward a conclusion that I and my colleagues have reached and then attempt to provide you with information in support of it. Readers are then deliberately left to draw their own conclusions from the views presented to them.

There is no such thing as a bad 4GL — just bad selection and use of it.

4   THE THREE LANGUAGES

To help readers unfamiliar with any of these languages a short introduction to each might be useful.

4.1   Pick

This is probably the oldest of the three environments. Developed originally in the 1970s by Dick Pick to provide an easy method for US soldiers to make enquiries on mainframe data.

Pick is really an operating system and 4GL combined. It is normally embedded in the computer hardware rather than being a separate downloadable piece of software. This was done to ensure "purity" between manufacturers' implementations and protect Pick's copyright. Initially available on minicomputers there are now versions running on PCs to IBM 43xx mainframes.

The basis of Pick is a form of relational database combined with (by 1970s standards) a user-friendly enquiry and reporting language. Although it has been around for quite some time it is powerful and flexible.

4.2   Oracle

Is a relatively recent addition to the DP tool set, being about five years old. Oracle was originally developed in the USA to make use of relational database ideas and the SQL (system query language) ideas of IBM and Tedd Codd. Oracle grew very quickly in the DEC mini market and have since expanded to cover PCs and most mainframes including IBM.

4.3   QuickBuild

This is the odd one of the three. QuickBuild only runs on ICL mainframes that use the VME operating system. However it is typical of a large mainframe 4GL development environment. QuickBuild is aimed at organizations which definitely need to build high volume or complex applications that will have many simultaneous on-line users.

QuickBuild is a proprietary system from ICL which incorporates application development tools, corporate data dictionaries and the IDMSX database management system.

I will compare these three products under a number of headings relating to their functionality and usability. In addition, I will briefly review their suitability as a means of development for a number of different scenarios.

5   APPLICATION DEVELOPMENT

This relates to the features provided for the development of various types of system such as on-line, or batch only, a mixture of the two, management information systems or complex processing systems. More detailed considerations would encompass editors, screen handlers, testing and debugging aids, report writing and enquiry-generation capabilities, standardization and maintenance.

5.1   Pick

Pick as standard uses DATA BASIC as its programming language for TP and batch jobs. Pick also has an enquiry language called ACCESS. ACCESS is extremely powerful and often used by "computer illiterates" without their realizing because it is designed around the concept of structured English. As an example, LIST CUSTOMERS WITH BALANCE > £3,000 will show all customers with an account balance greater than £3,000. It is important to realize that this PC type enquiry has been available on Pick minicomputers for some years. Users of conventional mainframes are often amazed at how easy it is to enquire on a Pick system when they first encounter it.

Programming big applications, although faster than using COBOL, is still dependent on a skilled programmer being available. Additional tools such as debuggers and screen painters are now becoming available from third parties.

5.2   Oracle

Oracle from Version 5 has very easy-to-use screen-painting facilities. It produces simple screens that are user friendly and take advantage of many modern hardware facilities. Enquiries are easy to produce using the forms generators, SQL statements or menu-driven SQL tools.

Batch work is best done (in my experience) using traditional languages such as COBOL and incorporating SQL statements as required to access the database.

5.3   QuickBuild

QuickBuild is ideal for high volumes of data and multi-user TP applications. Although much quicker than COBOL it requires a good understanding of the computer environment. QuickBuild cannot be used by novices to make simple quick systems as can the other examples. It is very powerful especially for large applications, but still very mainframe (cumbersome) orientated. Batch applications, if complex, are best written in COBOL if competent programmers are available.

6   DATA   MANAGEMENT

4GL-based systems depend on the quality of data structure design for their effective operation. There are a number of different structuring approaches including hierarchical and relational database systems, inverted files and flat files, each of which has its own relative strengths and weaknesses. In addition to the storage method there are a number of other important considerations such as whether the DBMS is an integral part of the product or interfaced to it, whether global data definitions are possible and physical size constraints.

6.1   Pick

Pick uses a form of relational database. In effect, indexed variable-length records are created as files. Individual fields can be accessed from the definition of another file. This gives the effect of "views" of data. All views are controlled by the data dictionary. However, this does not contain a common view of data. By this I mean there is no description of the use to which the data is put or an easy way of telling in what other views or programs it is used.

For small systems it is very quick and easy to build a database. Great care must be used if complex structures are needed or large amounts of data are involved. The integrity of data can be questionable in Pick. There are numerous examples of "group format errors" occurring especially during development. A "gfe" is where the system has lost track of where it is supposed to be storing a piece of data. Automatic recovery and the concept of success units within an application have to be programmed by the user.

6.2   Oracle

Oracle is a very flexible modern relational database system. It copes with the requirement to add fields, records or change their length at any time during the applications life. There are however penalties to pay in terms of increased processing overheads for this flexibility.

There are sophisticated integrity and security procedures right down to field level. Oracle, like Pick, has an integral DBMS but doesn't appear to suffer from size problems. With the release of new products Oracle can read information from databases on several machines that are networked together. It is relatively easy to construct a basic Oracle database but it requires considerable skill to get optimum performance from it if it is large or there are many users.

6.3   QuickBuild

QuickBuild relies totally on the ICL implementation of the powerful IDMS system. IDMS is a pure CODASYL hierarchical database. It is ideally suitable for handling extremely large volumes of data for many simultaneous users.

IDMS requires a very high level of skill to use properly and does not suffer fools well. Its integrity and security controls are second to none but rely on a skilled database administrator who will monitor and control what is happening.

217

7   EFFICIENCY

4GLs have a reputation for poor utilization of machine resources. This is probably an inevitability with higher and higher levels of facilities but it need not be an overriding problem with current and anticipated hardware price/performance ratios. It is prudent, especially in larger, multi-user mainframe systems to seek features which enhance the efficiency of resource utilization. These would include facilities for database tuning and optimization, memory utilization, control over data storage I/Os and whether an interpretive or compiled approach has been adopted. A number of marked differences are apparent.

7.1   Pick

As mentioned earlier, Pick is mainly implemented as part of the hardware of the computer. It is in effect its own operating system. As a consequence, in its pure forms it can be extremely fast, especially on systems like the Ultimate range (based on Honeywell mainframes) with speed-enhancement facilities. Unless considerable thought is given to the original design of Pick database and all the access paths are properly defined in advance it is difficult to optimize the database structures once implemented. For this reason, Pick can become relatively inefficient when large volumes of data or many users with different application programs are trying to access what is in effect the same data. Significant system degradation has been noticed on heavily loaded computers, ie when all twelve terminals on a small mini are working using complex sorts of the same type.

7.2   Oracle

All true relational DBMSs have an appalling reputation for efficiency. This is mainly because the route to a particular piece or combination of pieces of data can be long and cumbersome. Oracle, along with others of its ilk have tried to optimize the access paths wherever possible. Sophisticated optimization software sits in the enquiry systems (as part of the package) to interpret what the user has requested and find the fastest way of accessing the relevant data items.

There are a number of techniques such as indexing and clustering adopted in Oracle which allow regularly used groups of related data items to be dealt with efficiently. Indexing provides a direct access path to a number of related items without having to read all the items and then put them in order each time. Clustering physically places items commonly of use together in the same physical part of the storage device. These techniques can dramatically reduce the number of I/O transactions especially on large databases.

7.3   QuickBuild

Efficiency, especially in terms of data access, is a hallmark of a well-designed hierarchical CODASYL database. Given a high level of skill from the database designer it is possible to optimize IDMS in many different ways. The latest version of this DBMS and its IDMSX allows for sophisticated multiple indexes to be held, data items to be concatenated and used as one field rather than several in different circumstances, and data to be split across a number of areas which, in turn, can be split over a number of physical storage devices to optimise the hardware I/O channels and thus make the best use of the processor's power. However, the user is left to his own devices to determine the relative benefits of any of these techniques and because of the size of most IDMS databases it becomes extremely long-winded and therefore costly to reorganize in the event that extra fields have to be added or more space is required.

8   INTERFACES

4GLs do not exist in a vacuum — they may need to interact with a wide variety of other software and products, such as operating systems, DBMSs, data dictionaries, TP monitors and existing applications software. The flexibility and ease of use of these interfaces can have a fundamental impact on the usability of the product. A number of interesting differences in scope have come to light between the different examples:

8.1 Pick

Effectively, there are no interfaces from "pure" Pick to other environments. Certain implementations allow the reading of flat or index sequential files, but all of them require that either the ACCESS enquiry language or DATA BASIC is used to manipulate data. Although most users of Pick find its native facilities quite adequate, the majority have also made use of third party tools such as screen painters to simplify what can be the expensive, time-consuming and complex job of building an application.

8.2 Oracle

Originally Oracle only used the SQL system. Although powerful this had a number of problems when it came to complex processing requirements. Later developments of Oracle allow one to use a variety of programming languages, in particular COBOL, to handle complex or difficult tasks. Through COBOL it is possible to access other files, even to interface to such products as IBM DB2 databases and share information in a number of ways.

8.3 QuickBuild

Possibly because QuickBuild is a proprietary system to ICL and was designed to make use of their data dictionary and IDMS DBMS system it does not interface with other file structures easily. Later versions of Quickbuild acknowledge that 4GLs do not cope with every eventuality and therefore allow very easy interfaces for the programmer to use COBOL wherever appropriate. Both an attraction and a disadvantage of Quickbuild is its need to work through the data dictionary. It forces a set of conventions on the programmer which can greatly improve the maintenance aspects of the system but does not make it particularly user friendly for our friend the "computer illiterate".

9   ENVIRONMENTAL INDEPENDENCE

There are two considerations here, the products portability across different manufacturers systems and operating systems; and within one manufacturers product range and operating systems.

There are very significant differences between the products.

9.1   Pick

One of the main virtues of Pick, especially in its "pure" form, is its extreme portability. Almost without exception any application written in Pick can be easily transferred to another computer manufacturer's hardware. This was built into the original concept of Pick long before it became fashionable and as such makes it an attractive proposition.

9.2   Oracle

Being a later development than Pick, Oracle seized on this concept of portability. However, they were different to Pick in that they did not demand large licence fees in advance to port their development regime to particular hardware. This means that the major hardware suppliers can all offer Oracle (indeed Oracle sell it aggressively direct to end-users). With the latest version of Oracle it is true to say that an application developed on one machine, say a PC, can be picked up, recompiled and run on another and all differences such as screen handling are taken into account automatically. This is a major achievement considering the wide variety of TP monitors around in the market today.

9.3   QuickBuild

QuickBuild is completely environmentally dependent. By this I mean it only runs on ICL mainframes which use the VME operating system. It was developed by ICL and makes full use of their unique facilities. Despite its many other qualities if the requirement is portability across manufacturer's hardware then QuickBuild loses out heavily.

10 MANAGEMENT AND CONTROL

Management and control of the product and projects using it is vital. This would include the type and role of the data dictionary and the extent of its interface with users, whether multi versions of programs and data are possible for development, whether adequate audit facilities exist and, retrospectively, whether it is possible to monitor and control actual performance. We have found that:

10.1 Pick

In terms of managing the control of the product and projects Pick is virtually useless. Multiple versions of programs are only allowed in the sense that they have different names and it is virtually impossible to monitor and control actual performance.

10.2 Oracle

One of the later additions to Oracle is the DSD tool. It provides a highly defined development route but it only operates on Sun super workstations at present. The data dictionary allows adequate definition of data from a corporate viewpoint but this is not a mandatory requirement of using a 4GL.

10.3 QuickBuild

Possibly because of its mainframe origins QuickBuild scores well in this area. Management controls are extremely sophisticated — being limited only by the user's willingness to implement them. Development, test and live versions of software and databases are easy to control. Change and version control is automatically taken care of by the data dictionary. Most importantly a fundamental concept behind QuickBuild is the use of a global corporate data dictionary. In this, data is defined once and then used by many different people in many different ways.

11 MAN MACHINE INTERFACE (MMI)

The user interface is arguably the most important aspect of the 4GL. Some products return a COBOL-style language interface with a comprehensive syntax, verbs and conditions; others adopt the increasingly popular menu-driven approach which guides the user through simple selections until a blank form is eventually displayed for completion. A third approach is that of complex command words supported by strings of parameters. The type of user — DP professional, competent end-user, or novice — will determine which MMI is most appropriate.

11.1 Pick

For writing applications and batch routines the MMI is essentially DATA BASIC which is all right if you are a DATA BASIC programmer. The ACCESS query and reporting language is very easy to use once you understand it. It uses English-like sentences with verbs and operations but can be a little off-putting in the hands of a total novice. To this end a number of proprietary menu-driven products have been produced to simplify an end-user's requirements.

11.2 Oracle

SQL language is based on four simple commands. It then goes on to use a lot of operators and clauses to control what is happening to the data. Oracle have got round many of these limitations by developing in effect menu-driven forms painters, report writer and query languages, all of which ultimately write SQL statements. Systems in Oracle can be implemented very quickly and easily and depending on the hardware with a great deal of sophistication using pop-up windows, scrolling fields and even different colours to highlight functions.

11.3 QuickBuild

Although significantly better than COBOL, QuickBuild is definitely a programmer's language. It enforces structured programming with all the learning curve that that involves. If used properly QuickBuild programs are very simple to maintain as they all follow the same logical type of structure. Possibly because it is mainframe-based using block-mode terminals QuickBuild is not the easiest of languages to use. Later developments of QuickBuild — including Pathway — have attempted to redress this by providing high-level menu-driven interfaces to produce simple systems. These have proved acceptable for producing prototypes but invariably need considerable tuning after the first compilation.

12 ANALYSIS AND DESIGN

There are now two opposing views about the means of developing systems. The most well established, the structured analysis and design methodologies — SSADM, LSDM, ISDM, CACI, YOURDAN, GANE and SARSA etc — which have evolved over the last ten years, are really all about imposing adequate controls over the development of very large and complex systems by a staged and highly prescriptive approach. The more recent approach is prototyping, which has grown out of the availability of quick and easy-to-use microcomputers and 4GLs which allow the very speedy definition of screens, reports and data structures.

12.1 Pick

Pick encourages the development of quick systems. It was really designed as an end-user tool querying diverse data sets. The DATA BASIC language does not encourage the use of structured methods although they can be incorporated if required. Pick is all about getting fast answers to end-user's enquiries, not about building the most elegant systems.

12.2 Oracle

Oracle can be used as a very efficient prototyping system, in that it is quick and easy to develop screens and a database which sits behind them. It also allows the use of structured systems methods because of its use of the data-dictionary concept based very much on the SSADM principle. Recent developments with Oracle, especially to do with their design system, encourage formal software engineering techniques to be adopted for the management of large projects.

12.3 QuickBuild

QuickBuild was really developed to exploit techniques such as SSADM. The concepts of software engineering are virtually built in to QuickBuild. Indeed rushing into a QuickBuild development without doing a formal design is virtually a recipe for disaster. Maybe this is why QuickBuild excels at large complex systems which have to meet the needs of many different users and yet not demand phenomenal machine resources to satisfy them.

13   WHEN TO USE EACH LANGUAGE

With these various experiences in mind it is worth reviewing the circumstances under which we would recommend use of each product to develop a system.

13.1 Pick

In our experience Pick is ideal as a departmental machine, where relatively small, uncomplicated file structure are required. Wherever end-users need regularly to interrogate data in an *ad hoc* fashion Pick is ideal. Having said this, some massive systems with several hundred users running on mainframes have been developed under Pick to everybody's complete satisfaction.

13.2 Oracle

The latest developments of Oracle have removed many of the performance constraints surrounding relational database systems. For medium-size TP applications where there is a high proportion of *ad hoc* enquiries the Oracle-type product is ideal. Wherever there is a possibility of data structures, combinations or even data items frequently changing there is not much to beat a true relational DBMS.

13.3 QuickBuild

For high-volume heavy-transaction loads with many users where a stable environment is a prerequisite, QuickBuild scores heavily. It does not encourage frequent changes either to programs or to data structures. Its real strength is producing very large applications for many hundreds of users in a fraction of the time normally taken using traditional methods such as COBOL. Used correctly the programming side of a major development can often be reduced to a third of its conventional time by using QuickBuild.

14 CONCLUSION

By now you will have formed some idea of how each product has performed under different circumstances. I hope I have been able to give information which supports my conclusion that "There is no such thing as a bad 4GL — just bad selection and use of it".

You may have formed the impression from this paper that Oracle is my favourite development language. That is not always the case. Each of the environments has strengths and weaknesses. Pick has some data-integrity problems but is relatively cheap for a multi-user database system. Oracle is extremely machine hungry but very flexible in use. Quickbuild is often complicated but very efficient and reliable when used in large projects.

Finally let me remind you (as if you really needed it) that you are entering a minefield where no one product will cover all your likely needs. Great care must be taken in matching the product to the task to be performed. Do not fall into the trap of having a solution which is always looking for the right problem to solve.

Chapter 16

THE APPLICATION OF SOFTWARE ENGINEERING TECHNIQUES TO A MANAGEMENT INFORMATION SYSTEM FOR A WOOL TEXTILE GROUP

Keith Butler
Illingworth, Morris plc

1   THE COMPANY — BACKGROUND

Illingworth Morris and Company Limited was incorporated on 18 February 1920 from a collection of textile operations most of which evolved at, or soon after, the industrial revolution.

The group tended to be assembled in a piecemeal fashion without any clear strategy being pursued. The group suffered from a lack of direction and during the late 1970s and early 1980s was in deep recession, surviving only by heavy borrowing.

In 1983, control of the group passed to A. J. Lewis, the current chairman and chief executive. Through Hartley Investment Trust Ltd., Lewis controls 51% of the equity of Illingworth Morris plc. Lewis embarked upon a recovery plan:

- to rationalize the structure of the group;

- to strengthen the management;

- to produce high-quality products;

- to be marketing-led rather than production-led;

- to use the latest technology.

The group has achieved a considerable improvement during the last three years, although greater efficiency can be expected.

Today, Illingworth Morris plc consists of a group of totally UK-based companies in a vertically integrated textile business. The verticality necessarily means that the group is diverse, with companies in different sectors of textile activity starting with raw wool and extending through combing, spinning and weaving of cloth up to the manufacture of finished garments.

In addition to this diversity of process the companies vary widely in size, ranging from those with a turnover of £1m and 100 employees to those of £30m and 1000 employees.

Currently, Illingworth Morris is the largest wool group of its kind in the world with a stock market capitalization of approximately £65,000,000.

Group external turnover for the year to 31st March 1986 was very nearly £100,000,000 of which approximately one half represented direct and indirect exports. Group profit before taxation exceeded £6,000,000.

The new managements of the operating companies are aware of the need for the essential information with which to plan and manage their operations. This leads to a demand for systems to reflect the diversity of processes, size and methods of control for the companies.

2 PREVIOUS INFORMATION TECHNOLOGY EXPERIENCE

In 1984 the group attempted to meet this demand in the conventional manner of preparing a definition of requirements and selecting package software, written in COBOL, to meet these requirements.

This project both failed to produce benefits and to meet expectations of timescale and cost. The experience left a jaundiced view of information technology among the potential users, which could only be removed by a practical demonstration of the benefits.

The reasons for this failure were analysed and include:

User inexperience : many "grass roots" users in a traditional industry find it difficult to define their requirements.

Diversity of the group: a single package was unable to cater for the diversity of size and methods of control exercised within the group. As the package was written in COBOL the timescales and costs of amendment militated against acceptance of information technology.

Tradition: the woollen textile industry has methods and a terminology specific to each sector. The majority of packages have been developed to support engineering and the methods and terminology are very different. It proved impossible within one package to address this problem, which is fundamental to acceptance by the grass roots users in companies.

Quality of software: many problems were experienced in the quality of systems produced by the software house which originated the package. Programs failed frequently in operation causing a very high maintenance load on DP staff.

Despite considerable efforts it is primarily ledger systems which are installed within the group, albeit somewhat unsatisfactorily. In view of this traumatic experience the board commissioned Peat Marwick to assist the information systems department in a strategy review.

3   INFORMATION TECHNOLOGY STRATEGY

3.1   Definition and evaluations

Historically, the diversity of a large decentralized textile group has posed a significant challenge when attempting to determine a cohesive and effective strategy for information technology.

Following a detailed review of the experience of the group, the principles for the development of an information technology strategy were defined as:

- To provide systems suitable for each industry sector and size of company.

- To consider the adoption of packages, where applicable.

- To control IT costs through a policy of standard hardware, operating system and development methods.

3.2 The revised strategy

A review of alternative strategies was conducted against these principles.

A steering committee of users was formed to monitor progress of the development of the strategy.

It became apparent that the route of implementing packages (either single or multiple) was impractical. The alternative of allowing each operating unit to select their systems would be too expensive in capital and revenue terms. In addition, this option would result in a "shanty town" of information systems, with differing hardware and operating systems.

It was recognized that the development of bespoke systems using conventional languages could not meet realistic targets for cost and timescale.

Attention turned to the use of 4GSs. More than ten leading 4GLs were subjected to a formal evaluation, which resulted in Data Language's "Progress" being regarded as the leading contender. The basis for this choice rested on productivity, facilities, robustness, reliability, operational features, portability and cost.

This evaluation of leading 4GLs was conducted to pre-set criteria. These criteria are listed in Appendix 1 to this chapter.

It was felt that Progress was the most advanced and powerful of the 4GLs reviewed. In particular it provided one environment for the database, data dictionary, application language, formatting and editing facilities.

However, there was little practical experience and support within the UK and there were attendant risks of relatively unproven performance in the field. Experience of 4GLs had shown that there were more failures than successes and it was felt that the feasibility of the method should be established with a pilot project.

NCR equipment was selected for the pilot project as NCR were committed to using Progress internally.

4   THE PILOT PROJECT

4.1   Organization

In order to contain these risks an evaluation of Progress was undertaken. A clear definition of the objectives, milestones and project control methods was established prior to commencement. These can be seen in detail at Appendix 2 to this chapter. In summary these objectives were to prove the performance claims of Progress both in development and operation of a system. At the same time the performance of hardware and software suppliers was to be appraised in the support needed and provided.

4.2   Scope

A specification was prepared for a stock-control and material-traceability system. The programming effort was estimated using conventional languages (COBOL) and an objective of a 50% reduction in development time was set.

The major stages of the pilot project included:

- training in the use of progress;
- establishing the database;
- preparing 53 "programs" to include file maintenance, implosion;
- explosion, enquiry and reporting logic;
- system testing;
- performance benchmarking.

The project commenced on 17 November 1986 with three staff deployed. It was completed at the end of February 1987. The time spent on every activity was recorded against the estimate and all objectives were met, with many being improved upon dramatically. During this period 53 modules comprising 10616 statements were developed and fully tested.

4.3 Findings

A significant number of other benefits in terms of ability to prototype, robustness of code generated, user friendliness and ease of future enhancement and maintenance became apparent.

Upon reflection, it was recognized that these benefits would result in greater cost savings in the future than the originally perceived benefit of improved productivity.

The capability of the 4GL to be used for prototyping was impressive and had clear benefits in guiding inexperienced users to definitions of requirements.

It was noted that there was a longer learning curve for programmers experienced in 3GL, as they needed to trust the 4GL to construct a sound logic flow. There was a tendency for 3GL programmers to force the 4GL to perform to their preconception of program logic flow. This had lost some of the benefits of productivity. It was concluded that productivity would be higher than that achieved during the pilot project.

The initial experience of prototyping resulted in an excessive number of modifications to the database design, which whilst far easier to accommodate than traditional methods, resulted in disruption via rework of programs. It was considered that for a full project a balance between good standards and prototyping was required.

It was found that the system produced had a higher level of functionality than the COBOL equivalent planned. Considerable use had been made of extended help facilities by the programmers. In fact 1133 statements of the total 10616 were in this category (10.67%).

Whilst satisfied that all the objectives for the pilot project had been met, it was considered necessary to take up further references from users of Progress and to establish the performance of Progress under operational conditions.

4.4 References

References had been taken up in Europe prior to the pilot project. References were taken up in the USA during March 1987.

Visits were made to a software house, two users of Progress systems (at differing ends of the spectrum of transaction rates), the authors of the language and NCR.

Their experience confirmed the view of the benefits perceived and that such systems were capable of handling transaction volumes far in excess of those in Illingworth Morris Plc.

4.5 Benchmarking

It was clear that benefits through the development, implementation and maintenance cycle could be achieved.

The concern remained that these benefits were "bought" at the cost of operational performance.

In order to evaluate operational performance a benchmark was undertaken for the following configuration:

- NCR Tower 32/600;
- 12Mb memory;
- 23 VDUs;
- 2 printers;
- Unix Version 1.2;
- Progress Version 3.2;
- 2 x 85Mb Winchester disk drives.

The method used for the benchmark and results obtained can be seen at Appendix 3.

4.6 Use of structured analysis and design methods

The pilot project illustrated that there was a need to introduce formal methods to a prototyping approach, and research was undertaken into available methodologies.

A modified (reduced) version of SSADM was introduced together with a CASE tool (computer-aided software engineering). Learmonth and Burchett's

Automate + was selected as the most appropriate system for the Illingworth Morris environment and eventually introduced.

5 THE PROJECT

Integrated business systems are being developed to meet the needs of the companies which make up the group.

5.1 Objectives

To produce fully integrated business systems for the decentralized operating companies in a vertically integrated textile group.

5.2 Method

It was considered that certain key elements are required by all companies (for example the need to record inventory movements) and a specification was raised against this lowest common denominator.

This "core" system was developed using the 4GL (Progress) and used as a prototype to demonstrate to a representative company from each industry sector (ie a processing company, a spinning company, a weaving company and a garment manufacturer).

Core systems are being developed for:

- stock, traceability and purchase control;

- sales order processing, analysis and forecasting;

- material and capacity planning, production scheduling and documentation;

- work in progress recording and valuation.

Packages written in Progress were acquired for ledgers and net payroll. The core systems integrate with these packages.

The demonstration of the prototype was used to assist users in producing a formal definition of their requirements to be agreed.

A variant, specific to the industry sector, was produced using the core system as the foundation. This method can only be made available with the facilities of a 4GL to modify the database, programs and input/output processes rapidly.

The conventional process of producing operating procedures, staff training, data capture and parallel/pilot running was followed leading to the implementation of the system.

After a period of operation an implementation review will be undertaken to improve the package further, in the light of experience.

5.3   Project launch

Analysis of the requirements for sales order processing and stock control commenced upon receipt of board approval of the full project in April 1987.

In each industry sector a "major" site was nominated, at which extensive analysis was undertaken. A "reference" site was used for each sector to check the findings from the major site.

This analysis was initially performed to the existing departmental standards which did not employ any prescriptive data or function-analysis techniques.

The experience of the pilot project indicated the need for such methods and SSADM was selected as the methodology. The selection of the methodology was not as rigorous as for the 4GL. The influencing reasons for selecting SSADM were its pedigree (CCTA and NCC involvement) − thus providing reassurance on its prospective life − and the ready availability of courses in SSADM.

It was appreciated that SSADM was an extremely full and rigorous methodology that did not leave a place for the prototyping we wished to use. For these reasons a subset of SSADM was developed which preserved the essentials of logical data structures, data flow diagrams and entity life histories.

This belated introduction of a methodology initially slowed project progress. Acceptance of, and commitment to, the methodology varied by project team.

However, it became apparent that the team with the greater committment to the methodology consistently produced work of a higher quality. The process of quality review illustrated this difference and commitment to the methodology increased as a result.

The full project required that an additional five staff were recruited. Difficulties were experienced in recruitment as there was tendency for staff steeped in 3GL to mistrust a department comitted to 4GL.

Recruitment caused the more significant delay to project progress. Eventually due to these problems and the anticipated loss of an experienced member of staff on maternity leave (coinciding with the coding stage of the project) a trainee scheme was introduced.

A total of nine weeks' slippage (attributed as seven weeks due to recruitment and subsequent training difficulties and two weeks to rework to SSADM's standards) occurred at this stage.

As an essential part of project launch each company was requested to form their working party (see project control), issued with terms of reference and advised on composition.

The working party provided the form for discussion of the findings and initial design specifications and a method of communicating with end-users.

5.4 Communication and involvement

Previous standards required that business systems definition (BSD) be produced. This BSD would typically be voluminous, technical and remain unread by users. However, the users' agreement was required on the document and normally such agreement was contrived.

It was recognized that this conventional approach was based on false assumptions:

- that the user firstly was able to understand and specify his requirements;

- that the analyst could understand and faithfully record these;

- that they would be successfully translated through the process of design, specification coding and testing;

- that they would not be subject to modification in the light of increased user understanding or changing business environment.

An alternative method, using techniques from within SSADM was devised.

The process of producing a business specification was retained. However, it was "indexed" by a problem/requirement list which identified where and how a solution was proposed.

The BSD was the subject of a formal presentation to each working party. The BSD was considered as a means to an end, ie to improve the definition of the system.

These presentations rested on techniques of:

- describing and agreeing on the problems and requirements of the units;

- describing and agreeing the data flow in the organization;

- describing and agreeing the data elements utilized in this flow.

It was therefore possible to lead users from a description of their current system to the proposed computer-based alternative.

At this stage the working party was requested to agree that data and function were correct in principle.

It was clearly acknowledged that this agreement was subject to modification after a prototype had been produced and demonstrated practically.

5.5   Design of the database

Following this agreement in principle it was possible to use the normalization techniques of SSADM to produce the database schema.

A Progress database contains more than a description of the files, fields and indices. It can be used to store at a central point the validation rules to be applied, the help messages to be used during data entry and the error messages to issue in the event of validation failing.

The advantage of having a single set of validation rules when contrasted to expressing that validation in many programs was obvious.

The drawback was that such validation was a "program" in its own right which could not be fully tested until invoked by its calling procedure.

Thus, recognizing that change was likely to occur both from user request and during the programming phase, a change control procedure was specified.

5.6   Change control

With the information system department a change control board was established from the project leaders.

Requests for change were documented and evaluated by this panel who would concentrate on determining the effects of change both functionally and operationally.

This meeting would agree a plan for the introduction of such change in a controlled manner. This has been achieved by having revision levels of database and software. A limited form of automated change control has been introduced using the facilities of Unix. During the development stage of the project the database of 102 files, 168 indices and 2723 fields a total of 125 changes were implemented.

These have been analysed as

- 36 due to additions/amendments to secondary indices 29%

- 35 bugs in validation routines 28%

- 29 due to typing errors when setting up the dictionary 23%

- 15 changes to labels on screens (cosmetic improvements) 12%

- 10 changes to initial values/defaults 8%

5.7   Estimating and project control

In keeping with many projects, the overall timescales and resources for this project have been set by the board of directors. Therefore the project scheduling technique has been that of back scheduling and setting milestones. Project leaders are set annual and quarterly objectives which they translate into a rolling quarterly team plan. Establishtibing an accurate estimate for any task has been a persistent problem. In the absence of any obvious solution project control has been very tight. It is worth noting that motivation and morale have been high with a desire to meet targets.

Accuracy of estimates improved as control of tasks was exclusive to the department (eg programming). This is attributed to the factors of removing uncontrollable external influences and having more historical information on which to base estimates.

The techniques of discussing programming estimates, agreeing realistic staff utilization factors (75%) and obtaining commitment to achieve the estimate paid dividends during the programming phase. During this phase the period of project review was one week with any slippage having to be corrected within that week. Staff accepted this commitment and whilst overtime was required it was neither excessive nor demotivating. Two staff voluntarily worked overtime in order to beat their targets!

5.8   Programming

A team of six staff were used to produce and test the 121 programs which comprised the demonstrable "core" system.

Of these six staff:

- two were trainees who had only seven weeks' computing experience;

- two had been previously trained without the opportunity to practise coding "in anger";

- two had gained experience during the pilot project.

The estimates for programming were based on the experience of the pilot project. Typically a major program received an estimate as high as five days, reports and enquiries received estimates of 1.75 hours. It must be noted that the system developed has an extremely high level of complexity due to requirements unique to textiles. Programs have extensive help, documentation and code-look-up facilities. They are functionally more complex than their conventional 3GL equivalent for, say, an engineering company. Productivity improvements must be considered with these facts firmly in mind.

Appendix 5 tabulates the estimates and actuals achieved by person.

Productivity during the coding and system testing phases exceeded the targets set following the pilot project. Project slippage was reduced from nine to four weeks.

5.9 Environment in which this was achieved

During the late stage of design and throughout the programming stage the department head count was one short due to maternity leave.

In addition to the development of the core system the department was required to:

- maintain eight existing mini-computer systems;

- support 20 PC users;

- implement ledgers in three companies;

- develop and implement an accounting systems for an offshore bank;

- develop and install a cloth-costing yields and mending system;

- develop a laboratory-results-recording and certificate-of-conformity system;

- commission six computers ie install operating system, Progress software and housekeeping software;

- implement software upgrades to Unix and Progress.

5.10 An independent review

It was considered that an independent review would be advantageous of:

- the quality and efficiency of the database design;

- the quality and efficiency of the major update programs produced.

Consequently, a consultancy exercise was undertaken by Progress Software Corporation's technical support manager.

His report concluded that the desgn of the database provided an efficient base on which to work. This was attributed to the techniques of SSADM which had allowed us to develop the correct level of indexing for the database.

Using the data volumes collected during analysis, the performance of the major programs was investigated. The design aim was to achieve an average response time of three to four seconds. Whilst the review highlighted methods by which performance could be improved further, all programs achieved the level of performance set.

6   CRITERIA FOR SUCCESS

Targets have been set in two major areas in order to assess the success of the project. These may be considered to be the improvements in timescale, cost and quality of the systems produced; and the improvements in performance of the operating companies.

These include:

6.1   Improvements in timescale

Measured by comparison of development effort with Progress against an estimate for COBOL.

- Improvements in cost will be measured in the same way.

- Further improvements in the overall project timescale are anticipated from the prototyping method. These will be measured against previous estimates for system implementations.

- Improvements in the quality of systems will be measured by comparing the number of lines of code generated for a COBOL and Progress program. It can be assumed that the fewer lines produced the lower is the probability of error.

- Improvements in "user friendliness" will be measured by contrasting the facilities which can be provided by COBOL programs to those which can be provided under Progress.

6.2   Improvements in performance in the operating companies

A number of objectives have been nominated by the operating companies for the purposes of monitoring the success of the project. These include:

- reduced investment through lower inventory holding;

- increased sales potential — from reduced "past due" orders and better delivery performance;

- increased profits — from effective purchasing, scheduling and loading, operator performance;

- reduced losses — from cancelled orders, stock writeoffs and related losses.

Each site has set a monetary value on these savings to enable performance to be measured.

7   PROJECT CONTROL

Detailed plans were produced for the project which indicate the major tasks and resources required.

Three levels of control are used to monitor achievement against the plans.

7.1   Steering committee

A steering committee, chaired by the group finance director, and comprising two other main board directors and representatives from all the main users was established. Its terms of reference are to direct the group's IT operations, assess priorities, involve users in decision making and generally to monitor IT plans within the group. It presents reports to the board of Illingworth Morris plc, which relies heavily on it.

7.2   Working Party

Each operating company has established a working party to monitor progress within the company. It ensures that the neccessary user resource is applied and approves specifications of systems.

The milestones, deliverables and benefits set for the company are reviewed by this body. The terms of reference for these groups can be seen at Appendix 4

7.3   Project recording

The technical aspects of the project are managed by the information systems manager. The duration of all activities has been estimated and actual performance is recorded against this estimate. Projects are reviewed formally on a fortnightly basis.

8   CONCLUSIONS

Within a diverse group such as Illingworth Morris, the adoption of these methods will allow modern, effective information systems to be more readily accepted and utilized by staff in the operating units.

- Improvements in productivity during the coding phase are at least 50% for "complicated" programs and far greater for simple enquiries and reports.

- Future maintenance and enhancement are simplified as there are far fewer lines of code.

- System testing is speedier as errors can be corrected speedily.

- Where staff do not have extensive 3GL experience training of new staff is a speedier process. Experienced analyst/programmers have trained themselves and produced small systems within three weeks.

- Systems are more attractive to end-users both cosmetically and functionally.

- Prototyping is a valuable method to encourage user identification, improved communication and precise specification.

- Systems can be produced at lower cost allowing IT to be applied to operating units which would otherwise not show a payback.

- A smaller department was required than with 3GL. A structure based on analyst/programmer, rather than the segregation of the two disciplines was more effective with a 4GL.

- A single language can be used to offer facilities on Unix and MS-DOS-based machines. Systems have been ported up and down between such machines.

- A cost-effective, cohesive and rational approach can be taken to development methodologies, operating system, hardware and applications, resulting in cost savings in the Information System department.

However a balance must be struck between the benefit of prototyping and the need to have the database design "right first time". It is therefore essential to have a good analysis and design methodology, otherwise it is difficult to move from the prototype to the production model.

A CASE tool should be considered to support the chosen methodology. Good project control is even more essential as enthusiasm for the facilities and prototyping can lead to "overdesigned" solutions.

And above all allow for the learner curve for "traditional programmers".

APPENDIX 1
EVALUATION OF 4GLs:
CRITERIA USED

Measurement of software development tools

SELECTION CRITERIA	WEIGHTING FACTOR
A. DEVELOPMENT PRODUCTIVITY	
1. Data dictionary	5
2. Screen painting	4
3. Data independence	3
4. Ease of programming (including aids)	5
5. Debugging/testing aids	3
6. Ease of change/addition to structure	4
7. Learning curve	5
8. Training availability	4
9. Documentation generation	2
10. Data comparison	4
11. Ability to prototype	4
B. END-USER FACILITIES	
1. Query language	4
2. Report generator	4
C. SECURITY AND ROBUSTNESS	
1. Transaction logging/recovery	3
2. Access control	4
3. User views	2
4. Audit trail	2
5. Record locking/concurrency	5
6. Database error detection	4
7. Automatic update indexes/relationships	5

SELECTION CRITERIA	WEIGHTING FACTOR

D. OPERATIONAL FEATURES

1.	Multi-user/multi-task	5
2.	Direct access	5
3.	Alternate key, duplicate, partial	5
4.	Relational	5
5.	Full batch update and run facilities	5
6.	Limitations on volumes	4
7.	Compiler/interpreter	3
8.	Transfer in/out files	3
9.	System performance statistics	3

E. RELIABILITY

1.	Support	5
2.	Documentation	5
3.	User satisfaction	4
4.	Number of sites	3
5.	Target machine	2
6.	Development plan	3
7.	User group	3

F. COST

1.	Cost of package	3
2.	Cost of options	3

G. PORTABILITY

1.	Portability across range of hardware	5
2.	Expansion potential	5

APPENDIX 2
OBJECTIVES FOR THE PILOT PROJECT

Objectives, milestones, basis of monitoring and measuring

1.   Objectives

- The hardware provides a suitable development environment.

- The hardware will adequately handle the expected transaction throughput.

- The hardware will adequately handle the expect number of terminals.

- "Progress" provides a quick and efficient environment for the development of systems.

- "Progress" and the hardware provide a good runtime response.

- "Progress" provides an acceptable compile time response.

- Response for support for hardware, "Progress" and "Unix" is good and the support is of high quality.

- Test mult-disk version of "Progress".

2.   Milestones

- Install the hardware and "Progress".

- Train DP personnel in "Unix" and "Progress".

- Design the database.

- Develop a prototype of a section of the proposed stock system.

- User evaluation of the response of hardware and facilities for users in "Progress".

- Test and evaluate the performance of the Tower 32 hardware and "Progress" including high transaction environment.

- Test and evaluate the response of the Tower 32 and "Progress" with 22 terminals.

247

3. Monitoring and measuring

- The basis for overall monitoring and measuring will be fortnightly meetings.

- The amount of time supplied by support staff will be recorded.

- The Data Processing staff time will be recorded against each module of the developmnent phase; training and testing.

- All support calls will be logged and the response times noted.

- Growth of "Progress" expertise at NCR.

STOCK CONTROL SYSTEM

Modules to be completed during "Pilot" project

	Estimate of using time in traditional methods	Target time using "Progress"	Actual
File maintenance/audits			
1. System parameters	3		1
2. Stock types	5		1
3. Table file	6		1.5
4. Stock items	8		5
	22	10	8.5
File maintenance/audits			
5. Stock lots works order	5		2
Create/update	5		5
Stock issues	8		5
	18	9	12

248

	Estimate of using time in traditional methods	Target time using "Progress"	Actual
Stock receipts	8		5
Stock transfers	5		4
Reservations/allocations	5		3
Re-allocations	5		2
	23	11	14
Enquiries -			
Stock (5)	23	11	6
Enquiries-			
Traceability(2)	14		5.5
Reservations/allocations	3		1.5
Cost update	6		7
	23	11	14
Reports			
Stock file prints (3)	8		2.5
Works orders print	3	5	
Allocations print	3		1.5
Traceability reports	7		1.5
	21	10	6
Reports			
Stock valuation	4		2
Stock ageing	4		1.5
Stock exception	4		1.5
Lot variance	4		1.5
Period end traceability	4		-
	20	10	6.5
System Tests	10	8	4
TOTAL	160	80	75

249

APPENDIX 3
BENCHMARK RESULTS

Method

A calibration test was undertaken against Illingworth Morris's computer to eliminate variables such as Unix and Progress configuration differences.

Phase I

Objective: to determine the effectiveness of I/O

Terminals were successfully signed into Progress and a self-looping enquiry, involving two file accesses with no computation, were initiated on database of 2000 items.

Response times from initiation of the invoking key to the display of last character of a full screen being displayed were measured.

Average response times of between three to four seconds were observed with effective daily transaction rates of 69000 enquiries in a 7-hour day.

Phase II

Objective: to provide a mix of on-line enquiries to three data sets and to promote maximum of head movement.

Screens were logged in as self-looping enquiries of three different types. The load of enquiries was evenly spread over the screens. Alternate enquiries were made from each "end" of the database to promote head movement.

Database sizes were enquiry   a 2000 items
                                             b 4000 items
                                             c 2000 items

Average response times of between three to four seconds were observed.

Phase III

Objective: as Phase II with the introduction of sequential reads to search for unindexed items.

As for Phase II with enquiry "a" being changed to a two-stage process of indexed read followed by a sequential search of 4000 history items.

Response times of between three to four seconds were observed.

Phase IV

A relationship between terminal type (four different models were used) and response time was noted and a test of the fastest type was introduced as in Phase III.

Response times of between two to three seconds were observed.

Phase V

Objective: to introduce data entry tasks on six terminals, a batch process on one terminal, and enquiries as in Phase I on the remaining 15 terminals.

The batch task involved sequentially reading a file of 4000 items and computing the cost amendments.

The keyboard tasks were allocation of stock to orders and receipts of stock.

Response times on the self-looping screens remained between two to three seconds.

Keyboard responses were acceptable to all operators.

Phases VI

Objective: to simulate a product load.

Three screens were used for batch processes of reading, writing and deleting records from a data set.

Two screens initiated printing processes.

One screen initiated a computation loop of addition and subtraction.

Four screens initiated data-entry tasks.

The remaining screens initiated self-looping enquiries.

Some degradation of keyboard response was noted but all other responses were within three to four seconds.

Later investigation of the data-entry program revealed inefficient coding.

APPENDIX 4
TERMS OF REFERENCE — WORKING PARTIES

1. To agree plans for the implementation of hardware and systems within the company, having reference to the targets set by the information systems department but considering local conditions and resources.

2. To review, amend and authorize the business systems definition; prototypes or core systems; and company-specific requirements.

3. To determine priorities for systems implementation, within the constraints of the availability of systems and support from the information systems department.

4. To quantify, schedule and co-ordinate the resources of the operating unit and information systems department required for the project.

5. To monitor and report progress and constraints on the introduction of systems. To recommend action to remedy and shortfall of achievement.

6. To ensure that disruption and implementation workload is minimized.

7. To review plans for training.

8. To allocate operating unit resources to the establishment of procedures and coding systems.

9. To consider the organization of the unit against the criteria of accountability and responsibility for data accuracy.

10. To consider the security and privacy required for the operation of systems.

11. To establish external audit requirements and controls external to the computer system.

12. To authorize amendments and requests for other work and allocate relative priorities for work requested by the operating unit.

13. To control costs within the capability of the working party.

14. To review proposals and approaches taken by other working parties and consider whether these would be appropriate.

COMPARISON OF ESTIMATES AND ACTUAL TIMES ACHIEVED DURING PROGRAMMING

Notes: Estimates based on:

50% reduction on COBOL for difficult programs
60% reduction on COBOL for medium programs
75% reduction on COBOL for easy programs

Utilization Factors
50% for trainees
50% for supervisor
75% for all others

Programmer 1 - No previous Progress experience

No. of programs			23
Estimated duration	53.1	Actual	40.5

Programmer 2 - Trainee

No. of programs			16
Estimated duration	28.0	Actual	39.79

Programmer 3 - Experienced Progress programmer

No. of programs			13
Estimated duration	50	Actual	31.75

Programmer 4 - Trainee

No. of programs			42
Estimated duration	55.9	Actual	33.15

Programmer 5 - Experienced, supervisory role

No. of programs			16
Estimated duration	41.00	Actual	23.76

Programmer 6 - No previous experience

No. of programs			11
Estimated duration	47.5	Actual	31.67

Total

No. of programs			121
Total estimate	275.5	Actual	200.6

Chapter 17

DEFINING THE STRATEGIC USE, COSTING AND BENEFIT OF INTRODUCING FOURTH-GENERATION LANGUAGES WITHIN AN ORGANIZATION

Richard Williams
Richalis Computer Services Ltd

1   INTRODUCTION

The adoption of 4GLs by businesses has unquestioned implications and opportunities. The move to more business-orientated information systems, making wider use of corporately held data, can immediately be seen as an "end-user" benefit in terms of data access and flexibility. However, this tangiblt benefit is not the only advantage of the adoption of such a policy. It is now possible for new methods of data access to be undertaken by different types of personnel, who do not necessarily have to be as highly trained in computational techniques as has been the case in the past. Within the overall DP environment the commitment to extending the use of data by different types of people for different reasons has been a central objective. This paper attempts to assess this approach and recommend a strategy for its operational use based on an example of 4GL implementation in a commercial environment.

Over the past few years a number of 4GLs have been produced and used increasingly in the DP environment. This has had a number of effects in terms of the approach adopted to fulfilling business requirements in computer terms. With the arrival of 4GLs the need for skill and understanding on the part of users of programming techniques has been reduced, as the languages themselves allow the computer to make decisions on how to execute commands and present results without the degree of human interaction previously necessary.

Querymaster (QM) is one such product, designed by ICL to be used in direct business environments as an *ad hoc* enquiry tool. It is the second ICL reporting 4GL, and is intended to complement the previous package in this area, Reportmaster. Reportmaster (RM) has been widely used since its release in 1983, and is geared at producing report programs more quickly than the standard program language, COBOL. It has limitations compared to COBOL, but for general report requirements can cope with most user requests.

Many businesses have had RM programs produced, but the sheer volume of business uses for system-held data has precluded many requests being responded to. Currently an RM program takes two to three days to produce in a commercial environment, which is much quicker than its COBOL equivalent (c5+ days). However, programming resources within DP are not limitless, and valuable business developments often take a while to implement as a result. Consequently, support for businesses in terms of reporting, especially in the area of business modelling - the classic "What If?" report requests, are very hard to respond to. This is especially true where no guarantee of business improvement can be made before the program has been produced. It was this specific area that ICL developed and released QM. If the business modelling approach to data development and usage could be satisfied quickly, in terms of both time and resource usage, then more creative business uses of data could be the result.

A study on the applicability of COBOL, RM and QM to fulfil report requirements in a commercial computing environment was undertaken using a stock-control database system. This paper sets out a brief description of the survey, its results, and a strategy for the implementation of 4GLs in a commercial situation. The paper also draws attention to the limitations and the cost considerations which need to be taken into account if business areas wish to use such products. It must be recognized that certain systems will be inappropriate for the use of the QM type of 4GL, and this paper attempts to identify when this situation can arise.

2 ASSESSING FOURTH -GENERATION LANGUAGES IN A COMMERCIAL COMPUTER ENVIRONMENT

2.1 The test environment

The development of a strategy for efficient product implementation was necessary if better use of DP facilities in association with the 4GL tools was to be achieved. It was felt essential that a project to assess the real business value of the products should be undertaken using a real processing system. The one chosen to evaluate the product was the warehouse control system. This was felt to be representative of database systems within the company concerned, and in terms of the outstanding user requirements in the business it was felt that QM might well fulfil a proportion of them. There were worries within senior DP management about the amount of machine processing power that might be needed to support such a product, and consequently a working party reflecting the interests of all areas of DP in 4GLs was convened.

The working party had input from all areas of DP within the company. Interest was centred on a number of considerations, including the products' extra use of machine resource and the impact of using Contents Addressable Filestore (CAFS) in association with them. CAFS is an ICL product directed at extracting data directly off disks. The CAFS product is vended by ICL as a major method of reducing processing costs, and is therefore of potentially strategic importance to computerized businesses. Other interests were concerned with the potential cost reduction for business areas due to the increased programming requests that may be "farmed out" to them directly. As well as the programming and machine-environment impacts on the implementation of the 4GL product being assessed, a third area of DP interest in the evaluation was concerned with the strategic value of 4GLs to businesses to improve modelling, and its value in encouraging people to adhere to corporate standards of documentation, analysis and design. This is because the 4GL products rely on Data-Dictionary-sourced information to operate. Thus corporate standards of documentation were shown to have direct business benefit, as the Data Dictionary is the recognized medium for recording all business and computing information within the company.

The method of assessment chosen to undertake the evaluation was to replicate existing report programs for the stock-control system in COBOL, RM and QM and test their total costings using a copy of the live database. The time taken to write the various programs using the different languages was to be included in the evaluation results, combining program production with their costs to run. These running costs were to be identified for a five-year period, which is the standard system life for any development (in terms of accounting purposes). Extrapolations were made based upon the likely frequency of program use, as reports are produced on different timescales. These timescales are normally, often (weekly), regularly (monthly) and occasionally *(ad hoc)*. As a result of this each programming method had three overall running costs to reflect the varying timescales.

The study wished to examine the impact of the CAFS product on run times, as the vendors, ICL, had indicated dramatic savings by its use. The business focus of the study was determined as being QM and consequently this was the language the CAFS product was linked to. This was because QM was the heaviest user of machine resource of the three, so the savings using CAFS could be expected to be the greatest, and secondly because the emphasis of the whole survey was to use the latest technique to reduce business costs of computing. Since COBOL and RM require much more training to implement than QM, if more end-user computing was to be achieved within the company then QM was the language most likely to achieve the goal.

2.2   Results of the evaluation

The evaluation was undertaken using a number of RM programs currently on the live stock-control system as the basis for the comparison. These were replicated in COBOL by a trainee programmer as part of his education (and, therefore, at no cost to the user). The reports were then reproduced by the members of the working party using QM. The costs of production of the RM programs were already known, but were recalculated at current unit rates so as to be on the same basis as the COBOL and QM equivalents.

Each individual run was monitored to obtain machine-resource cost comparisons. Particular attention was paid to the processing power (OCP use) necessary to run each job, because of the impact of this factor in the charging algorithms, and concerns about the increased requirements of such power that 4GLs themselves need in order to operate properly.

A specific computer environment was created for the evaluation, together with a CAFS-searchable copy of the live database. This allowed searching to be applied without affecting normal work on the live database, permitted CAFS testing and ensured all tests were directly comparable.

The results are presented in tabular form, and all of the unit costs quoted in the tables are at the unit-cost levels relevant to the company in question. No assumptions concerning either future inflation or changes to costing algorithms were made.

The programs were run in RM, COBOL and then QM 210, which was the version supported at the time the evaluation began. The results obtained are given below in Figure 17.1.

Prog. No.	COBOL		Reportmaster		Querymaster	
	Prod.	Run	Prod.	Run	Prod.	Run
1	480	0.73	120	1.09	10	1.40
2	240	5.94	120	8.18	5	10.91
3	240	0.93	120	1.63	5	2.23

Note: Prod. = Unit Production Cost.

Figure 17.1 Program unit costs for the stock-control system used in the 4GL evaluation.

As these figures stand, the results are misleading. In order to quantify the cost differences more objectively, a life of five years was assumed for each report. The next table, (Figure 17.2 overleaf) indicates the run costs for the programs, if they were run weekly and monthly over this system life.

Run No.	COBOL		Reportmaster		Querymaster	
	Weekly	Monthly	Weekly	Monthly	Weekly	Monthly
1	189.8	43.8	283.4	65.4	364	84
2	1544.4	357.4	2126.8	490.8	2415.4	557.4
3	241.8	55.8	415.8	97.8	579.8	133.8
TOTAL	1976.0	457.0	2826.0	654.0	3359.2	775.2

Figure 17.2 Unit run for the stock-control report programs given a five-year system life.

Whilst these figures include system life and run frequency, they exclude development costs. These were then incorporated into the costings and the combined results are given in Figure 17.3 below.

Run No.	COBOL		Reportmaster		Querymaster	
	Weekly	Monthly	Weekly	Monthly	Weekly	Monthly
1	669.8	523.8	403.4	185.4	374	94
2	1784.4	597.4	2246.8	610.8	2420.4	562.4
3	481.8	295.8	535.8	352.8	584.8	138.8
TOTAL	2936	1417	3186	1014	3379.2	795.2

Figure 17.3 Rationalized unit costings for stock-control report programs given a five-years system life.

As discussed earlier in this Section, 4GLs require extra processing power to run than standard COBOL programs (measured in OCP seconds). To assess this increased overhead in using such products as QM the OCP times of the runs were also monitored. We were informed that the linkage of QM with the CAFS product could significantly reduce the OCP time used to produce reports, and since each OCP second costs in unit cross charging terms this was felt to be a major aspect of the whole assessment. Therefore the effect of using CAFS on the enquiries made with QM was now considered, still using QM210. The results are shown in Figure 17.4 below.

Run No.	QM210 Without CAFS		QM210 With CAFS	
	OCP	Unit Cost	OCP	Unit Cost
1	-	1.4	179	0.88
2	146	10.91	85	7.2
3	16	2.23	- CAFS ERROR -	

Figure 17.4 Comparison of the effect of CAFS when using QM210 in the stock-control system.

The reduction in the costs by using CAFS with QM210 was quite dramatic in the two cases where the reports were capable of being produced. The third program failed because of a QM210 / CAFS problem, solved by QM250.

Also of interest here is the effect on the normal workload of changing the database page format, as required for CAFS searching. ICL had estimated an OCP overhead of approximately 2%, but the study determined this to be an 11% overhead for non-CAFS work. This was identified when a standard stock-control-statistics production run was undertaken against both the live database and the CAFS-searchable copy with identical data.

At this stage, the QM250 product was introduced into the evaluation and the last set of criteria reapplied. Figure 17.5 below shows the results.

Run No.	QM250 Without CAFS		QM250 With CAFS	
	OCP	Unit Cost	OCP	Unit Cost
1	154	1.60	136	0.97
2	232	15.52	94	9.63
3	25	5.43	23	3.31

Figure 17.5 Comparison of the effect of CAFS when using QM250 in the stock-control system.

As can be seen in both Figure 17.4 and 17.5, the CAFS runs show savings over non-CAFS in all cases, with some instances of dramatic reductions in OCP utilization.

At this stage confidence in the QM250 product was so great that QM210 was decommissioned. Figure 17.6 below is a replication of Figure 17.3, to allow comparison of the overall costs with QM250 replacing QM210.

Run No.	COBOL		Reportmaster		Querymaster	
	Weekly	Monthly	Weekly	Monthly	Weekly	Monthly
1	669.8	523.8	403.4	185.4	262.2	68.2
2	1784.4	597.4	2246.8	610.8	2508.8	582.8
3	237	147	260	108	863.1	201.1
TOTAL	2691.2	1268.2	2910.2	904.2	3634.1	852.1

Figure 17.6 Revised rationalized unit costings over five years using QM250 (with CAFS).

These results are considered in comparative terms in Figure 17.7, where COBOL is used as the benchmark.

Weekly		Monthly	
RM	QM	RM	QM
+8%	+35%	-28%	-33%

Figure 17.7 Percentage difference in costs for the reports given a five-year life (COBOL=100%).

As can be seen from this summary, significant overall savings can be made for programs run on a monthly basis, using either RM or QM as against COBOL. The surprising result was that the RM weekly runs cost slightly more than their COBOL equivalents. Whilst it was anticipated that QM would be significantly more expensive for frequently run programs over a five-year system life, RM was expected to achieve runtime efficiency very much closer to COBOL.

Further analysis of this apparent anomaly showed that the data area, and therefore mainstore requirement, for RM tends to be large but remain fairly constant whilst, for COBOL, it increases with the complexity of the program. Except for Run 1, none of the programs was particularly large and, therefore, the mainstore requirements were less for the COBOL programs. For Run 1, RM costings came out at only 60% of of their COBOL equivalent for the weekly run over five years, which illustrates the point very clearly. It is the other, smaller, COBOL runs which compare favourably to RM for weekly runs.

It is felt that these results do have important implications for future system developments. These implications, and a strategy to maximize the benefits available from the analysis are considered in detail in Section 3.

3   CONCLUSIONS AND RECOMMENDATIONS

3.1   A strategy for the use of fourth-generation languages

This paper recommends that the use of 4GLs in commercial organizations IS best implemented by functionally splitting their introduction between new and existing systems.

The recommended approach to new systems development is as follows:-

- A full analysis of the business requirements for data and processing will always be undertaken to installation standards. Currently this requires proper use of structured analysis, including user participation.

- The findings of the analysis will be recorded on the Data Dictionary and used to generate a prototype solution via application generators (like the ICL Quickbuild product set, including an end-user query language, such as QM).

- The prototype will be demonstrated to and checked with the user, to ensure its support of identified needs and to reveal any latent requirements.

- The user will be advised of the possibilities of supporting his reporting requirements using the appropriate available methods (COBOL, RM or QM etc.). Advice will also be provided on the cost implications for production and support of the proposed solution. Particularly, the user will be guided towards reducing complexity so as to minimize costs.

- Data structures will be designed with the use of 4G techniques in mind, and vetted by DP to ensure they provide for the effective use of these products.

- Users without prior experience of 4GL techniques will always be provided with full training in their use when any part of their reporting requirement is to be satisfied by such products.

In terms of the analysis on the ICL products detailed in Section 2 the company recommended the following approach be adopted:

(A) Standard report programs that are to be run more frequently than monthly will be produced using RM.

(B) COBOL will only be used for reports which are both standard and frequently run:

- where the user insists on a level of complexity not supportable by RM;

- for very small report programs; and

- for those easily derived from existing COBOL programs.

(C) QM will always be the first choice for *ad hoc* reports and for standard reports run monthly or less frequently, unless the product is incapable of meeting the user requirement. If this should be the case, RM should be chosen in preference to COBOL.

(D) All post-implementation requests for additional reports will, wherever possible, first be satisfied by a QM solution. Once the user is clearly able to identify the usefulness of the report and the required frequency of its production, the above criteria will be applied to establish the means of its ongoing production.

The experience of other organizations where QM has been made available to users is that the user will normally have initiated this process before approaching DP.

Whilst the above strategy is ideal for entirely new systems, it needs to be modified where such products are being considered as an enhancement to an existing system: all requests will be "post implementation" by definition, and users will have had little direct involvement in the production of the system. Suggestions for this type of situation are as follows:

- DP staff are to be trained in the use of the 4GLs.

- These staff will also be provided with training in the exploitation of 4GLs on systems not designed with its use in mind, with particular reference to those systems for which they provide support.

- The activities specified above for new systems will be performed by these staff, with paragraph (D) as the start point.

If these strategic guidelines are adopted, the view of this paper is that the outcome will be much greater effectiveness in the use of resources, both human and financial.

3.2 Potential limitations on the use of fourth-generation languages

For historic reasons, the dictionary documentation of business data and processing for existing systems is frequently inadequate, if not entirely absent. This deficiency makes it much more difficult for users to be involved with the production of their own reports and, in all probability, will prevent them from using products such as QM without considerable training in the detail of the system implementation.

Whilst this is not an insurmountable problem, it will require a greater degree of DP involvement than new systems developed with end-user access in mind. This needs to be planned for because, once the knowledge of such products as QM becomes widespread their potential for the satisfaction of *ad hoc* reporting requirements will unquestionably increase further, and more requests for information will be made.

It must also be recognized by business areas that certain systems may be too large for QM-type products to be applied to directly. In the company discussed in this analysis any system with over 250,000 records only had an aspect, or subset of the data accessible using QM, (a "Query View" which was not the whole record structure, but a grouping of data of interest to the business for specific purposes).

Because such products have a number of set needs and identified limitations, they cannot provide a universal solution to reporting needs. The recommendation for the technical implementation of QM in the company in the study was along the guidelines given below;

QM, as a mainframe facility, was designed to be operated by end-users. Consequently it was to be utilized primarily during the normal working day – at peak machine-loading times. In order to provide a usable service, whilst ensuring the minimum possible interference with other applications, it was recommended that the following controls on machine and data access be adopted:

- No user area should be given direct access to the product for 12 months.

- During the intervening 12 months the DP staff who will support users of the product to be trained in its exploitation.

- An "enquiry desk" to service user requests during the 12 months be set up. Initially, users requests limited to set times of the day.

- The enquiry desk to provide a "same-day" response. However, requests which involve excessive run times should be submitted in batch mode for overnight running and next-day delivery. The user to be informed when this is necessary.

- The use of the product to be closely monitored to provide accurate estimates as to its impact on capacity management.

- To permit the use of CAFS by QM without incurring extra overheads for non-CAFS work and to minimize the impact on production TP, queries to be undertaken only on copies of live databases.

- Because a CAFS-searchable database can only be constructed from a non-CAFS version via IDMS dump and restore software, the security strategies for production databases on which it is required to use CAFS to be reviewed, and the additional costs identified to users.

- Query Views providing access to relevant subsets of data are defined by DP. These take account of operational and performance criteria, plus any restrictions required to comply with the Data Protection Act registration for the system.

During the period before the product was made generally available, demonstrations to potentially interested users were undertaken. This allowed those users who required to use QM themselves to include any necessary financing in their Business Plans.

3.3   Fourth-generation languages and business areas

The first consideration which needs to be addressed in this context is user education. Potential users must be informed of the implications for their business of the adoption of such products. This includes their capabilities and their limitations, together with the costs of implementation and use. The 4G techniques are not a universal panacea for existing system deficiencies, nor are they the whole answer to reducing the costs of future systems. We must ensure this is well understood by end-users.

Optimally, consideration of the applicability of such products would occur in the context of identifying the information requirements of the business area, as part of the analysis for a new system design. The structured analysis methods require user involvement in understanding the business data and processing from the earliest stage. Having stored in the Data Dictionary the results of this analysis, together with a comprehensive understanding of the requirements for a system to support the business, the production and demonstration of a prototype may be seen as an early deliverable of the analysis. Its purpose is, to cross check the analysis with the users, prior to undertaking real systems design.

Prototype production from the results of thorough data analysis is a relatively simple and speedy exercise. In a linked study in the company mentioned in this paper a prototype took less than a month to produce, using limited manpower resources and no application generation tools. The use of a products like Quickbuild for prototyping can reduce this time by about 75%.

An approach of this style enables users to see an outline of how their system will work to support their business, before real design work is undertaken and, thus, further validate the analysis. As well as assisting in increasing user participation in decisions on the eventual implementation, the approach gives users an early opportunity to see if 4GL tools have the type of capabilities they will require for reporting on their data.

In this way, user involvement in the implemented system may be encouraged, where this is an appropriate option. Here it must be recognized that not all systems will be suitable for end-user interrogation, particularly those involving very large data volumes.

User participation of the type suggested above is occurring on a number of new systems, where it is estimated that report production by the users via such techniques will reduce the report-program-production timescales and costs by some 70%. This estimate is based on the figures given in Section 2.

Savings in development will, of course, be tempered by increases in machine running costs, due to the extra demands placed on those resources. However these increased charges will be offset by reductions in programming support costs, resulting from the users themselves satisfying a large proportion of their report production requirements, with DP staff acting in a consultancy role.

The tangible benefit of this approach to any single user system is a reduction in the charge for increasingly expensive human resources in exchange for additional, but continually decreasing (in proportional terms), computing costs. This will provide an overall lessening of costs over a system life of five years. The currently less tangible benefits should be the increased availability of manpower for new systems development and increased use and development of the data asset by business areas.

Chapter 18

EXPERIENCES WITH A FOURTH-GENERATION LANGUAGE: TELON WITHIN AMRO-BANK

J.A.P.G. Verbraak
AMRO-Bank

1   INTRODUCTION

During the spring of 1984, the Automation and Organization department of AMRO-Bank decided to build the AIRS system *. A preliminary calculation of the required manpower needed to realize the functionally developed concept showed that the project would grow to unacceptable proportions.

This in addition to the already existing software backlog, was the reason to investigate 4GLs. The project team and development support centre were required to find a product that would

1.   give sufficient productivity increases to ensure a payback within the life of the project; and

2.   preferably fit in with the existing knowledge and procedures.

The investigation was finished within six weeks and shortly thereafter a trial agreement was signed for Telon. Apart from Telon the other on-line IMS generators investigated were: MAPK V, ADF II, UFO and Delta. Although each product had pros and cons, the deciding factors in favour of Telon were:

---

* AIRS is an on-line IMS system for registration and information supply concerning all automation equipment and software tools of the AMRO-bank. It also supports a number of operational functions (purchasing, logistics, budgeting and contract management)

- High acceptability by programmmers because of the fit with and likeness to the TSO-ISPF working method.

- Small risk to AMRO in case of a trial failure. Telon generates COBOL source is not present in the production environment.

- Integrated and interactive test facility.

In this chapter I will outline the integration process since 1984. How smoothly did Telon really integrate? What kind of management action has been taken?

The experiences discussed are based on my period as project manager of the AIRS pilot project and a small research carried out in 1988 in which various medium-scale projects were observed.

2   AMRO-BANK IN BRIEF

2.1   General information

Amsterdam-Rotterdam Bank NV — AMRO Bank for short — recorded total assets of f 143 billion at the end of 1987 and a net profit of f 480 million.

The bank is engaged in all areas of commercial and investment banking, for corporate customers and private individuals, for governments and institutions.

AMRO has over 23,000 employees and about 800 branches in the Netherlands, besides substantial international operations. Its customers include about two million private individuals and some 175,000 corporations.

In view of the liberalization of the European market after 1992 AMRO-Bank and Generale Bank NV of Belgium have announced a close cooperation in order to become ultimately one banking unit.

2.2 EDP poiicy

AMRO's large-scale EDP organization consists of about 800 employees. At the branch-offices Philips terminals are installed which are connected to the central IBM-mainframes in the computer centre of Amstelveen.

Since the early 1970s electronic DP forms an integrated part of almost all financial services AMRO offers to its clients and of its internal processes and administrations.

AMRO's information policy nowadays adresses the need to enhance the commercial product range based on information technology such as those already existing: electronic funds transfer, treasury management services and security services. Within the automation department this type of system is called "external integration": this indicates the fact that our customers have a direct connection to AMRO's computers by means of data communication.

Therefore huge investments in information technology are made: about 250 million guilders a year until 1990.

To further utilize the information technology as a strategic weapon a lot of work has to be done.

Key tasks are:

- turnaround from batch systems to on-line real-time systems;
- security of the systems-complex;
- diminishing the software backlog.

2.3 Information systems department

About 400 employees are working in the information systems departments, at the top level organizationally allocated to the business sectors they work for.

The following business sectors are identified:

1. Domestic market and branch offices.

2. Corporate customers and foreign offices.

3. Corporate staff and central services.

Each ISD is divided into three departments :

    1. Information planning: information strategy / project-definition.

    2. Systems development: system design / programming /
       implementation.

    3. Information center: end-user computing.

The standard programming language is COBOL: Method/l is practised as system development method.

Centrally organized are STIO (system, telecommunication, information organization) and NCF (network and computer facilities).

STIO is the technical research department which supports NCF on hardware matters and the ISDs on the application developments areas such as data management, CASE, methodology etc.

NCF operates the computer centres of AMRO, both in Amstelveen and Tilburg and the entire data communication network which includes a.o. all 800 branch-offices, gateways to international networks (SWIFT), Automated Cash Terminals and connections with large clients. NCF will extend its operations to 7 days a week and 24 hours a day.

3   TELON

3.1   Characteristics

The package on-line version release 1.4

TELON is a program generator that is used to develop conversational IMS applications. The development is carried out interactively under TSO control, whereby the developer describes the following:

- data-acces preprogram (this information can partially be copied from existing IMS control blocks which reside in AMRO's Data Dictionary);

- screens with the aid of screen painting;

- the relationships between database fields and screen labels;

- validations;

- dialogue structure;

- if necessary extra processing routines, eg in the form of COBOL statements (= custom code).

Using these descriptions Telon generates COBOL-source and MFS source to serve IMS screens. Aside from the development facilities Telon has a test-facility with which a program can be interactively tested under TSO. The generated source code is structured according to the Jackson-technique.

Telon has also a prototyping facility which allows the developer to show screen-to screen flow, with or without data. Simple screen or field checks can be easily changed at the user's request.

Telon was released by Christens Systems in 1983. Pansophic acquired Christensen at the end of 1984. Worldwide the package has over 200 customers, of which about 20 in the Benelux.

3.2 Application area

The area in which Telon-online is being used within AMRO is very broad. Telon has become the standard language for all conversational IMS-DC programs (operating under IBM 3270 mode).

Starting with ten programmers in 1984 the current situation is that about 100 to 150 developers are working with Telon. The total number of Telon-programs produced is between 2000 and 2500.

Although Telon was originally designed for IMS databases, some pilot projects with DB2 have nevertheless been undertaken.

The functional areas remain restricted to the transaction systems at the head-offices such as:

- back-office banking systems (stocks, insurance, financial mgt);
- logistic systems (personnel, office equipment, warehouse);
- maintenance functions of front-office applications.

This restriction is due to the fact that AMRO's hardware policy is based on Philips terminals at the branch offices. This PTS-6000 system has it own DC-monitor which is non-compatible with Telon. Therefore the mass of AMRO's front-office applications is closed for development with Telon.

3.3 Knowledge level

Telon is a fairly complex package and the learning process is relative. One has to know quite a number of commands (choices within menu-driven Telon) to be able to develop a program. Consequently, after a period of non-involvement it takes a little while to get back into it. This is not fully offset by the fact that less IMS/DC and MFS knowledge is required. IMS/DB knowledge remains necessary in order to make optimum use of the Telon test facility.

At least one project team member should have VSAM-knowledge in order to manage the Telon datasets.

The learning time for a starting project amounts to three weeks for a simple application and six to eight weeks for a fairly complex application. This time was taken from the finish of the four-day course given by the supplier. Within AMRO a specific designers course has been developed.

3.4 Performance

With the use of Telon, almost all of the programming activities and an increasing part of the analysis and design activities need to take place at the terminal. It is therefore important that this working environment on the one hand and the performance of Telon on the other hand do not become factors that influence speed negatively. Any possible productivity improvement stands or falls by this basic condition.

As a result of a project called TSO-PROF that took place in 1985, the availability and performance of TSO in the AMRO test computer has been upgraded drastically. Good foreground response, short turnaround times for the batch jobs and personal or PC-terminals for virtually every system developer influence the the capacity to develop in a positive way. This efficient environment obviously does justice to a product such as Telon.

The performance of the package is surprisingly good. The average response time is comparable to that of, for instance, the normal TSO-editor. The efficient storage of VSAM files probably ensures this.

The only increase in the use of resources compared to Telon in the test environment is in the extra generation step during which the Telon source is transferred into COBOL source. Measurements have indicated an increase by a factor of 1.5 compared to a normal compilation.

No good comparison is possible for the production environment. Although in the AMRO situation the influence of Telon on the total response time is negligible, it has to be noted that none of the developed systems has had extremely high transaction volumes yet.

4   IMPACT ON SOFTWARE DEVELOPMENT

4.1   Productivity increase

IMS

A classic symptom manifested in the use of different program generators is the relationship between the possible productivity increases and the complexity of the application.

After the experience of nearly four years and more than 2000 programs, it is also possible to establish this relationship with Telon.

Table 18.1 is a comparison between Telon and COBOL development in an IMS-DB/DC environment in man days per program (= per screen).

	TELON				COBOL		
	System Analyst	Progr	Total		S/A	P	Total
Simple	1.0	0.5	1.5		2.5	4.5	7.0
Medium	2.0	2.0	4.0		3.5	6.5	10.0
Complex	5.0	4.0	9.0		5.0	7.0	12.0

Table 18.1: Telon-COBOL Comparison

For a correct interpretation of these figures it is important to realize:

1. The productivity increases start when system design is done and finish upon completion of the user test. The transfer from test to production isn't affected.

2. The distinction between simple and complex applications. Key characteristics of simple applications are:

   • no multifunction screens, ie add, update and list functions;

   • hierarchical dialogue structure, no horizontal crossing between dialogue branches;

   • dialogue structure is in line with DB structure;

   • one occurrence of a database segment insert or update per screen.

3. The number of programs developed under Telon will exceed the number of COBOL programs for a typical system. Applying above guidelines will lead to splitting up functions into more simple ones. Rough estimates indicate that the number of programs grow by some 30%. This factor should of course be subtracted to determine the overall increase in proouctivity.

DB2

For the projects in which DB2 databases were used the increase in productivity was far less than with IMS databases. This is due to the fact that release 1.4. doesn't support DB2. Therefore all SQL statements had to be written manually as embedded custom code. Only a very few facilities of Telon-test could be utilized.

A comparison between the size of the added lines of custom code between a comparable IMS-DB and a DB2 project showed the following:

	CUSTOM CODE	GENERATED CODE
IMS-DB	15 %	85%
DB 2	70 %	30

Table 18.2: Comparison of Size of Added Lines of Code

Since beginning of 1988 version 2.0 which supports DB2, is installed at AMRO.

4.2 Maintenance

Within AMRO the preferred methodology as suggested by Telon is adhered to as much as possible. Complex applications are avoided when possible, not so much due to the expectation that development will take longer compared to COBOL, but rather to the maintainability of the application in the system maintenance phase.

Whereas development with Telon will always be faster than in COBOL, with maintenance it is not as straightforward. Simple applications show an even higher increase in productivity during maintenance. However, with complex applications we expect an adverse effect. The addition of substantial custom code and the opening of "the box of tricks" deliver a program, despite the Jackson program structure, whose function is not always sufficiently clear. Another risk we faced was the fact that new releases were not always 100% compatible with those parts of the program where work-arounds in custom code had been applied.

Another aspect related to maintenance was the fast-growing number of modifications. Many more user requests for light or heavy modifications were honoured than would be the case in a COBOL system. Because modifications are so easy and quick to implement the discipline taken in to account both by the user and developer is apparently declining.

4.3   Shift in function

System analyst / programmer

The productivity increases with Telon are especially effective in the programming phase. The use of Telon speeds up the work of the programmer to such an extent that the traditional task separation between systems analyst and programmer becomes somewhat unbalanced. The delivery of and communication on the program specifications very quickly becomes too heavy an overhead. Within AMRO a combined function has been created: system analyst/programmer. Analysis and programming can now be performed by the same person without loss of quality. At the same time the acquiring of new programmers was stopped: nowadays only candidates with growth potential to system analyst are adopted at AMRO-Bank.

System designer

In the design phase the system designer is responsible for both functional and technical design aspects. The design qualities of the system designer need to be focused on data analysis and database design, being the only fundamental aspects to be influenced. The IMS database structure strongly determines to what degree the "Telon preferred solution" can be used. This in turn will determine the level of productivity increases.

Moreover the system designer uses the Telon-provided tools for documenting screen layouts, field checks, and dialogue structures. This eliminates the duplicate effort of re-entering design input in later stages.

Practical implementation

The integration process does not always work out in the above way. In some system-development groups we see that the former systems analyst completes the job by himself: he or she writes the program specification fully in Telon, generates the program and performs the testing. In other groups the programmer gets his change to perform the entire job.

In the more conservative groups, however, nothing has changed yet: only the quantitative division has been adapted. The systems analyst gets only one programmer instead of two or three.

As far as the system designer is concerned we see two aspects. The first is a practical one: many of our functional system designers were not used to working with automated TSO-like tools. They missed the "hands-on" ability, which initially put them behind their collegues.

Another aspect was more fundamental. Being aware of the Telon-preferred solutions is not enough; the design should also be adressed to them. This invokes that already in the functional design phase a set of concrete design guidelines is applied. Most rules are often so simple that even users can apply them. Most system designers regard it as positive development; they can now spend their time on the real user-problems and by doing so they shift to the information-analysis and information-planning phase.

Conclusion

It will be obvious that the highest increase in productivity can only be reached if traditional task separation is abolished in an active way. Project management should be aware of this and emphasize it to each development group manager.

4.4   Development support centre

It is preferable to have a central Telon support function. Within AMRO this function is performed by the development support centre, a sub-department of STIO.

Tasks:

- Direction supplier: focal point for new releases, package-information, communicating problems and wishes.

- Direction STIO: coordinating the installation of new software releases and corrections.

- Direction NCF: organize procedures for the transfer from the application-program to the production environment.

- Direction project groups:

  - give demonstrations and courses (programmers and designer);
  - introduce new releases;

- build common utilities;
- support on individual practical problems (re-active);
- support the start-up of new Telon projects (pro-active);
- maintain a Telon-manual containing procedures, solutions, workarounds, users-list and design guidelines;
- represent the Benelux user-group.

Practical implementation

At the start of Telon in 1984/85 this task was performed by two persons. As Telon becomes more and more familiar nowadays one person can manage it.

Despite its central role it seems not so easy for DSC to create knowledge transfer between the various groups. Apparently every project group in the beginning faces the same "irritating" problems, without seeking for structural solutions on other groups. When asked many system developers said that they regarded it as the best way of learning the new tool. "By merely asking we don't learn it ourselves."

4.5 Spin-offs

By spin-offs I mean positive consequences which have not arisen on purpose.

1. 80% solution/user participation

The most important one is the breakthrough of what we at AMRO call the "80% solution". The "80% solution" is a system which contains only that part of the functional requirements of the user which really, quantifiably, contributes to a more efficient or effective situation. Functions which are nice to have but do not have a significant added value are no longer included in the first release of a system. As Telon forces one to think in primary functions and its complexity means the developer is far better equipped to discuss with the user the real need of a function than before. Thus project control is eased.

Despite the move towards 80% solutions our users seem to be quite satisfied with the new approach. Now they know far earlier what is really possible and what is not. In the conventional working method functional designers spend months in interviewing and writing down requirements, wishes, restraints, procedures and translate that into a functional design, usually an enormous report as end product. It was the primary job of the technical staff to judge the functional design on feasibility and "stupidities".

When using Telon in the functional design phase technical feasibility can be judged far earlier. This improved user participation is positively influenced by the panel presentation facility which enables dialogue prototyping. Utilizing the Telon test facility cuts the delay prior to the user being confronted with the final system by several weeks.

2.   Pressure on potential new critical factors in the technical infrastructure

As outlined before Telon is especially active in the programming phase. Components of the system-development process which ultimately came under pressure were: all activities related to the data dictionary and all activities needed to transfer an application system from the test computer to the production environment.

5   CONCLUSION

Telon can be seen as a reliable aid in the development of on-line IMS applications. Although odd cosmetic changes could be made to the package, it is well liked and realizes considerable — though not the promised — spectactular savings.

The smooth integration into the AMRO development environment, aimed at continuity and reliability, has been the most critical success factor. Telon characteristics made it possible but management action had to finalize it. An optimal benefit certainly requires adaptation in the development organization and lifestyle, as I have tried to explain in this chapter.

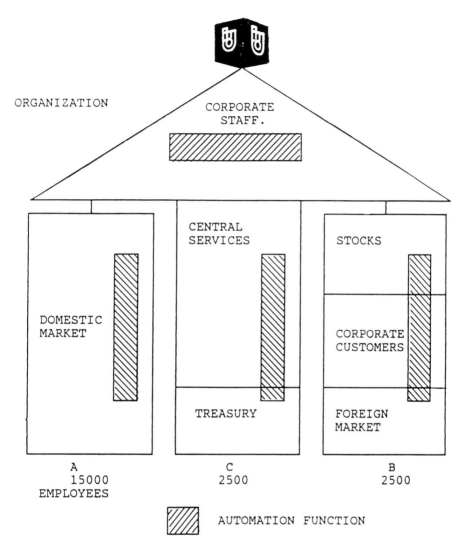

ORGANIZATION

CORPORATE
STAFF.

CENTRAL
SERVICES

STOCKS

DOMESTIC
MARKET

CORPORATE
CUSTOMERS

TREASURY

FOREIGN
MARKET

A
15000
EMPLOYEES

C
2500

B
2500

AUTOMATION FUNCTION

Figure 18.1   The AMRO-bank in brief – organization.

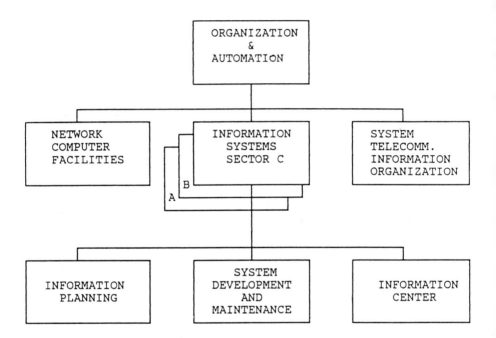

Figure 18.2 The AMRO-Bank in brief – information systems department.

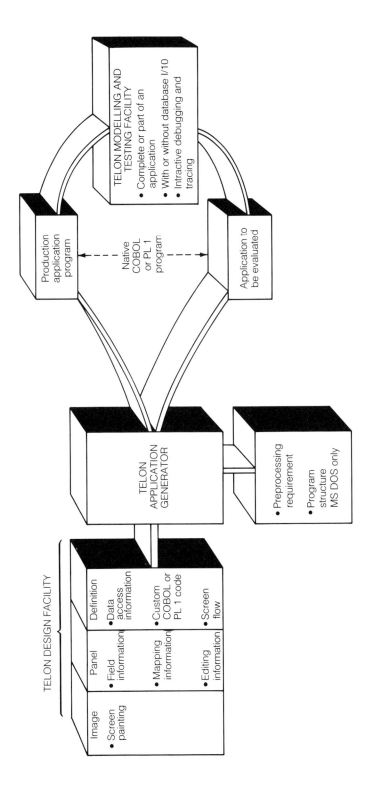

Figure 18.3 Telon.

283

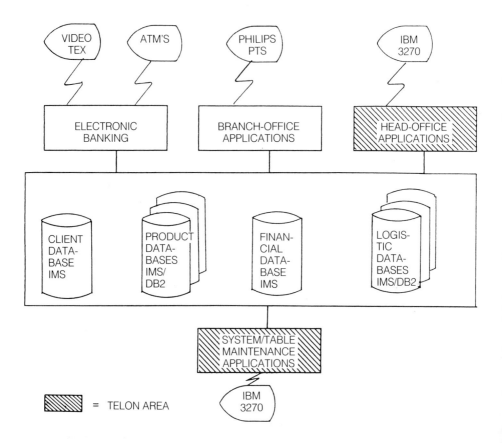

Figure 18.4 Telon experiences within AMRO – functional area.

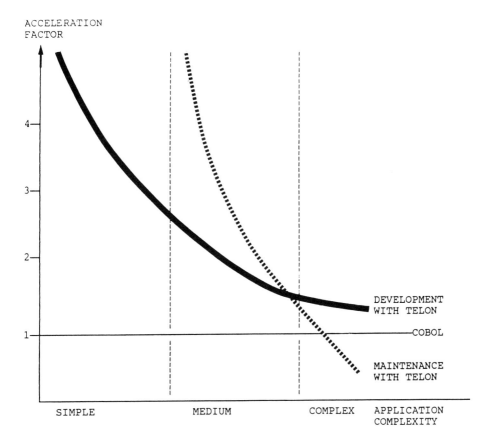

ACCELERATION
FACTOR

4 —
3 —
2 —
1 —

DEVELOPMENT
WITH TELON

COBOL

MAINTENANCE
WITH TELON

SIMPLE   MEDIUM   COMPLEX   APPLICATION
                                       COMPLEXITY

Figure 18.5   Impact on software development – productivity increase.

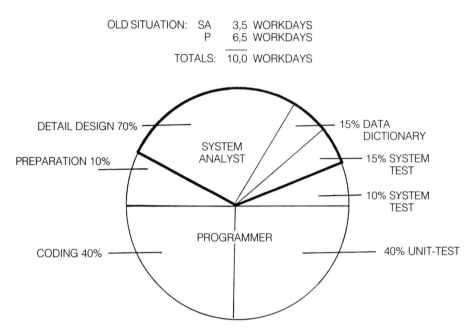

Figure 18.6 Impact on software development – division workelements.

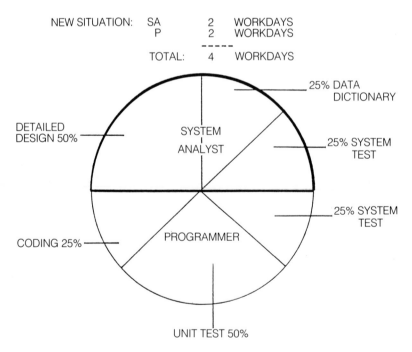

Figure 18.7 Impact on software development – division workelements.

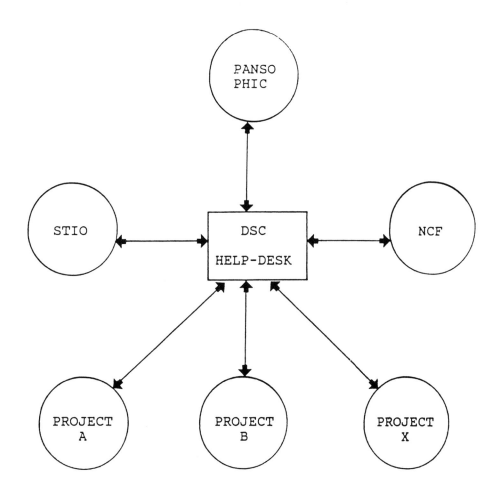

Figure 18.8 Impact on software development – development support centre.

NEW PRODUCTS:
THE VENDOR'S DETAILS

Chapter 19
FOURTH-GENERATION SOFTWARE TOOLS —
THE NEW OPPORTUNITY ?

R.S. Raizada
Limrose Software Limited,

What is 4G software, and why does it offer new opportunities claimed by 4GL vendors and software houses ? What is in it for you, the end-user ?

These and many other questions about 4G software are continually being asked and this chapter is an attempt to answer them briefly. First of all, 4G software is not the half-way solution to 5G computing so often talked about (eg the Alvey programme, expert and knowledge-based systems etc) and does not actually involve too many new radical directions in computing. It is the "pragmatic" solution to problems facing software developers working with 3GL "procedural" programming languages such as COBOL, BASIC, Fortran etc. 4G software enables the end-user to develop customized software without requiring massive resources in terms of time and financial support.

1   RELATIONAL VIEW OF DATA

4G software tools fall in various categories, all of which at their heart accept the "relational" view of data. The relational database concept provides greater flexibility to manipulate data than is possible with conventional database software. The relational database, in its essence, uses simple tables of data which are "linked" together with the application software to achieve the desired results. The application programme is isolated from the database structure. This is not possible with the older type of databases, using the hierarchical or network approach. Although none of the products currently available actually satisfy all the requirements of the relational model as postulated by E.F. Codd (the relational guru who first formally postulated the concept), the relational database is at the heart of many 4GL products.

The "pure" relational database concept, however, has been compromised by software vendors in the interest of development speed, faster data retrieval and greater flexibility in data organization. However, it has now been widely recognized that having a relational database structure incorporated within a 4GL framework is no guarantee of its usefulness and practicality. For a 4GL product to be successful, it must in addition be user friendly, flexible and thoroughly proven.

The fourth-generation programming languages (4GL) are just one aspect of 4G software. Numerous 4GL products are currently on the market with varying degrees of integration with their own databases, data dictionaries, report generators, form generators, graphics processors and other software tools.

2   4GL AS NON-PROCEDURAL LANGUAGES

As yet, no universal definition of 4GLs has been accepted. The UK Institute of Data Processing Management prefers the formal definition which states that "4GLs are non-procedural languages. That is, they are specification languages rather than programming languages ... and are suitable for describing what is to be done but not how it is to be done by a computer." In other words, 4GLs provide facilities which free the user from having to consider the way the computer will process the work. According to this definition, programs which simply speed up software generation, such as COBOL speed-up tools, are not 4GL. However, even a fairly basic code generator would be classified as a 4GL. Other 4GLs include complex application generators and complete system development environments suitable for both end-users and professional programmers.

3   THE 4GL TEMPLATE APPROACH

The pure 4GL is a language for describing the parameters of a job — a template, with which the end-user can develop his software and achieve twentyfold or more gain in development speed. Not all products are "pure" 4GL, and some rely heavily on a procedural approach. However a good 4GL would avoid "procedures" and can be entirely "menu driven". Although an overall query language interface is often used with 4GLs, it is not necessary and end-users find a menu-driven program easier to use in many situations. However, IBM's SQL query language is likely to become a prerequisite for all 4GL products in the near future.

The "pure" 4GL (which ideally is totally non-procedural) end-user does not have to be a professional programmer, although he must be computer literate to some extent. No actual programming is involved and the end-user communicates with the computer by answering a series of questions about the application to complete the "template" which in essence drives the 4GL. The "templates" can include the data dictionary, forms generation, link table, report writers and graphics processor.

In some 4GLs, the template is not actually provided and is "created" by the end-user himself by another menu-driven program. The main reason for the success of 4GL is the template approach. The rationale behind the template approach is the success of "packaged" software, because users cannot afford "customized" software which meets their requirements exactly. The packaged software is a compromise, and the template approach offered by 4GLs takes the user nearer the ideal solution at a cost similar to packaged software. If a 4GL cannot meet all requirements by itself, often a subroutine written in a 3GL can be linked to the application.

Small parts of a system are developed at a time, updated and improved until they meet user requirements and then "linked" together finally to produce the "integrated" software. Report generation and graphics output is usually added at the last stage to complete the "package". However, the finished product can still be altered, and management control of systems development becomes more in line with general requirements and corporate budgets. Smaller components can often be developed as "prototype" systems after a day or so, without the need for detailed specifications and large budgets.

However, using a 4GL is not always a substitute for proper analysis of user requirements, and it is absolutely essential that a thorough analysis of these requirements is undertaken at some stage.

4 PROGEN 4GL — THE TOTAL NON-PROCEDURAL SOLUTION

PROGEN 4GL is a "non-procedural" 4G programming language developed by Limrose Software Limited, Wrexham, Clwyd, UK PROGEN 4GL is non-procedural and menu-driven throughout. It incorporates a multi-dimensional relational database structure, but has additional features to increase its speed and practical usefulness particularly in microcomputer systems. It uses a "flexible relational" approach so that the linkages between data files can be made as relational as necessary to meet user requirements.

It is not often realized that a truly relational data structure is neither necessary nor desirable in some applications, whereas it is absolutely necessary in others. For example, in an invoicing application it would be unacceptable to permit a customer address to be altered or edited after an invoice has been created, even though the customer has moved elsewhere afterwards. On the other hand, in insurance policy software any changes in the customer address must be reflected automatically in all related files. The "relational" linkages therefore must be controllable in a practical package and it should be possible to alter the linkages significantly without affecting data file structures and referential integrity. Loss of referential integrity results in loss of data and can corrupt a database significantly to make it unuseable.

PROGEN 4GL uses a "relational flag" in the data dictionary for linked fields to control data transfer between tables. This flag can be altered without affecting the data already stored in the computer, or affecting its reliability in any manner whatsoever. All indexes, except those used for defining relational linkages, can be edited at any time without affecting referential integrity. PROGEN 4GL, thus offers a very flexible relational structure. It also incorporates "write-forward" and "write-back" facilities and up to 50 "tables" can be linked together relationally to form an "integrated" database and transaction-processing environment.

To facilitate data recovery in case of hardware or software failure, each record is stamped with the date and time of last update, irrespective of how the data has been updated. Data can be updated by simple editing of the record, or by a transaction anywhere in the computer network to which the particular table is linked.

As PROGEN 4GL is fully menu-driven, columns, views and transactions can be added to existing tables at any time. Adding extra columns to a table is done via a menu-driven program, which is also used to create new tables, transactions and views.

PROGEN 4GL also provides facilities for "large chunk" data retrieval and unlimited numbers of text files can be relationally linked to any table. To facilitate keyword search on large fields, such as titles of books, an automatic "major word indexing" flag can be used with any field. In the major-word-indexing mode, every single word in the title (except minor words such as an, at, on, the etc) will be automatically indexed. This facility is particularly useful in library applications, in which availability of keyword search can make a world of difference.

PROGEN 4GL also offers an "auto-run" mode, in which data from several tables can be combined together for transaction processing for unattended runs, such as overnight production of invoices in a commercial environment. This facility has been found to be very useful in practical commercial applications.

In addition to most of the usual facilities necessary in a practical 4GL software tool, PROGEN 4GL features "multiple input" fields and extensive input data validation − all without using "procedures". Multiple input fields can be used as "keywords" in addition to their numerous practical usages in all types of applications. A 3GL interface is also provided to make PROGEN versatile enough to solve almost any business or other problem.

Random access files and binary search is used throughout in PROGEN 4GL to produce a fast response time, even in moderate to large databases. PROGEN 4GL also has its own built-in data dictionery, applications generator, report writer, forms generator and graphics processor and provides the end-user or system developer with a complete program-development environment.

PROGEN 4GL uses an SQL type of query interface for making selections. Selections criteria can be entered in the computer via a menu-driven program, or as an .SQF file. The menu-driven query programme creates a .SQF file, which can be read by the computer later if necessary. The .SQF file, however, can be created by another program, and sent to the PROGEN 4GL database to make enquiries. This can be done over a network, or in a multi-user system, without having to understand how PROGEN 4GL works, or where the data is stored, to make an enquiry.

A process control interface for PROGEN 4GL, together with an ability to handle additional facilities such as trigonometric and mathematical functions, timers, interrupts etc is under development. Utility programmes are available for PROGEN 4GL to input data generated by most other databases and spreadsheets, and it can also output data files compatible with other software packages.

PROGEN 4GL is available on all IBM-compatibles, the IBM-PS/2 and the Apricot computers in single-user and multi-user versions. Versions for Unix/Xenix and several mainframe computers which support a "C" Compiler are also available. It is highly likely that an IBM DB2-compatible SQL interface will be added to the multi-user and networked versions of PROGEN 4GL at a future date.

5 HOW 4GLS ARE USED – SOME CASE HISTORIES

The following case histories relate to use of PROGEN 4GL in the business environment only, and are an attempt to answer the question "What types of applications are being developed using 4GLs ?"

5.1 Printer's costing package

Most small printers provide a range of services, some of which, such as finishing, are actually contracted out. The workload is shared between a number of printing facilities which are often rented or leased and operational costs are known or can be calculated quite easily. Accurate cost control, and adequate profit margins are essential for a successful operation. This package was developed using an early version of PROGEN 4GL and is linked to "standard" business software (also written in PROGEN) such as sales ledger, purchase ledger, nominal ledgers, stock control etc. The package has been in use for over three years now.

5.2   PROGEN solves consultant's nightmare

A firm of industrial consultants, employing about 50 consultants, needed a reliable costing and invoicing package customized to meet their specific requirements. A search through available packages proved fruitless, and a special package was written in PROGEN 4GL to meet their requirements. The package includes consultant, project and client registers, and consultant "time sheets" which are fed into the computer for cost analysis and invoicing purposes. This package has also been in use for over two years and was written in an earlier version of PROGEN 4GL.

5.3   Multi-company accounting

A multi-company accounting package, involving some foreign currency transactions and "factoring" has recently been developed to meet the requirements of a specific client.   The software will eventually be extended to cover other associated companies located in Europe so that data can be exchanged between companies using a system of networked computers. The software has been customized to meet the specific requirements of the client and has now been in use for about 12 months.

5.4   Cylinder rentals resolved

A company in the West Midlands, which sells industrial gases, uses a number of IBM-PC/AT machines spread over several sites. Using PROGEN 4GL, they developed the necessary software which is now being used throughout the company. The software was entirely developed by the customer, with only an occasional reference to Limrose. A further enhancement to the software in the company has been to control cylinder movements. Cylinder control is vital to the company as the cost of the cylinder often exceeds the gases supplied in it.

5.5 Mail-order supplier under threat

A supplier to a large national mail-order company was told to get computerized or risk losing further orders. A frantic search revealed that software and hardware costs would be very substantial if a conventional approach was used as the software had to be custom written. The chosen solution was to use PROGEN 4GL to generate the necessary software, and use a microcomputer to run it. The software, which deals with mainframe-generated paperwork, is also used for order processing, compiling loading lists, stock control and invoicing. Software was developed by the customer with some help from a Limrose applications consultant.

5.6 Stockbroker systems

A fairly complex suite of software for a firm of investment consultants has been developed using PROGEN 4GL. This application makes extensive use of the "flexible-relational" feature of PROGEN and is already running.

5.7 Citizen's Advice Bureau logs enquiries

A relatively simple, but typical small application, is the use of PROGEN 4GL for data collection and analysis in a Citizen's Advice Bureau. All enquiries are logged using a database written in PROGEN for further analysis. Local information is also catalogued and retrieved in some CABs using PROGEN 4GL.

5.8 Library software uses "keywords"

Various versions of software for library automation have been developed to meet requirements for multi-media libraries. This software features "keywords" for high-speed data retrieval and is suitable for use in schools and colleges, as well as industrial and technical libraries. Using this software package, you can dispense with subject and author indexes and search for books using "keywords". A more elaborate version of this package including facilities for handling book loans, return and cash fines has also been developed.

5.9 Members of Parliament tune into IT

PROGEN-generated software is currently being used by some MPs to help them keep track of their large postbags and to get in touch with voters selectively. Electoral registers have been downloaded as PROGEN files from mainframe computers, so that selected and personalized letters can be sent to constituents; this also helps with address labels, canvassing lists, postal votes register etc.

5.10 Integrated accounting package

One of the first "guinea pigs" for PROGEN 4GL was Limrose itself which now uses purpose-written, integrated software for handling the day-to-day requirements of the company such as invoicing, accounting, cash-flow management, mailing list, quotations, stock control etc. This software, which has a total of 18 interlinked applications, has now been in use for over three years. The experience gained has enabled Limrose to produce accounting packages for general use.

5.11 Timber stock control

Small timber yards have one of the most difficult problems in stock control. Logs, and other stock items, are often sawn off to produce a multiple of further items and it becomes practically impossible for a small operator to keep track of his stock and costings. For large timber yards, solutions have been available for some time now at about £30K for software alone. For small yards, a stock control written in PROGEN 4GL in now available.

5.12 Design crossword puzzles using PROGEN

One of the problems facing crossword-puzzle designers is to find words which fit into the spaces left when there are already certain letters filled in. For example, using the Oxford Dictionary, just try finding even a few words with seven letters which have an "i" in the fourth position and end in an "e". A program written in PROGEN 4GL solves this problem easily.

5.13 Indexing a book or catalogue ?

This is not a particularly difficult problem to solve using a modern database, however a program to do this can be written in PROGEN 4GL in just a few minutes.

5.14 Managing magazine "bingo" cards

Most trade magazines use "bingo" cards to handle advertising enquiries. Readers fill in the tear-off card and post them to the publisher. Details from the cards are keyed into the computer as they are received. The computer then sorts them out and prints enquiry lists/labels to be sent to individual advertisers. Further analysis, such as the number of enquiries received for a particular advertisement, are also obtained automatically.

These are only some of the many possible applications in which PROGEN 4GL is being used. A large number of applications using PROGEN 4GL have been written by end-users themselves, and many of them are very ingenious indeed. A small software house, in the North West, has written a complete software package to handle newsagents' business, and there are numerous software packages written in PROGEN 4GL for estate agents which automatically match buyers and properties.

6 HOW PROGEN AND OTHER 4GLS WORK

Although all 4GLs are different, and use different approaches in attempting to solve the same problem, they all have certain underlying similarities. PROGEN 4GL consists of the following modules:

6.1 Data dictionary

PROGEN data dictionary is a proprietary product and holds all information about the database structure, screen displays, search fields, validation procedures etc. This is the most important "parameter" file in PROGEN-based applications. The data structure used in PROGEN permits every field to be designated a "multiple entry" field if required, and data is validated as entered. This file also contains the "relational" flag and controls editing of "link" and other content-sensitive fields.

6.2   Relational linkage files

Relational links in PROGEN 4GL are refered to as "postings" due to the historical connection with accounting software. Postings are used in PROGEN to "link" applications together. This consists of two parts, a postings generator and a run-time processor. Using the run-time processor, data from a "source" file can be simply passed to a "destination" file, or can be added, subtracted, concatenated, multiplied, divided etc by the source data or constants during postings.

6.3   Relational database

PROGEN uses a "flexible-relational" database and provides facilities for adding, searching, editing and deleting records. Referential integrity is maintained by not permitting the major "link keys" to be edited, however linkages can be altered without affecting data structures. PROGEN uses sorted binary files and binary-search for data retrieval throughout making it very fast as compared to packages using sequential or indexed sequential files. Optional sequential and string search is allowed at the expense of speed if really neccessary. PROGEN allows an unlimited number of indexed keys and uses both "single-entry" and "multiple-entry" data fields. All data is indexed automatically, and all index fields (except those used as relational links) can be edited at any time.

6.4   Report generator

The built-in report generator can mix text strings and files with data, and perform mail-merge functions. Field totals can be printed and trailing spaces automatically removed from data fields, if required. It also includes facilities for controlling printing from "multiple-entry" fields, and printing-system date and time automatically. Printer control codes can be embedded in reports to control printer output for compressed, expanded, emphasized printing etc as shown in the attached sample printout of an invoice from a PROGEN-generated application. Output can be redirected to Laser printers if required.

6.5 Graphics generator

PROGEN 4GL has a graphics processor which can analyse data to produce line graphs, bar charts and pie charts in full colour automatically. The graphics processor is also menu-driven and no programming is necessary. See attached examples of graphics output.

6.6 3GL interface

Programs written in 3GLs (such as BASIC and "C") can be automatically "chained", and control returned to PROGEN afterwards, for integrating complex functions not provided in PROGEN 4GL.

6.7 Data security

Access to PROGEN applications is security coded and three different levels of access control have been provided. The multi-user version provides record-locking and file-locking automatically and can be used with networked or multi-user systems.

As PROGEN 4GL is a complete systems-development package, no software execpt a wordprocessor is necessary for providing total office automation. Bar-code readers can be interfaced to PROGEN-generated applications for point-of-sale and other applications. Some 4GL products do not provide the complete system interface and a substantial part of the development gain is lost.

PROGEN 4GL can save up to 80% in software development costs. This is hard to believe, but true. It is realistic to save 80% or more in software development costs using PROGEN 4GL provided that the user really understands how PROGEN 4GL works. For successful implementation of 4GL-based solutions, it is advisable to include a systems develoment expert from the vendor company as part of the team to achieve savings of this order.

As PROGEN 4GL is a "non-procedural" language, it is fairly easy to use for simpler applications and most end-users can develop their own solutions to many problems quite easily. In many cases, sufficient learning has been achieved by novice (but otherwise intelligent and computer-literate) end-users in a couple of days to produce an acceptable "prototype" solution to many long standing problems using PROGEN 4GL. Some fairly complex software, such as payroll written to full PAYE specifications has been written using PROGEN 4GL in just a few weeks as compared to several months using BASIC or COBOL. For complex "integrated" applications, however, substantial professional skill in system analysis and a thorough understanding of PROGEN 4GL is necessary for successful implementation.

Most 4GLs, including PROGEN 4GL, are usually suitable for "data-intensive" applications only. For example, PROGEN 4GL is ideal for most database and business applications, however it cannot really provide the universal solutions which 3GLs generally can. It is primarily for this reason that a 3GL interface is included in most 4GLs — including PROGEN 4GL — to make the 4GL as widely applicable as possible.

```
********************************************************************************
JOHN'S  OFF  LICENCE,  LLAY,  WREXHAM
********************************************************************************
PETER HARGREAVES                            Invoice Date 22/06/84
192 CHESTER DRIVE                           INVOICE NO.   2
MANLEY
WARRINGTON WA8 4HT

TERMS : CASH ON DELIVERY, Surcharge of 2% per month on overdue accounts
_____

ITEM       DESCRIPTION                  QTY    PRICE    GOODS     VAT
_____

VER-R      VERMOUTH RED SWEET            2      3.25     6.50      .98
VER-W      VERMOUTH WHITE DRY            1      2.50     2.50      .38
SH-D       DRY SHERRY                    1      2.50     2.50      .38
SH-MD      MEDIUM DRY SHERRY             1      2.59     2.59      .39
GIN-QB     QUARTER BOTTLE GIN            1      2.00     2.00      .30
WHS-FB     BOTTLE OF WHISKY              1      6.50     6.50      .98
COFF8      INSTANT COFFEE 8OZ            1      1.95     1.95     0.00




_____
THANK YOU FOR YOUR CUSTOM - HAVE A GOOD DAY    Totals    24.54     3.41
_____
                                             INVOICE TOTAL    27.95
```

SPECIALS THIS WEEK:

> Gordon's Gin - Full Bottle £4.75 ONLY !!! CHEAPEST IN TOWN. BUY NOW
> Instant Coffee 8 oz Jar - £1.80 if you buy two at a time.

WE ARE CLOSED FOR CHRISTMAS FROM 20TH TO 28TH DECEMBER. MERRY CHRISTMAS!!

Figure 19.1 Typical printout using PROGEN 4GL report writer.

301

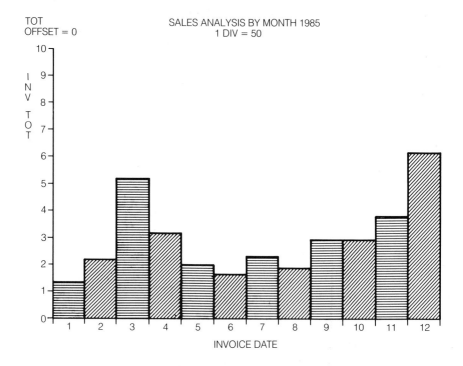

Figure 19.2 A bar chart showing sales analysis.

FREQ SALES ANALYSIS BY MONTH 1985

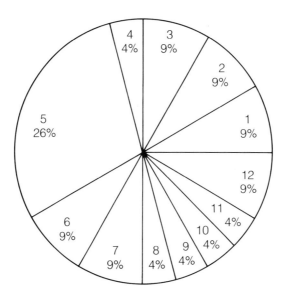

Figure 19.3   A pie chart produced from PROGEN 4GL.

```
type culist.prr
47,-1,0,0,"C[CUTB]>[0]",0,"",0,"",0,"",0
"CUDAT",1,6,0,0,"Date Entered",0,3,17,3,-1,0,0,0,0,"",0,"",0,"",0
"CUREC",1,6,0,0,"Record No.",51,3,62,3,0,0,0,0,0,"",0,"",0,"",0
"CUCOD",1,8,0,0,"Customer Code",0,4,17,4,-1,-1,0,0,-1,"",-1,"",0,"E",0
"CUNAM",0,30,0,0,"Invoice Add",0,6,17,6,-1,-1,0,0,0,"",-1,"",0,"",0
"CUAD1",0,30,0,0,"Add Line 1",3,7,17,7,-1,-1,0,0,0,"",0,"",0,"",0
"CUAD2",0,30,0,0,"Add Line 2",3,8,17,8,-1,-1,0,0,0,"",0,"",0,"",0
"CUTOW",0,20,0,0,"Town, County",3,9,17,9,-1,-1,0,0,0,"",0,"",0,"",0
"CUPC",1,9,0,0,"Post Code",3,10,17,10,-1,-1,0,0,0,"",0,"",0,"",0
"CUTEL",0,15,0,0,"Tel. No.",3,11,12,11,-1,-1,0,0,0,"",-1,"",0,"",0
"CUCON",0,20,0,0,"Contact",28,11,36,11,-1,-1,0,0,0,"",0,"",0,"",0
"CUGRP",1,3,0,0,"Cust Group",51,4,62,4,-1,-1,0,0,0,"",0,"",0,"",0
"CUARC",1,3,0,0,"Area Code",51,6,71,6,-1,-1,0,0,-1,"",0,"",0,"",0
"CUREP",1,3,0,0,"Rep Code",51,7,71,7,-1,-1,0,0,0,"",0,"",0,"",0
"CUCTI",0,1,0,0,"Invoice same as Delivery (y/n)",6,12,37,12,-1,-1,0,0,0,"",0,":I
[1][yn]:C[CUCTI]=[y]O[CUDNAM_CUNAM]O[CUDAD1_CUAD1]O[CUDAD2_CUAD2]O[CUDTOW_CUTOW]
O[CUDPC_CUPC]O[CUDTEL_CUTEL]O[CUDCON_CUCON]O[CUDCTY_CUCTY]G[CUVAR]",0,"",0
"CUDNAM",0,30,0,0,"Delivery Add",0,14,17,14,-1,-1,0,0,0,"",0,"",0,"",0
"CUDAD1",0,30,0,0,"Add Line 1",3,15,17,15,-1,-1,0,0,0,"",0,"",0,"",0
"CUDAD2",0,30,0,0,"Add Line 2",3,16,17,16,-1,-1,0,0,0,"",0,"",0,"",0
"CUDTOW",0,20,0,0,"Town, County",3,17,17,17,-1,-1,0,0,0,"",0,"",0,"",0
"CUDPC",1,9,0,0,"Post Code",3,18,17,18,-1,-1,0,0,0,"",0,"",0,"",0
"CUDTEL",0,15,0,0,"Tel No.",3,19,12,19,-1,-1,0,0,0,"",0,"",0,"",0
"CUDCON",0,20,0,0,"Contact",28,19,36,19,-1,-1,0,0,0,"",0,"",0,"",0
"CUVAR",0,60,0,0,"Comments",0,20,9,20,-1,-1,0,0,0,"",0,"",0,"",0
"CUPRI",1,10,0,-1,"Products of Interest",51,12,59,13,-1,-1,23,0,0,"",0,"",0,"",6
"CUDC",1,8,0,-1,"Date",0,3,0,4,-1,-1,24,0,0,"",0,"",1,"D",0
"CUDN",0,70,0,-1,"Contact Notes",9,3,9,4,-1,-1,24,0,0,"",0,"",1,"",0
"CUDNC",1,2,0,0,"Next Contact Wk ?",51,8,71,8,-1,-1,0,0,0,"",0,"",0,"",0
"CUDNCS",0,6,0,0,"Unused",79,3,79,3,-1,0,0,0,0,"",0,"",1,"",0
"CUDIS",0,5,0,0,"Sett.Terms%",0,6,15,6,0,-1,0,0,0,"",0,"",2,"",0
"CUDPE",0,2,0,0,"Discount Period",23,6,40,6,-1,-1,0,0,0,"",0,"",2,"",0
"CUDDU",0,2,0,0,"Days Due",0,7,15,7,-1,-1,0,0,0,"",0,"",2,"",0
"CUZV",1,1,0,0,"VAT Exempt (Y/N)?",0,9,19,9,-1,0,0,0,0,"",0,"",2,"",0
"CULIM",0,10,0,0,"CREDIT LIMIT",0,3,15,3,0,-1,0,2,0,"",0,"",2,"",0
"CUTO",0,10,0,0,"Net Turnover",47,3,61,3,0,-1,0,2,0,"",0,"",2,"",0
"CUCP",0,10,-1,0,"This month",0,14,0,15,0,-1,0,2,0,"",0,"",2,"",0
"CUP1",0,10,0,0,"1 Month",12,14,11,15,0,-1,0,2,0,"",0,"",2,"",0
"CUP2",0,10,0,0,"2 Months",23,14,22,15,0,-1,0,2,0,"",0,"",2,"",0
"CUP3",0,10,0,0,"3 Months",33,14,33,15,0,-1,0,2,0,"",0,"",2,"",0
"CUP4",0,10,0,0,"4 Months",45,14,44,15,0,-1,0,2,0,"",0,"",2,"",0
"CUP5",0,10,0,0,"5 Months",56,14,55,15,0,-1,0,2,0,"",0,"",2,"",0
"CUP6",0,10,0,0,"6 Months",67,14,66,15,0,-1,0,2,0,"",0,"",2,"",0
"CUP7",0,10,0,0,"7 Months",12,17,11,18,0,-1,0,2,0,"",0,"",2,"",0
"CUP8",0,10,0,0,"8 Months",23,17,22,18,0,-1,0,2,0,"",0,"",2,"",0
"CUP9",0,10,0,0,"9 Months",34,17,33,18,0,-1,0,2,0,"",0,"",2,"",0
"CUP10",0,10,0,0,"10 Months",44,17,44,18,0,-1,0,2,0,"",0,"",2,"",0
"CUP11",0,10,0,0,"11 Months",55,17,55,18,0,-1,0,2,0,"",0,"",2,"",0
"CUP12",0,10,0,0,"12 Months +",66,17,66,18,0,-1,0,2,0,"",0,"",2,"",0
"CUTB",1,10,-1,0,"Total Due",0,4,15,4,0,-1,0,2,0,"",-1,"",2,"",0
```

Figure 19.4 A sample printout of PROGEN data dictionary.

Chapter 20
THE DATA INDEPENDENT LANGUAGE

Bharat M Mistry
Cognos Limited

1   THE DATA INDEPENDENT LANGUAGE

The term 4GL is often used to describe any modern program-development tool, with no consensus on definition amongst   DP professionals for end-users. Indeed it is a common misconception that a single 4GL will meet all the development needs of a particular organization.

It is therefore hardly surprising that many people have experienced difficulties when applying their chosen 4GL to a broad range of business applications. After all nobody would seriously suggest that a single 3GL such as Cobol should be used for all applications development, and most mature DP departments are equipped with a selection of compilers, assemblers and report generators.

2   4GL CATEGORIES

It is possible to divide today's 4GLs into two broad categories: information centre (IC) or table driven versus development centre (DC) or syntax driven. In addition, around 50 percent incorporate a proprietary, usually relational, database.

It is worth taking a few moments to examine the importance of this categorization in an attempt to uncover pointers which will allow us to narrow down the multitude of 4GL solutions which might be applied to a business application.

Firstly, IC 4GLs are designed with the needs of the end-user or business analyst in mind. The primary design goal is ease of use — depth of capability is often sacrificed as a result. In contrast DC 4GLs are designed to provide productivity gains for DP professionals who demand the same degree of flexibility and levels of performance as can be achieved using 3GLs. As a result DC 4GLs often appear to lack some user-friendly features of their IC counterparts.

If we move on to consider the trade-offs between syntax-driven and table-driven architectures it can readily be appreciated that the table-driven, form-filling approach, which so readily lends itself to end-user development, would become extremely tedious for an experienced programmer. On the other hand, a syntax-driven 4GL demands that the programmer should fully appreciate the wide range of optional commands at his disposal and this tends to extend the learning curve beyond the reach of most end-users.

3   RELATIONAL DATABASES

Finally, many people believe that the relational database management system (RDBMS) is a mandatory feature for any 4GL. Indeed the boundary between 4G programming languages and relational database management systems has blurred in the recent past through the trend for independent database vendors to offer "bolt-on" productivity tools. These "first generation" RDBMSs provide the basic functions of relational databases; the ability to join data from different relations together in a single view, and the ability to restructure databases easily. The "second generation" relational databases available these days are products of the late 80s and they deliver new, additional capabilities like distributed processing, on-line transaction processing, greater performance, industrys-tandard interfaces and more.

Clearly then anyone who purchases a table driven, IC-oriented 4GL in conjunction with a RDBMS is going to be disappointed if he expects to successfully develop a major transaction processing system, with the same degree of flexibility and performance as might be achieved using 3G methods. Difficulties will also arise if senior managers are presented with a syntax-oriented, DC 4GL, which ties directly into the corporate hierarchical database.

It is a fact of life that DP professionals are still required to build the most important corporate systems. Unlike end-users, they have the skills to analyse a business application and to translate it into a database design, with rules and procedures which can be successfully implemented within financial constraints on appropriate or available hardware. These professionals need DC 4GLs to increase their productivity but they are not prepared to sacrifice flexibility or performance along the way. Most organizations also realize the gains to be made by allowing users outside the DP department limited development capability and access to corporate data. This can often be achieved by introducing an IC 4GL together with "snap-shots" of corporate data down-loaded into a separate RDBMS.

The market for 4GLs and RDBMS is growing rapidly and the buyers are becoming more demanding. With increasing regularity we are encountering organizations that are purchasing their second or even third productivity tool, and in the main, they are asking for DC 4GLs. This is hardly surprising, since IC products have often been hurriedly purchased to meet management demands for more information and, whilst they may have sometimes been successful in this role, they have proved unsuitable for developing major applications.

The foregoing may lead us to conclude that because the market for 4GLs falls naturally into two parts, the IC and DC 4GLs will continue to co-exist side by side, much in the same way as Fortran and COBOL have endured for nearly 30 years. There is however an opportunity for major IC and DC vendors to extend the appeal of their respective products towards the common ground in the middle. One of the most striking examples of this can be seen in the continual quest for improved performance amongst competitors in the RDBMS market. They are recognizing that whilst the great flexibility of their products makes them ideally suited to IC applications, the rate of transaction throughput that can be attained using current technology is insufficient for major corporate applications such as on-line order entry. Similarly DC 4GL vendors are offering user-friendly front ends and interfaces to the hardware manufactures RDBMSs in an attempt to make their products easier to use.

Ultimately this should mean that today's IC 4GLs will incorporate the necessary performance and depth of capability to tackle even the most demanding application and DC 4GLs will become more and more user friendly, to the point where they can be used by the computer illiterate. There may however be flaws in this assumption.

Firstly whilst it is relatively straightforward for a DC 4GL vendor to add higher levels of user interface to a product which already meets the demands of the DP professional it will be more difficult for an IC 4GL vendor to back fill end-user tools with deeper capabilities.

4   HARDWARE VENDORS INFLUENCE

Secondly hardware manufacturers find the IC concept more attractive than the DC. This is because they can see a great opportunity for selling processors to a wider market by taking control of applications development away from the DP department. This trend can readily be identified by the increasing number of hardware manufacturers who are introducing their own RDBMS and the scramble to develop or acquire suitable IC front-ends.

The hardware manufacturers also have the ability to solve the performance problems inherent in a wholly soft implementation of RDBMS architecture. Already we see signs that they are developing database back-end processors and micro-coding RDBMS instructions into intelligent disk controllers. This will effectively remove the RDBMS market from the control of independent vendors. Also the growing acceptance of SQL as a standard for RDBMS access and the ability of individual hardware manufacturers to offer a complete range of processors from micro to mainframe will diminish the attraction of portable third-party RDBMs solutions.

On the other hand DC 4GLs, which interface to the hardware manufacturers DBMS, have the ability totally to replace 3G programming techniques and will quickly react to changing database environments.

Thirdly, we are discovering that end-users rapidly outgrow the very high-level, fill-in-the-forms approaches to development. This suggests that a layered 4GL environment may well prove the most attractive. At the outset users would work with a menu of options, then as their experience increases they can start utilizing high-level non-procedural statements, extending their repertoire to keep pace with the demands they are making. By building a great deal of intelligence into the front-end components, we can foresee the ability of the DC 4GL to question the user about his application and to make significant decisions about matters such as physical database design, validation rules and procedures.

5   PORTABILITY ISSUES

Finally, it is worth examining the market penetration of IC and DC 4GLs. IC products are generally easy to port onto new hardware and operating system architectures because they create an environment which is almost wholly independent of the host; most are therefore available on a very wide range of manufacturers' hardware. By contrast DC 4GLs need to integrate fully with the targets systems, detailed performance tuning is required and above all, the product must appear as a totally transparent part of the native software architecture. This makes DC 4GLs expensive to port and all are restricted to a small range of manufacturers hardware, often only one. It is therefore surprising that the leading DC 4GL vendors are achieving unit sales and revenues which are equivalent to or greater than those of their IC counterparts who can address a much wider market. This surely indicates that the DC solution has wider appeal than the IC alternative. It follows that as DC 4GL vendors slowly move their products on to new hardware they will stand a greater chance of dominating the market. In addition if they can also provide a "second generation" relational database, or an interface to one, which conforms to industry standards, and provides greater performance and portability, their position in the market will be even stronger.

Chapter 21
USING
FOURTH-GENERATION LANGUAGES
WITH UNIX
OR THE PRICE OF
PROGRAMMER PRODUCTIVITY

Dominic Dunlop
Sphinx Ltd.

1   WHAT 4G TOOLS DO

The tag "Fourth-Generation" has, over the last few years, been applied by more marketing departments to more products than you can shake a stick at. The old chart:

Figure 21.1. Evolution of languages — authorized version

has been repeated ad nauseam. Actually, the true picture is nearer to

Figure 212. Evolution of languages — actual situation

In fact, the only safe definition for a 4G feature is "something that a third-generation language doesn't do (or doesn't do well)." As the diagram begins to show, this definition leaves the field wide open: there are all sorts of things that 3GLs don't do, so any product which does one or more of them has some claim to being called a 4GL.

Despite this difficulty, it is necessary to formulate some broad definitions of the features that 4G products are likely to have. Without these definitions, it is not possible to identify the type and quantity of computer resources needed during the development of applications with these products, and during their subsequent running.

310

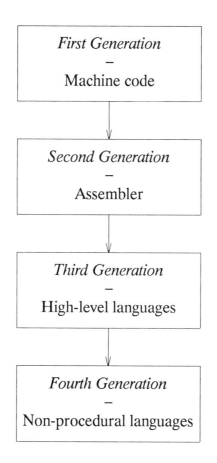

Figure 21.1 Evolution of languages – authorized version.

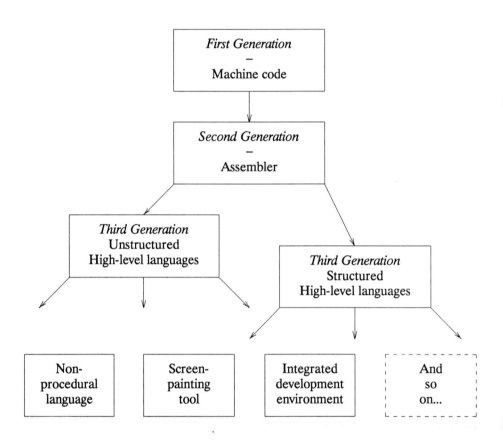

Figure 21.2 Evolution of languages – actual situation.

Data-based approach	Easy access to a (more or less) relational database, usually with a (more or less comprehensive) data dictionary
Transaction-based	Ability to treat a sequence of data-approach manipulations as a unit which are applied to the database in full, or not at all
Data structuring	Facilities (at least) for handling programmatic data as records (database rows) and/or arrays (collections of rows)
Type independence	Extension of "representation independence" from database records to program statements
Data validation	Extensive (and more or less automatic) checking of the validity of entered data
Security facilities	Both to control access to data, and the ability to run particular parts of an application suite
Program structuring	Requirement for or encouragement of "good" programming practices
Code reusability	Facilities for keeping track of the function and interface of working modules in order that they can be reused
Extensive library	Many common requirements (validation, screen painting, accumulation ...) already catered for, eliminating need to re-invent wheels
Form-building	"Screen painter" for building approach dialogues, reports — or applications "codeless" removal of need to generate line-programming-oriented source programs using a text editor
Documentation/help	Tools or procedures for the production facility of (possibly multi-lingual) on- and off-line documentation
Debugging facilities	Tools to identify and quickly correct programming errors
Change control	Means for tracking different variants or revisions of an application
Binary portability	Provision for porting of binary application code and data across different hardware and operating systems.

Table 21.1 Attributes of 4G tools.

Of course, no one 4G tool provides — or can provide — all of these features. Sometimes a feature is precluded because of a design decision by the implementor of the tool. Alternatively, a feature may not be provided because it is difficult or expensive to support, given the facilities offered by the host hardware and operating environment. This paper is intended to show the environmental factors which can influence 4GL design decisions, and good and bad solutions to particular implementation problems.

2   WHAT 4G TOOLS NEED

A basic premise underlying the design of most 4G tools is that some or all of the following resources are in abundant supply:

Memory	Needed for large libraries, multiple processes, buffering, screen images, inter-process communication ...
Disk storage	For flat databases and dictionaries, logs, on-line help, source control, libraries, program images, self documenting code ...
Disk speed	For fast access to all of the above
Execution speed	For interpretation of "semi-compiled" code (P-code) and/or database access statements
Process switching	Facilitates the support of modular applications, possibly with multi-user access; speeds application development and debugging
Inter-process comms.	For file and record locking and other concurrency controls; also for communication with back- and front-end programs

Table 21.2   Requirements of 4G tools.

It's a sad fact of life that not every operating environment can fill all these needs. When creating a 4G tool for a single specific environment, such as MS-DOS or UNIX, a developer can optimize the tool heavily to make the best use of the features of that environment. However, it is increasingly the case that 4G products are designed to operate across a range of different environments. This enables application developers to create software for many different classes of computer without the need to learn a variety of languages, and allows users to move those applications between machine classes without retraining operators.

Faced with this requirement, the temptation for the developer of the 4G tool is to use the minimum set of operating system facilities common to all the target environments, and to optimize for none of them. This approach seldom leads to satisfactory performance, as, while a particular action may be supported in more than one environment, it may be cheap in one but expensive in another. The only way to get satisfactory performance in more than one environment is for the developer to provide at least some level of environment-specific optimization in each case.

An interesting side-effect of the necessity of optimization is the fact that the first implementation of a product in its second target environment seldom performs anywhere near as well as the parent product does in the environment for which it was originally developed. For example, a tool moved from UNIX, which performs best running a large number of comparatively small processes, is unlikely to be a good fit on MS-DOS, which runs a single comparatively large process.

It is also worth noting that there are two activities which 4G tools tend not to address, but which, nevertheless, are important to all practical applications in a production environment:

Printer control	Maintenance of spool queues; forms management; problem recovery
Back-up facilities	Both as an insurance against disaster, and to allow selective archiving and recovery

Table 21.3 Things that 4GLs don't provide.

Developers of 4G tools have a good argument against providing specific support for these activities. It is that the facilities provided vary greatly even among different implementations of the same operating system, never mind across different operating environments. As an example, in the UNIX world, NCR systems provide reasonably comprehensive printer forms control, and back-up to sequential-access cartridge tapes, while AT&T machines have no forms control, and use randomly-accessible cartridge tapes.

This lack means that the user of a 4G tool is faced with a choice: either applications must contain environment-dependent code to handle these activities, or they must be handled outside the application.

3   WHAT THE UNIX OPERATING ENVIRONMENT PROVIDES

The following is a brief summary of the facilities offered by UNIX:

User management	Validation of user log-ins, leading to controlled access to specific command interpreters, applications, directories and data files
Process control	Creation of multiple concurrent processes up to a fixed limit per user, and for the whole system
Memory management	Allowing processes to expand (and occasionally to contract) dynamic stacks and static data storage areas
File access	Concurrently to a (hard or soft) maximum number of files per process, and to a hard limit for the whole system. Arbitrary portions (records) of files may be locked (details of locking currently vary slightly between implementations)
Inter-process comms.	Through pipes, and, in System V implementations, via message passing, semaphores and shared memory. Alternatively, in Berkeley-derived variants, via sockets
Networking	Transparent access to some or all of the facilities of one or more remote computers. (Networking is at least an option on all recent implementations)

Table 21.4   Facilities provided by the UNIX operating system.

An implementor with an intimate knowledge of UNIX attributes, and of the likely cost of each type of operation that it supports, can create software which, in addition to running efficiently, is easily portable across different implementations of the operating system. If the knowledgeable implementor is developing a 4G tool, the trade-offs between efficiency and ease of use can be balanced so as to create a product which, while allowing applications to be developed much faster than would be possible with tools of a previous generation, does not make unreasonable demands on system resources. The remainder of this chapter discusses specific instances where well-informed design decisions can increase performance or reduce the resource usage — or both.

4   UNIX MEMORY MANAGEMENT

The UNIX process model can be traced by direct descent from that of the PDP-11 minicomputer:

Figure 21.3. UNIX Process Model

A fixed-size block of machine instructions[1] [2] manipulates static data in an area which grows (or contracts) when an explicit request for more (or less) memory is made to the operating system. Dynamic data and subroutine linkage information is held on a stack, which grows and contracts dynamically.

(Paging and virtual memory, provided in most recent implementations of UNIX, have little effect on this picture and the discussion which follows.)

---

1. In some Berkeley-derived implementations, it is possible to pass execution control into the data area, allowing, in effect, run-time expansion of the instruction block. Few practical applications apart from debugging tools use this facility.

2. Historically, UNIX supported a marginally useful code-overlaying facility. Few recent implementations support this link with the past.

317

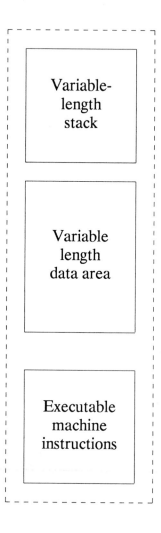

Figure 21.3 UNIX process model.

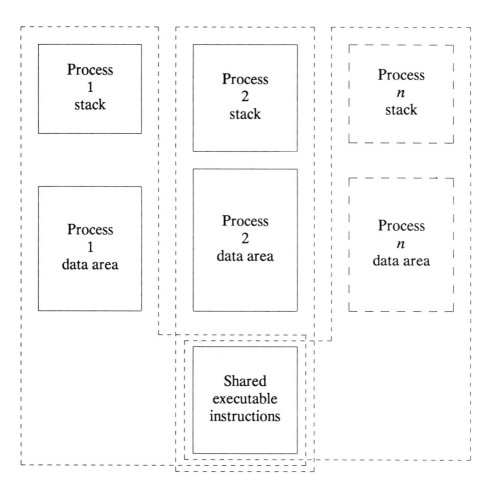

Figure 21.4 Multiple UNIX processes sharing instructions.

319

In general, each distinct process running under UNIX will require a separate area of memory to be allocated for each of its three portions. There is, however, an important special case which occurs when two or more instances of a single application module are running concurrently:

Figure 21.4. Multiple UNIX processes sharing instructions

Only a single copy of the instructions is held in memory. For each concurrently executing process, a separate data and stack area is still allocated. This code-sharing facility (known in the jargon as shared text) is provided because, as a multi-user operating system, UNIX is quite likely to be executing the same program on behalf of several users at once, so the system automatically minimizes memory usage when this situation arises. A side-effect of this optimization is that the second and subsequent users of a given program see a more rapid start-up because there is no need to fetch the instructions from disk before execution can commence.

These properties hold however the program was created — whether from a 3GL, a 4GL, or even an assembler, provided that its code consists of binary machine instructions. Many 4G tools do not produce binary code, but instead produce pseudo-code which is interpreted by a run-time interpreter[3]. It is worth examining what is in memory when UNIX is running multiple instances of the same interpreted program:

Figure 21.5. Multiple instances of interpreted application

---

3. Many suppliers shy away from the term "interpreter" because everybody knows that interpreters are slow. However, the speed penalty of using an interpreter may be minimal, and the advantages considerable (see below).

4. In contrast, Pick, a fully-interpretative environment, has a sophisticated scheme for sharing memory copies of pseudo-code between processes. In theory, the shared memory facilities of System V UNIX allow the development of similar strategies in user-level code outside the operating system kernel, although I am not aware of any implementations of this type.

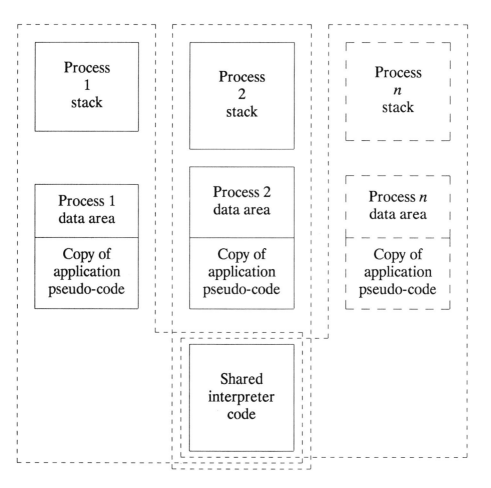

Figure 21.5 Multiple instances of interpreted application.

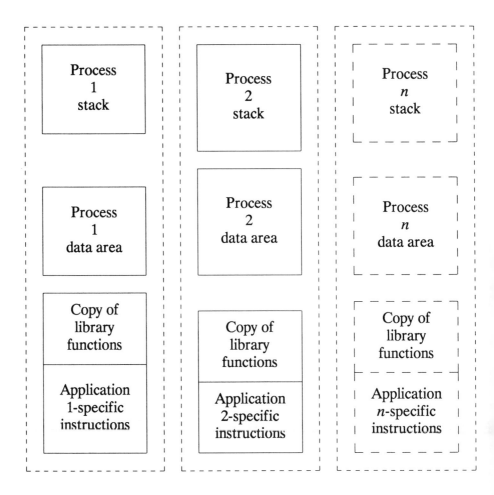

Figure 21.6 Different applications running simultaneously.

While the interpreter, which consists of binary machine instructions, is still shared, each instance of the application must devote part of its data area to holding a copy of the pseudo-code for the application. It is a penalty of the interpretative approach that the application instructions can no longer be shared[4].

While pseudo-code is usually considerably more compact than binary machine instructions, the necessity of maintaining multiple copies in memory offsets this advantage to some extent. However, the balance of advantage shifts back when the running of a number of distinct, but similar, binary programs is examined:

Figure 21.6. Different applications running simultaneously

Here it can be seen that the binary code for each program contains a copy of a set of library functions. In binary programs generated by 4G tools, these functions are typically large subsystems responsible for screen handling, data validation, report generation and the like. They can easily add a hundred kilobytes to the size of the code for each module. In an interpreted scheme, there would be just one memory copy of these functions: in the interpreter itself.

In order to avoid wasting memory − and increasing program start-up time − through loading duplicate copies of library functions, some means of sharing these functions between modules is needed. Such a facility has been late in coming to UNIX, but has arrived in the last year:

Figure 21.7. Several applications sharing library

Shared-object libraries are provided in UNIX System V, release 35. In fact, in the standard release, each application can access up to four shared libraries. A further benefit of shared libraries is that they may be updated in order to enhance functionality, improve performance, or fix bugs without the need to relink application programs.

---

5. OS/2 provides shared libraries as a matter of course. In fact, it supports no other type of library.

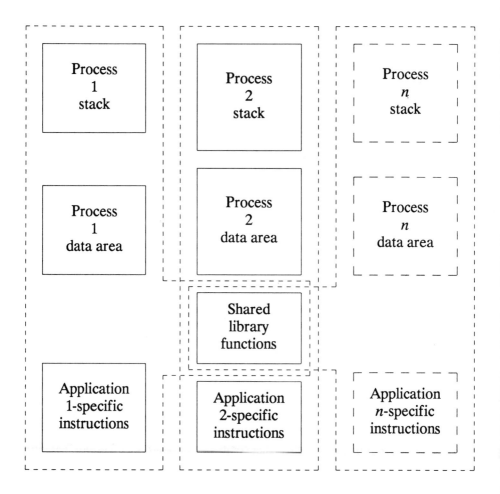

Figure 21.7   Several applications sharing a library.

4.1 Informix-4GL and memory usage

Informix-4GL is unusual among 4G tools for UNIX in that it compiles applications all the way to binary machine code. This is done both to maximize run speed, and to allow easy integration with modules written in other languages − particularly in C. Consequently, the remarks in section 4 about interpreters are not relevant.

The current state of applications created with Informix-4GL is shown in Figure 21.4 for multiple instances of the same module, and in Figure 21.6 for distinct modules. Informix-4GL has yet to take advantage of shared libraries.

A newly announced product, Informix-4GL Rapid Development System (RDS) provides an interpreter as an alternative to full code generation. While this will change the picture to that of Figure 21.5, the main reason for the adoption of an interpreter is to speed the development cycle. This is discussed in section 6 below.

5   ASPECTS OF SHARED DATABASE ACCESS

Almost all 4G tools are built around a database manager. Indeed, some have databases which go so far as to keep track of the programs which can operate on the data, as well as the data itself.

Given the process model of the previous section, how can a process access records which are under the control of a database-management package? The most obvious answer is that each program module should contain copies of library functions which can manipulate database files. These functions must, of course, be capable of managing concurrency and the associated user-access permission checks and locking protocols:

Figure 21.8. Multiple access to a database

There are several problems with this approach. Firstly, the library functions are likely to be very large, particularly if they implement a structured query language interface to a fully relational database. Query optimization, becoming more and more necessary in a competitive market, only adds to the size and complexity of the functions. Of course, this size problem could be mitigated by using a shared library.

325

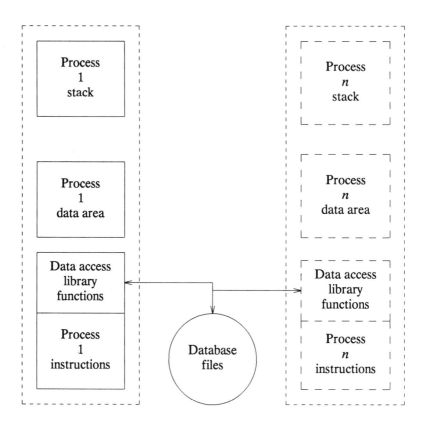

Figure 21.8 Multiple access to a database.

Unfortunately, there is another difficulty: a database manager is conceptually a privileged program: it can allow or deny each user on a system access to particular fields in particular database tables. This access control operates at a considerably more detailed level than does the file access control provided by the operating system itself.

Examination of the diagram shows that there is no process which is identifiable as a manager. Consequently, each process which accesses the database must somehow implement the necessary permission checks. While UNIX incorporates mechanisms which allow processes to gain more privilege, the safe use of these mechanisms in interactive programs is a tricky task best left to skilled systems programmers. To use them as a matter of course in 4GL-generated code would constitute a considerable security risk.

Finally, direct access by applications to the files which make up a database limits an implementor's options when the time comes to address new computer architectures. For example, in the diagram above, it is difficult to see how the local files could be replaced by a hardware database engine capable of processing SQL statements directly. In order to do this, it would be necessary to rewrite the data-access library functions, and relink the application code with the new library. Similar considerations apply to implementations on multi-processor, networked or distributed systems, or those which provide support for alternative file layouts.

All of these problems may be overcome by partitioning the task database access into a back-end program which is separate from the application program:

Figure 21.9. Multiple database access with multiple servers

The traditional version of this diagram has a single server task (perhaps referred to as a transaction-processing monitor) fielding requests from a large number of application processes. This model has traditionally been difficult to implement under UNIX 6 both because of the comparatively low limit on the number of files which any one process may open (typically 20), and the semantics of the UNIX pipe inter-process communication channel. Consequently, it is preferable under UNIX to move to a halfway house where there is one server (back-end) process per application process. Each application contains a small interface library function (possibly shared) and communicates with its own private server. The servers in turn may communicate with each other either by means of system file locks, or, in more advanced implementations, through shared memory areas. Because all instances of the server can share a single set of instructions, memory usage is likely to be less than that required by multiple copies of large library.

The separation of the server from the application allows the server, which is not an interactive program, to apply user permission checks, and provide controlled access to data which is not accessible to unprivileged users by other means. Additionally, because the server hides the low-level structure of the database from the applications, that structure can be changed, or removed to a remote system, provided only that the high-level interface between the application and the server is preserved.

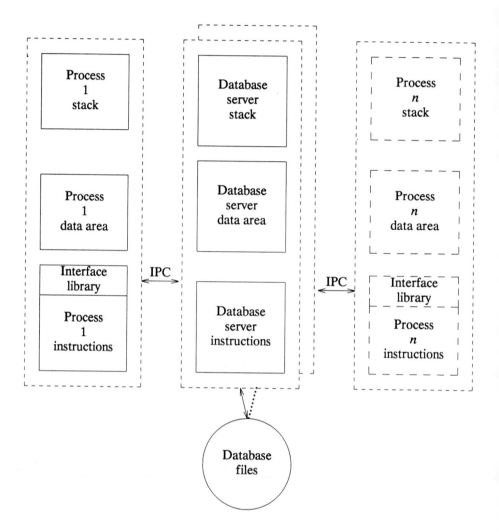

Figure 21.9 Multiple database access with multiple servers.

5.1 Informix-4GL and database access

Early Informix products adopted the strategy of Figure 21.8. Because of the limitations of this approach, the Informix-SQL product family (of which Informix-4GL is a part) moved to the server-based approach of Figure 21.9. The original server maintains databases in collections of standard UNIX files, which are accessed through the standard read-and-write system calls. Recently, a high-performance product, Informix-Turbo, has been introduced. This is an alternative server which maintains the database on a dedicated disk (or disks). This brings improvements in performance, security and reliability, yet requires no changes to application programs because the command interface of the server has been preserved unchanged.

---

6. Although Berkeley sockets and System V, release 3 streams overcome most of the outstanding problems

6   SPEEDING THE DEVELOPMENT CYCLE

Another well-worn diagram is that of the software development cycle:

Figure 21.10. The software development cycle

While a number of 4G products claim to break this loop, two more realistic expectations are to minimize the number of circuits taken around it in the course of application development, and to reduce the amount of time taken for each circuit.

Achievement of the first goal may be aided either by conventional line-oriented, but very high-level languages, or by screen-oriented fill-in-the-blanks applications generators. High-quality development tools are paramount in satisfying the second. Here, tools which run batch compiles all the way down to machine code for each circuit of the loop are clearly less than optimal:

Figure 21.11. Software development with full compilation

Each circuit is time-consuming and expensive in terms of hardware resources, firstly because a considerable number of separate processes must be executed, and secondly because the compilation phase uses the system heavily for a possibly considerable period.

Clearly, while binary machine-code applications are likely to be efficient in production use, they are less than perfect during development and debugging. During this phase of an application's life, it is more important to minimize the cost of any change than to achieve maximum run-time efficiency. A highly-integrated interpretive environment with an incremental (statement at-a-time) compiler can deliver great benefits:

Figure 21.12. Software development with incremental compilation

The integration of the various functions of the development suite can minimize the number of separate processes needed to make a circuit of the loop, and an incremental compiler need reprocess only changed statements, vastly reducing the cost of incorporating changes. Problem identification can be further speeded if the suite incorporates a powerful debugger to help the developer to identify the source of unexpected behaviour.

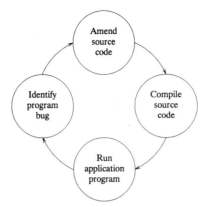

Figure 21.10 The software development cycle.

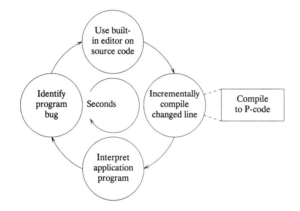

Figure 21.11 Software development with full compilation.

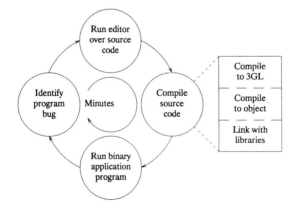

Figure 21.12 Software development with incremental compilation.

6.1 Informix-4GL and application development

Because its language is compiled all the way to binary machine code, Informix-4GL currently conforms to Figure 21.11 above. Recognizing that interpretative environments have a clear advantage during software development, Informix Software has just announced its Rapid Development System (RDS), which will follow Figure 21.12.

The following trademarks and registered trademarks of the named companies have been used in this document: Informix, Informix-4GL: Informix Software; MS-, OS/2: Microsoft; PDP: Digital Equipment Corporation; UNIX: AT&T.

Chapter 22
PROGRESS:
THE FULL PROCEDURAL APPROACH

P R Whyman
Slinn Computer Group Ltd

1   INTRODUCTION

This chapter is a case study in the experiences of two different systems houses in utilizing the procedural 4GL PROGRESS supplied by Progress Software Corporation, 5 Oak Park, Bedford, Massachusetts, USA.

It starts by describing the product in general terms and gives the reason for its selection.

It gives detailed examples of the language and its data dictionary, to make it clear what is meant by the term "very high level procedural 4GL".

It discusses the types of projects for which the language has been used, and its advantages and drawbacks.

It concludes with the effects which the language has had on the operations of the systems houses.

The Organizations are:-

1. Slinn Computer Group Ltd

2. Dataspeed Ltd

2   PROGRESS: GENERAL FEATURES

PROGRESS is a complete self-contained programming environment. It is *not* a set of tools designed to interface with another DBMS or language (eg SQL).

A recent independent survey by Datapro Research Corporation concluded that its structure gave significant advantages to PROGRESS (Table 22.1), in relation to the other major international 4GLs:

DATAPRO & PROGRESS

HOW PROGRESS RATES	MARKS OUT OF 10	POSITION OVERALL
RELIABILITY	9.36	1
EFFICIENCY	8.30	1
EASE OF INSTALLATION	9.33	1
EASE OF USE	8.52	1
DOCUMENTATION	8.21	3
TRAINING	8.79	1
MAINTENANCE	8.83	1
TROUBLESHOOTING	8.84	1
OVERALL	9.21	1
HOW PROGRESS COMPARES		
PROGRESS	9.21	1
INGRES	8.74	2
ORACLE	8.55	3
UNIFY	8.21	4
FOCUS	8.07	5
INFORMIX	7.60	6

Table 22.1   Data pro-progress comparison.

The general satisfaction of these users is easily recognizable simply by viewing the mean average user rating — 9.21 — for the overall satisfaction category. The reason for this satisfaction could possibly be summed up by the following statements from two of the respondents: "Other packages in its (PROGRESS) class may have a feature or two that are "better" or "more advanced" but PROGRESS at least has "a way to do it". I never have to ask the question "Can I do it with PROGRESS?" The answer is always yes. "We searched for the right development tool for over five years. This tool had to provide portability across operating systems, be transaction-oriented with rapid crash recovery, be fully featured and powerful, and allow us complete control over all modifications for later users. PROGRESS (met these criteria)."

This sums up very well the conclusions of the two organizations described in this chapter.

3   PROGRESS: ELEMENTS AND REASONS FOR CHOICE

PROGRESS consists of a relational database system, a data dictionary and an application language (of which more later) with its editor.

It is useful to the system developer in that it supports MS-DOS, PC-DOS, UNIX, XENIX, CENTIX, ULTRIX, AIX, VMS and LAN (under NetBIOS and Novell), and has been ported to many machine styles. Applications can be developed on a micro and re-compiled on to a supermini.

The system generates its own "r" (run-time) code which operates very quickly compared with most 4GLs. Compilation times are also very rapid, enabling a prototype to compile in seconds as programs are called up. The language is very robust, with before-imaging (incomplete transactions are automatically backed-out after system failures) and optional after-imaging (allowing "roll-forward" of transactions). Since the applications considered are real-time, multi-user, this was considered very important in the selection by the two organizations.

Multi-user operation itself is also largely transparent to the programmer under PROGRESS.

PROGRESS procedures can include "C" and SQL code. Interfaces with many different languages and databases are currently under development, many having been realized since the paper was first written. However, it is PROGRESS's independence of the need for such interfaces in order to perform a given task

335

(rather than specifically to interface with existing systems) which is illustrated below.

Screen painting, "fast" report generation and "query (including file maintenance) by forms" are now being made available: whilst these will certainly improve the PROGRESS environment even further, they were not used (or missed) for the applications described.

A later release level (Version 4, released November 1987) gives a 20–30% increase in run-time speed: references to response times should be seen in this light.

We will start by describing the data dictionary, then give examples of program code.

4   PROGRESS: DATA DICTIONARY

The data dictionary can define all of the following for any field within a file:

1. Field name for referring to the item within a program.

2. Sequence number ("order") for this item within a file. By default, the dictionary numbers the items in tens as they are entered, but this can be overridden. If the programmer tells the program to "display" a file name, all the items in that file record are displayed on the screen, according to this sequence. The sequence can be changed in the dictionary and items can be added and deleted: the program will automatically reflect this.

3. Label (or title) for the item, to appear on a screen or report automatically (can be ignored or overridden by a given program).

4. Help message for the operator when keying in this field (message appears at foot of screen).

5. Data type choices:

alphanumeric	:	character
numeric	:	integer
		decimal
		date
logical	:	(ie, Y/N?)

6. Number of decimal places (if relevant).

7. Format. Examples:

general	- how many characters or digits?
	- specific presentation (eg (999) - 99/9999)
alphanumeric	- enforce alpha only, in capitals
	(auto-changing lower case to capitals)
numeric	- position of any commas, minus signs etc
	- preceding zeros: show as zero?
	fill with spaces?
	fill with security characters?
logical	- format of answers if not "Yes/No", eg:
	"True/False", "Active/Inactive", "Action/Ignore".

8. Extent (for arrays).

9. Initial value (if relevant).

10. Mandatory? Will the operator be forced to key something into this field?

11. Validation expression (if any).

12. Validation message to operator if 11 not complied with.

13. Description of the field (for the programmer)

The characteristics are defined once only and then apply to all programs. Taken together, they dramatically reduce the amount of coding needed in a 3GL approach.

The validation expression can be as complex as required. If the length of the expression would exceed the space available on the screen, a validation program can be cross-referenced on this line. This will automatically be compiled into any program referencing the field.

Based on the above definitions the data in programs is very intelligently formatted on to screens in a "user-friendly" format.

A key can be just one field, or a combination of several fields.

Any number of keys can be set up, of which one must be designated the primary key, and will be used if no key is specified in a program.

5   PROGRESS — LANGUAGE

The programs themselves are keyed in through a simple editor.

This verifies syntax very thoroughly during compilation. Invalid entries in the program generate a message at the foot of the screen, taking the cursor to the point in the program where the error occurred.

The message is backed up by a screen full of information accessed via the "help" (F2) key. In fact, a bank of "recent help screens" is retained by the system.

Some programming examples follow. The files and programs are based on examples in the test drive supplied by Progress Software Corporation.

6   EXAMPLES

6.1   Display sales representatives

Program

        FOR EACH salesrep:

        DISPLAY salesrep.

Results

| Rep | Name | Region | | |
Title		Yearly quota		Sales to-date
JRB	Bullen, Jane	South		
Trainee			200,000	86,000
PF	Fennell, Peter	South		
Sales representative			600,000	420,000
PWA	Ainsworth, Paul	East		
Sales representative			500,000	580,000

- etc -

If left entirely to its own devices, the language creates a box or "frame" for a record, and arranges fields from left to right across the screen or report with titles above the fields.

It will repeat records down to row 22 on the screen. If the combined length of the fields (or their titles, if these are longer) exceeds the available width, then there will be two or more rows of fields for each record.

This can be avoided by using the option to display fields vertically ("with one column", "with two columns" etc), and therefore with labels at the side ("side labels").

Centering on the screen ("centered") can also improve the appearance, as can titling ("title").

6.2 Create/amend sales rep records

Program

REPEAT:

        PROMPT-FOR salesrep.rep-code.
        FIND salesrep USING rep-code NO ERROR.

        IF NOT AVAILABLE salesrep THEN DO:
                MESSAGE "Creating new rep.".
                CREATE salesrep.
                ASSIGN rep-code.
                UPDATE name region title quota sales.
        END.

        ELSE DO:
                MESSAGE "Amend details".
                UPDATE salesrep.
        END.
END.

(The "key words" are shown in upper case. This is merely for clarity).

Results

Sales Reps	
Sales Rep:	PWA
Name:	Paul Ainsworth
Region:	East
Title:	Sales representative
Yearly quota:	500,000
Sales to-date:	580,000

Amending sales rep details. (Highlighted)

Sales rep's initials (help for each field).

6.3 Sales report: reps sorted alphabetically within region. Totals by region

Program

```
FOR EACH salesrep BREAK BY region BY name:
          DISPLAY      region
                       name
                       quota  (TOTAL BY region)
                       sales  (TOTAL BY region).
          END.
```

Results

Region	Name	Yearly quota	Sales to date
East	Ainsworth, Paul	500,000	580,000
East	Williams, Bob	400,000	310,010
		900,000	890,010 TOTAL
North	Jackson, Anne	200,000	256,700
North	Young, Mike	500,000	410,000
		700,000	666,700 TOTAL
South	Bullen, Jane	200,000	86,000
South	Fernell, Peter	600,000	420,000
South	Roberts, Alan	600,000	710,820
		1,400,000	1,216,820 TOTAL
West	Marshall, John	900,000	920,000
		900,000	920,000 TOTAL
		3,900,000	3,693,530 TOTAL

(To print, precede the program by "OUTPUT TO PRINTER").

6.4 Multi-file enquiry program

The next program performs the following:

- Key in customer number.

- Display certain customer fields in vertical format, centered on the screen, with a title.

- Highlights if customer balance exceeds £1,000.

- Finds each order for the customer (allows scrolling through).

- Allows scrolling to next page of lines.

- Finds item description from item (product) file.

- Generates line value as (qty times price), and gives this a title.

- Totals the order.

The arrangement of the boxes on the screen is done automatically.

Program

```
REPEAT WITH 1 COLUMN TITLE "Customer Orders" CENTERED.
        PROMPT-FOR customer.code.
        FIND customer USING code.
        DISPLAY code name address curr-bal.
        IF curr-bal 1000 THEN COLOUR DISPLAY MESSAGES  curr-bal.
        FOR EACH order OF customer WITH SIDE-LABELS  NO-BOX
        CENTERED:
                DISPLAY order-num date-prom  date-sent.
                FOR EACH order-line OF order WITH CENTERED:
                        FIND item OF order-line.
                        DISPLAY line-num item.num
                        item.desc qty price
                        qty * price label "Value"  (TOTAL).
                END.
        END.
END.
```

This handles four files (customers, orders, order lines and product item, from which the description is looked up).

Results

Customer Order

Customer No:	1053
Name:	Jade Electronics
Address:	17 Farrar Avenue
Unpaid balance:	1700.00

Order num: 1761   Promised 14/12/87   Sent 14/12/87

Line no	Item no	Desc	Qty	Price	Value
1	00761	Filing units	10	23.00	230.00
2	01042	Lettering machine	2	16.50	33.00
3	02011	Desk tidy	1	45.00	45.00
		TOTAL 308.00			

7 THE EXPERIENCES

7.1 Slinn Computer Group

Slinn's initial problem was to convert 600,000 lines of COBOL packages into 4GL. They chose PROGRESS after a long evaluation process and began in 1985 by benchmarking three systems:

1. An order -processing system with a multi-warehouse, multi-batch stock file.

2. A data import/export system, batch printing despatch notes remotely.

3. A complex decision-aid system to arrive at optimum product pricing in the printing industry.

All these proved satisfactory. The response times on the order-processing system (on UNISYS XE550 equipment) were indistinguishable from similar programs written in COBOL.

The decision-aid system was however twice as slow as its predecessor written in BASIC (although the latter took six months to develop and the former three weeks). Code optimization subsequently reduced this gap.

The original conclusion that programs such as the latter must inevitably be slower than 3GL equivalents has not been borne out by subsequent experience in developing a complex estimating system for the metal-manufacturing industry. This would seem to indicate that programmer inexperience is the major factor, and that this can be magnified by a 4GL on more intricate applications.

Slinn were sufficiently impressed with PROGRESS to decide to convert all their package applications to PROGRESS and become temporary UK distributors at the end of 1986. PROGRESS is now distributed in the UK by:

7.2   Programs produced

During 1987, the following package programs have been written:

- Sales ledger.

- Purchase ledger.

- General ledger.

- Asset register.

- Payroll.

- Sales order processing.

- Materials management.

- Purchase ordering.

- Costing.

- Estimating.

In all cases, the functionality of the COBOL programs has been improved upon.

The system is built round a starter pack:

- Menus customized for each operator.

- Operator priority code determines functions available in file maintenance programs.

- Help key allows cross-accessing other menus from within a particular screen, temporarily freezing that screen. Can jump out for enquiries or to create an account when in the middle of posting. Cursor on posting screen stays where it is.

The programs are very highly parameterized, featuring eg:

General ledger

- User-defined nominal code structure alpha or numeric (up to four elements).

- User-defined nominal report layouts (horizontal and vertical design).

- User-defined sequences of reporting based on the four elements of the nominal code.

Sales ledger/Purchase ledger

- User-defined account number (eg 3A + 2N, or 8N or 4A etc).

- User-defined interfaces to general ledger.

- Whether to keep history of transactions in nominal, and if so, whether in summary or detail form.

Payroll

User-defined payslip items:

- Position on payslip.

- How the item is calculated.

- Allowing for subtotals, percentages etc.

- Allowing for minimum/maximum costs.

- Allowing for comparisons with other fields.

- Allowing addition/deletion of items on payslip.

7.3 Advantages and effects

1. New projects can be prototyped quickly, enabling much better input from the end-user, and a much better specified job. Slinn's problem of designing packages is to agree requirements with several "key" users. In the traditional "study this written specification" format, this is an extremely long-drawn-out operation, which still misses much that could go into the system. Speeding up this part of the project through prototyping has been one of the most valuable aspects of using a 4GL.

2. Programmers are now coming more closely into contact with end-users through the use of prototyping, and this is mutually beneficial.

3. There is a blurring of the tight distinction between programmers and systems analysts, giving more flexibility of response to a given situation.

4. Very complex software had previously been provided by Slinn to "restore" disks after system crashes in the 3GL environment. This now proved unnecessary.

5. Applications are of course generated much more quickly. Coding time is reduced by typically up to 90%, depending on how much the coder is able to take advantage of PROGRESS's automatic formatting. The use of predefined skeletons for eg file-maintenance programs can increase this speed even further. Slinn's attitude has been to spend relatively more time on perfecting the design and user interface of the programs: PROGRESS gives considerable scope for this.

6. The amount of documentation has been greatly reduced. The largest programs might be 600 lines of code, compared with perhaps 10,000 lines of COBOL for a similar result.

In addition, detailed programming specifications are now the exception rather than the rule.

7. The clear procedural nature of PROGRESS has been of benefit in the following areas:

- The listings are very easy to follow by virtue of their compactness and the "English-style" language. This is very important for package maintenance.

- It was seen as a significant advantage by Slinn that for a given program all the code is present in the one listing, however complex the program may be, that there are no other languages involved to "do the hard bits", and the program can be quickly read through from start to finish.

- The following detailed features are of great importance:
    - There has proved to be no practical limit to the complexity of programs, whether in terms of "if ... then ... else" programming, cursor control, testing on any key on the keyboard, screen colouring/highlighting, mathematical formulae etc.
    - The ability to "nest" pre-written modules (to any level) greatly reduces the time needed to create a program, and makes documentation easy to follow.
    - Any amount of annotation can be added to the listing, to facilitate this further.

- "Career programmers" do not feel threatened by PROGRESS, but on the contrary find it very easy to relate to. Concepts of "files" and "fields" are retained, and again the "language" nature of the product proves easy to assimilate.

8 Given all the above, Slinn are now more prepared to take on "one-off" projects whereas previously they had only dealt in packages for closely defined industries.

7.4 Drawbacks

Elements of the language would benefit from improvement, especially for the package developer.

1. There was no system to log compilation levels (although one has now been written in the UK — in PROGRESS).

2. No "pictures" of screens are generated by the system (although it has to be conceded that it is a simple matter to print off a sample screen once the program has compiled).

3. There is no line numbering on the listing to cross-refer to. In practice, this has proved to be less of a drawback than had been expected: most programs are only two or three pages.

    Also compilation errors put the cursor on the listing at the point of the error. (Note: under Version 4 there are now line numbers and many other useful documentation options.)

4. When code has been compiled into "run-time" versions, changes to the database structure involve recompiling programs even when these do not use the file in question, (although recompilation is extremely fast: it takes one hour on an XE550 to compile several hundred programs in Slinn's ledgers package).

8   DATASPEED: PROJECTS MECHANIZED

1.   System already specified (ie, not designed for PROGRESS) yet using the data dictionary to enable quick translation into different languages

An international company required a complex high-speed sales-order processing system with extremely detailed history of the maintenance history of each product sold.

This project proved to Dataspeed that everything which they could program in COBOL could be done in PROGRESS, but also they were able to put in features which they would not have considered in COBOL.

Careful design of the programs meant that all the prompts and messages came from the data dictionary, thereby making it very easy to translate the whole system into French, German and Italian.

As a result of this and many other successes, Dataspeed have gone on to develop two packages:

2. An international warehousing system.

3 A well-featured word processing system.

It would be difficult to imagine a better tribute to the functionality of PROGRESS.

9   SUMMARY

1. Two different types of software house have found great increases in productivity with PROGRESS.

2. The following frequently-heard criticisms of 4GLs do not apply to PROGRESS:

   - "Systems run slowly."

   - "Systems have limited functionality."

   - "Systems are not very portable."

   - "Programmers dislike 4GLs."

   - "Programmers cannot discard 3GL habits, so write poor 4GL code."

   - "The fourth-generation 'language' is not a language at all, but a set of different tools which still only do 90% of the job."

3. The tool covers all the features of COBOL and allows more to be done, more elegantly than had ever been achieved with 3GLs.

4. It has led to a dramatic increase in business for both organizations.

ACKNOWLEDGEMENTS

Progress Software Corporation: PROGRESS Test Drive.	5 Oak Park Bedford Massachusetts USA
Datapro Research Corporation: Report SW25 - 262 WM - 107	Delran New Jersey 08075 USA
Dataspeed Ltd	Unit 12 Broomfield House Bolling Road Bradford BD4 7BG UK

Chapter 23

INFOEXEC
THE FIRST PRACTICAL
IMPLEMENTATION OF A SEMANTIC
DATABASE

A. Balfour
Unisys, Europe-Africa Division

1   INTRODUCTION

Four years ago, Unisys (Burroughs) began an exercise to develop new data management software for its A Series family of computer systems. The Unisys A Series is one of the widest, families of totally compatible mainframe systems in the computing industry today, spanning a relative performance spectrum from 25 to 3600. The phrase "totally compatible" applies, not only to object code, but also to data storage and to the operational environment.

The existing database management system DMS II, developed in the early 1970s, is an excellent product, particularly for on-line transaction-oriented production systems. However, the computing world has changed a great deal during the past 15 years. For example, there is a growing requirement to provide *ad hoc* access for casual end-users to centrally resident mainframe databases and files. Customers are seeking increased integrity and security for the information in their central databases. They are also trying to hold down aggregate costs by improving the productivity of staff, not only DP personnel, but a wide variety of individuals within their organizations. There were therefore several reasons why it was felt necessary to look again at the data management software available for A Series systems.

2 RELATIONAL STRENGTHS

Not surprisingly, going back to 1984, the starting point was to examine relational technology. The relational approach provides many advantages. It is conceptually simple and easy to use. Casual end-users find it attractive in that they see the information in a relational database as a collection of simple independent tables, clearly a major step forward from the older hierarchical and network (CODASYL) approaches.

There is significant run-time flexibility associated with relational technology. Casual end-users, provided they are clever enough, can dynamically join together information from different tables to produce a report. It also provides powerful "set at a time" retrieval capabilities — you do not have to possess programming skills to go into a relational database and retrieve all the records which satisfy some particular retrieval criterion.

In addition, SQL is becoming an industry standard *ad hoc* query language. Last year an ANSI standard emerged for SQL. It is now available as a front-end to many different relational systems, enabling end-users to go into different relational databases using the same *ad hoc* inquiry and reporting facility — a significant development.

Finally the structure of a relational database may be altered dynamically, for example by adding a new attribute to a table. Older database technologies are much less flexible with respect to structure changes, an "off-line" reorganization run often being required.

In summary, the main reason why relational technology is so popular today is, of course, its end-user orientation. For the first time, end-users have access, in a reasonable manner, to information resident in central databases.

3 RELATIONAL WEAKNESSES

However, the relational approach is by no means flawless. A fundamental weakness, for example, is that it is really too simple to reflect the complexities of the real world. Real-world situations do not map, or mirror, very nicely into a collection of simple independent tables. As a result, database designers often find that they have to distort the real world to make it fit relational technology.

The second fundamental weakness of the relational approach is that the meaning or "semantics" of real-world situations cannot be incorporated into the database schema. Much of the knowledge possessed by the database designer fails to be captured. As a result, those who access the database later must possess additional knowledge in order to initiate, for example, meaningful *ad hoc* inquiries.

A third weakness of many current implementations of relational technology centres around the lack of capabilities for specifying integrity constraints in the database definition — constraints that the system will then automatically apply. As a result, the burden is placed on application programmers to code integrity checks, reducing significantly their productivity and introducing the possibility that important checks are either omitted or, possibly even worse, specified by different programmers in an inconsistent fashion.

SQL is also by no means an ideal tool for casual end-users, despite the fact that it is becoming an industry-standard *ad hoc* inquiry and reporting capability. The syntax for inquiries can become quite complex, particularly when dynamic joins are involved. This has led to the development of various user-friendly front-ends for SQL, a welcome step but introducing again non-standard components into the arena.

Another problem with current implementations of relational technology is that, to date, they have not performed as well as the older database technologies in high volume on-line transaction-oriented environments. This, in turn, can force organizations into a "dual database" strategy, in that they use one database management system for high-volume on-line transaction-oriented production work, and another database management system to provide *ad hoc* casual end-user access.

Such an approach is far from ideal. For example, it introduces the need to extract and transfer information between two incompatible sets of file structures.

The normalization process associated with the relational approach also tends to fragment real-world entities over several tables, introducing significant reconstruction overheads at run-time when the database is accessed. Finally there are various problems related to the use of primary and foreign keys, a fundamental aspect of the relational approach.

4   SEMANTIC DATA MODELS

It is clear from the previous two sections that, although the relational approach possesses many positive features, major flaws do exist. On balance therefore, it was concluded that it would be inadvisable to base new advanced data management software for the Unisys A Series on relational technology.

It was also concluded, after further investigation and study, that the database management systems of the 1990s would be based on the semantic data model. The decision was therefore taken to use this approach when developing the new data management software for Unisys A Series for release to customers in the late-1987, early-1988 timeframe.

What is the basis for the semantic approach? For a start it is not a Unisys creation — there are many research papers in the literature of computer science dealing with various aspects of semantic technology. It is an active research area, with many parallel and related strands. There is no ANSI standard yet for semantic databases.

The Unisys implementation is based primarily on the work of Hammer and McLeod [1]. To quote from this paper:

Our goal is the design of a higher-level database model that will enable the database designer to naturally and directly incorporate more of the semantics of a database into its schema. Such a semantics-based database description and structuring formalism is intended to serve as a natural application modelling mechanism to capture and express the structure of the application environment in the structure of the database.

Note the key phrases "natural application modelling mechanism" and "enable the database designer to naturally and directly incorporate more of the semantics of a database into its schema". In other words, the main objectives of the semantic approach are to rectify the fundamental weaknesses of the relational approach.

The key concepts in the Unisys semantic database implementation are:

1. Entities.

2. Classes and sub-classes.

3. Generalization hierarchies.

4. Attribute inheritance.

5. Entity-valued attributes.

To illustrate these concepts, a simple example will be used.

5   A SIMPLE EXAMPLE

Consider the real-world situation of running a small library lending books to its customers.

An **entity** is any "object of interest" in the real world. In the library situation "person" entities and "book" entities are clearly of relevance and, in line with the relational approach, appropriate **data-valued** attributes will be defined for both kinds of entity eg:

person = < family-name, first-name, address, date-of-birth, ... >

book   = < title, author, publisher, publication-date, ... >

At database description time, strong data-typing capabilities are also available similar to those provided in the programming language Pascal.

The next step is to gather together entities of the same type to form classes. In this case, there are two classes to consider, namely PERSON and BOOK, which van be represented diagrammatically as in Figure 23.1.

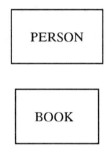

Figure 23.1 The classes PERSON and BOOK.

A slightly more detailed analysis of the real-world situation, however, shows that there are really two sub-classes of PERSON which are of interest, since there are those who work in the library and those who come in to borrow books, so that it is too simplistic to think merely of a PERSON class, if the real-world situation is to be modelled accurately. Two sub-classes of PERSON are therefore created, namely EMPLOYEE and BOOK-BORROWER, as illustrated in Figure 23.2.

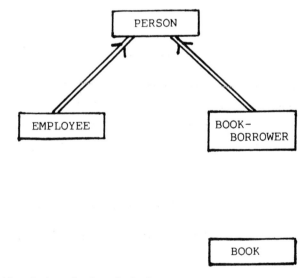

Figure 23.2 After the introduction of sub-classes.

In this case, a two-level hierarchy of classes and sub-classes has been created, but the Unisys implementation is much more general in that a multi-level generalization hierarchy may be defined.

Within a generalization hierarchy the principle of **attribute inheritance** applies. Any attribute defined in the "super-classes" of a given class are automatically inherited by the entities in that class. For example, in the library situation, the attributes defined for PERSON entities are automatically inherited by EMPLOYEE entities and BOOK-BORROWER entities so that, for example, there is no need to define again family name, first name etc for employees and book-borrowers.

Another interesting aspect of generalization hierarchies is that it is possible for a particular person to be both an employee and a book-borrower. On the other hand, consider the generalization hierarchy in Figure 23.3 below.

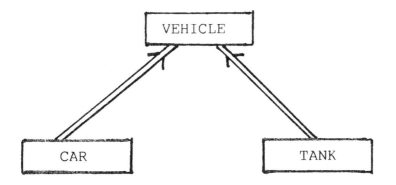

Figure 23.3 Alternative generalization hierarchy.

In this case the semantics are different in that a particular vehicle can be either a car or a tank but not both, and it is important that the appropriate semantics can be specified in the database description. The Unisys implementation allows this to be done. Relational systems, on the other hand, rely on application programmers to code the necessary checks.

Finally, in this simple example, books out on loan must be associated with the individuals who have books out on loan. This is achieved in an extremely elegant way using semantic technology as follows. For the BOOK class, one more attribute is defined called "borrowed-by". However, borrowed-by is not a data-valued attribute. It is an **entity-valued** attribute, the value of which is an entity in the class BOOK-BORROWER. In other words, a 1:1 relationship has been established between a book and the person who has borrowed it.

Similarly when attributes are being defined for BOOK-BORROWER, one additional attribute is defined called books-on-loan. Again this is an entity-valued attribute, but now multi-valued, whose values are in the class BOOK. In other words, a one-to-many relationship has been established between an individual and the several books he/she has out on loan. Thus it is as easy to define one-to-one relationship, one-to-many relationships and many-to-many relationships using entity-valued attributes as it is to define a person's family name, first name etc. In addition the integrity of inverse relationships so defined is automatically maintained by the system.

Figure 23.4 shows the incorporation of EVAs (entity-valued attributes) into the diagrammatic representation of the library situation. Note the use of single and double "arrow heads" to represent 1:1 and 1:n relationships.

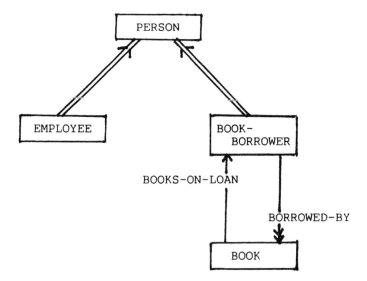

Figure 23.4   After the introduction of EVAs.

To summarize at this stage, the semantic data model approach provides all the advantages of the relational approach but, at the same time, eliminates the disadvantages. In particular, it provides a natural modelling mechanism for real-world situations and enables the semantics of real-world situations to be captured at database design time.

6 INFOEXEC – THE UNISYS IMPLEMENTATION

In its implementation of the semantic data model concept, Unisys has created not just a new database management system but a whole new family of products. This family of products is called the InfoExec family.

The new database management system is called SIM (Semantic Information Manager). In addition to the usual activities performed by a database management system, SIM is responsible for maintaining the integrity constraints specified at database definition time. There is no procedural language for defining integrity constraints nor indeed SIM databases. Instead such activities are performed in an interactive, menu-driven manner using ADDS (Advanced Data Dictionary System), the second major product in the InfoExec family.

Two new *ad hoc* inquiry and reporting capabilities have been provided. IQF (interactive query facility) is an extremely powerful tool designed for "DP literate" individuals. WQF (workstation query facility), on the other hand, is designed for casual end-users and requires, as the name suggests, the use of either a workstation from the Unisys B25 family or a PC. Both IQF and WQF are non-procedural menu-driven products. However, WQF exploits workstation capabilities such as colour, graphics and the use of a mouse to provide an extremely user-friendly environment. An interesting exercise is to undertake a number of inquiries of varying complexity using SQL, then to repeat the process using WQF. End-users have no doubt which they prefer !

For application programmers, host-language interfaces to SIM have been provided initially in COBOL 74, Algol and Pascal. In each case "set at a time" retrieval is the norm and care has been taken to provide appropriate syntax in each language so that, for example, a COBOL programmer will feel that he/she is working with COBOL even when accessing a SIM database.

The next member of the InfoExec family is called OCM (Operations Control Manager). OCM is a menu-driven product sitting above 14 different database utilities. Through OCM, 22 different database operational activities or functions may be performed, for example, database initialization, dumping, non-automatic forms of recovery etc. In each case, the database administrator or member of the operations staff selects the function he/she wishes performed and is then guided through its specification by menus. Traditionally, to perform such activities, a knowledge of procedural syntax with multiplicities of sub-options has been required and even skilled technical staff have had to consult the relevant technical reference manuals.

The concept of providing menu-driven access to activities or functions has been carried one step further by the final member of the InfoExec family, called the InfoExec Manager. This product sits above ADDS, IQF and OCM and hides their existence from the user. Again he/she specifies an activity or function to be performed and, as a result, will be guided into ADDS, IQF or OCM, but the user is unaware that this has happened, or indeed that separate discrete products exist. This approach of hiding complexity and the existence of individual pieces of software has been adopted consistently on Unisys A Series since 1985.

7   CUSTOMER BENEFITS

The first benefit that Unisys A Series customers will obtain from the InfoExec family of products is enhanced ease-of-use and enhanced productivity for a wide spectrum of personnel. Application programmers will be considerably more productive since it is now no longer necessary to code data-validation checks and referential integrity constraints.

IQF will be of considerable benefit to "DP literate" staff as will WAF to casual end-users accessing a SIM database.

The definition of databases may be carried out in a highly productive manner through the use of ADDS and, finally, OCM will bring significant benefits to database administrators and to operations staff.

The second major benefit of the InfoExec family lies in the area of superior information integrity. It is too dangerous to leave it to application programmers to remember to code check and to code them correctly. Erroneous information in a central database leads to bad decision-making based on bad information. Modern business is becoming too competitive to be able to survive on the basis of poor decisions.

The third major benefit is that the InfoExec family of products is suitable both for on-line transaction-oriented production work and for the provision of casual end-user access to information. As a result, A Series customers will be able to avoid the "dual database" strategy which has been forced on to many organizations.

Finally, and very importantly, it will be possible for existing DMS II users, particularly users of the Unisys 4GL LINC, to migrate to SIM in an evolutionary manner. To assist users, two additional pieces of software have been provided — DMS.View and LINC.View.

8   SPECIFICATION OF INTEGRITY CONSTRAINTS — A TEST CASE

To compare SIM with current database technologies, the same "Project, Personnel, Department" database was specified using (a) DMS II, (b) DB2 and (c) SIM. In each case, wherever possible, integrity constraints were specified at database definition time.

The results of this test case are shown in Figure 23.5.

SYSTEM	DATA ITEM VALIDATION		REFERENTIAL INTEGRITY	
	DBMS	APPLICATION	DBMS	APPLICATION
DMS II	77	25	4	86
DB2	66	36	0	90
SIM	102	0	90	0

Figure 23.5 Results of test case.

In this case, all 192 integrity checks can be specified in SIM at database definition time. With DB2, on the other hand, only 66 could be specified at database description time, leaving 126 for application programmers to code. Clearly a considerable amount of productivity significantly. Also ensuring the correctness of these coded integrity checks is far from trivial. There is a distinct possibility that some checks will be omitted or specified incorrectly.

9   SUMMARY AND CONCLUSIONS

With the availability of the InfoExec family of products today, Unisys believes that A Series customers have available to them the first practical implementation of semantic technology in the computing industry. Furthermore there are strong indications that the relational approach will be superseded by the semantic approach in the 1990s

The foundation has therefore been established for Unisys future developments in the data management area as far as its A Series mainframes are concerned.

10   REFERENCES

1   M. Hammer, D. McLeod. "Database Descriptions with SDM: A Semantic Data Model". *ACM Trans. Database Syst.* Vol. 6, No. 3, September 1981

Chapter 24
INTEGRATION OF
DATA-PROCESSING APPLICATIONS
AND
OFFICE AUTOMATION

T Jacobs
Belgian Institute for Automatic Control

1 INTRODUCTION

The purpose of this chapter is to describe the principles and functionality of Software AG 4G technology. More specifically, we will insist on the kind of information existing within an organization, like data, texts, images, CAD/CAM and the importance of a common language to manipulate them.

First of all, it is important to mention that 4G technology is not just a 4G language but rather a whole environment which defines the functionality of a computer at a level which makes it completely independent from the underlying systems environment.

A 4G environment can be implemented with identical functionality for the user in all systems environments, ie, IBM, MVS/XA, DOS/VSE, VM/CMS, DEC, VMS, UNIX, SIEMENS: BS2000, etc.

All computer functionality implemented following the principles of 4G technology can also embrace existing system-dependent functions and make them available to the user following the main principles, ie system transparency, portability, integrated/interactive application development and documentation.

The open integrated software architecture (ISA), in which 4G technology integrates defined basic functions in a visible manner, yields four major aspects:

- it allows a user to customize the environment;

- it allows the system developers and the users to extend the environment;

- it provides system-independent interfaces to a wide range of functions;

- it is based on accepted industry standards for its integration of architectures, operating environments and protocols.

A computer installation in the future will consist more and more of multiple computer nodes connected in a network, allowing any user to get to any function and/or data object in the system, irrespective of where it may be located.

Computer networks will be vertically structured in a three-tier architecture where an application will operate in a vertical, as well as horizontal integration of multiple computer nodes within the same application function.

For the support of a distributed computer network, Software AG has database (ADABAS) and 4G technology (NATURAL) available. These provide identical functionality across a variety of hardware, operating-system and TP environments on mainframe and departmental computer nodes. The NETWORK architecture supports the distribution of transactions and databases using various communication protocols, from channel-to-channel communication to SNA/VTAM, and even the connection across heterogeneous hardware using HyperChannel and/or VTAM protocols.

In the same three-tier computer configuration, Software AG has implemented an office-automation environment, CON-NECT, which is available to every user within the distributed three-tier computer network.

The Software AG 4G open integrated software architecture (ISA) is supported by various Software AG products based on the software components and interface available in the underlying systems architecture provided by the hardware manufacturer.

Software AG fully recognizes the requirements of structuring the system functionality in a well-defined framework of function blocks and is able to deliver additional benefits and productivity improvements complementing the manufacturers' software offerings.

In the following description, we will discuss the various components of open ISA in more detail starting from the "system layer" and going up to the "user access layer".

Description of the open ISA architecture with the layers:

- Operating systems.

- Database management.

- Dictionary.

- Application development.

- Common application.

- Session management.

We will insist on the database management and application development layers.

For the processing of data from all supported data-management systems such as VSAM, DL/l, IMS/DB, DB2, SQL/DS and ADABAS, and even system resources (via NATURAL PROCESS), NATURAL provides one common programming interface where the same processing statements can be applied to data managed by different systems. The common programming interface allows the creation of applications which:

- are portable across different data-management systems and operating environments through a common data-management interface;

- can be integrated across different systems via distributed databases;

- can be implemented with greater productivity as the system aspects are masked from the application logic;

- do not require error-prone source modifications for porting to a different environment.

2   DATA STRUCTURE

In addition to the basic DBMS functions available in different forms in ADABAS, DL/1 and DB2 database systems, many applications require advanced DBMS functions for complex data structures.

3   FREE TEXT RETRIEVAL/DOCUMENT DATABASE

Many applications today, besides the processing of formatted data, require unformatted data, such as textual documents, to be stored. They also need to be able to select text based on its content, using logical selection criteria including synonyms, word roots and proximity processing.

ADABAS TRS is an extension to ADABAS capable of managing text documents and performing free text retrieval on stored documents.

The free-text-retrieval functionality can be used from both a NATURAL, CON-NECT and a 3GL programme.

4   ENTITY RELATIONSHIP DATABASE

Relational theory requires all data objects to be defined in the form of flat tables.

While this approach is very easy to understand for the end-user, it nevertheless ignores the requirements for storage of more complex data objects, such as textual data, graphical objects or structured CAD/CAM objects.

The theory for the entity relationship data model is currently being discussed in the academic field as the NF2 (not first normal form) model. This will, in the future, also have to be integrated into the relational model, especially as far as the SQL language interface is concerned.

5   THE KNOWLEDGE BASE

The ADABAS knowledge base uses the ADABAS E/R DBMS as a base for the management of knowledge rules.

Rule interconnections are automatically maintained and can be queried dynamically during the creation and maintenance of the expert model as well as during execution.

Software AG, with the NATURAL EXPERT system, approaches the technology of rule-based expert systems as an extension to database technology.

Since in the future rule-based expert systems will not exist as isolated black boxes, but rather will be integrated into real business applications, they must be able to access data stored in production databases as well as special user-information bases.

6   THE SYSTEM ENVIRONMENT DATABASE

The operating system and TP environment represent in broader terms a database where data about the systems environment is stored. The systems database can be accessed via NATURAL PROCESS and processed through the same common programming interface (CPI) which is used for other databases.

Resources   accessible to a NATURAL programme via NATURAL PROCESS include:

- the SNA VTAM environment;
- the JES2/JES3 input and output queues;
- datasets stored as PDS, sequential or VSAM files;
- the systems catalog and VTOC information.

NATURAL PROCESS presents this system information in the form of data views similar to those for data files.

The NATURAL PROCESS extension of NATURAL allows the same NATURAL common programming interface to be used for data processing and system-control applications.

All these kinds of datas will be handled within a common application development environment: NATURAL.

NATURAL has three dimensions:

- NATURAL language;
- NATURAL application development facilities;
- NATURAL environment.

The NATURAL family products include many options for many needs. Application development, end-user computing, office support are part of the integrated capabilities of NATURAL.

CON-NECT is the office-automation environment integrated with NATURAL. What we are seeking to do with CON-NECT 2 and this is something nobody else is able to do is to provide a means of fully integrating all the various DP functions, whether they are office system functions, business functions, manufacturing functions or any other DP function.

There are many standard objects defined to CON-NECT, eg text, but also a PC object, source programmes, spreadsheets, and digitized images. Also the internal objects which are only of interest to CON-NECT — a CON-NECT menu or new CON-NECT command which you have written can be distributed too.

CON-NECT has to be able to distinguish between these different objects to know how the user is allowed to manipulate them.

In order to give to the user a maximum of flexibility in handling different kinds of objects, we integrated in CON-NECT a command processor.

With the command processor, it is possible to create new objects, new commands and adapting current programmes written in NATURAL.

For CON-NECT open architecture is the ability to interface to the applications area. What we are offering, and this is unique in CON-NECT, is the ability to invoke NATURAL applications directly from CON-NECT. But we are also offering you the converse concept. Within your applications programme, you can invoke individual CON-NECT functions.

What we have done is to allow CON-NECT to be fully integrated with NATURAL. Now we are using ADABAS, not just as a database but as an information base.

CON-NECT merges traditional office functions with traditional data processing to make it possible to create a new category of application: "office applications".

7   EXAMPLES OF APPLICATIONS

We have seen a first example of creation of a specific object: insurance policy.

One of our customers, an insurance company, has decided to create a new object: an image. This image is generated by a scanner system, from letters coming from their customers, from accident schemes. The images are considered by CON-NECT as documents and integrated with the standard documents such as policies, contracts.

Due to the fact that CON-NECT is a NATURAL application, it was easy to integrate the current applications like commercial applications, invoicing, etc with CON-NECT. The employee will have one specific environment tailored to his needs and giving him access to the data (texts, contracts folders), to office-automation functions (electronic mail, textprocessing), to end-user computing and to DP applications.

Thanks to this integrated access to the applications and the information, the employees are able to manage their job in a more effective and speedy way. For the company itself it means more effectiveness and it gives it a more competitive edge.

A second example of integration comes from a public administration which was looking for a system of creation and tracking of folders. For each activity it was necessary to create a folder and afterwards to complete and to modify it according to the time and the situation. The users were really "end-users" and the needs were a mix of office-automation functionalities like wordprocessing (in PC and mainframe), folders tracking, activity creation (a loan for example or a building authorization), steps within an activity etc. Thus there was a mix of thousands of objects, different kinds of activities by object, relations between objects and activities. The customer was also asking for dynamic generation of programmes.

The system was developed using NATURAL, CON-NECT and ADABAS.

It was based on three kind of integrations between CON-NECT and NATURAL:

- CON-NECT as an application command processor giving the dynamic aspects;

- connection between the application and the CON-NECT filing system;

- access to OA functions (fill-in documents, wordprocessing).

Software AG is absolutely convinced that the integration of DP applications, office systems and end-user systems will considerably increase the productivity within current organization.

This goal will only be reached within DP architecture integrating 4GT tools and DBMS accessing to all kinds of information.

APPENDICES

Appendix A
LIST OF
FOURTH–GENERATION SYSTEM
PRODUCTS

This list provided by the editor, is not exhaustive, but is put forward as a guide to the reader of the current products in the market.

A.1 BY MACHINE TYPE

IBM Mainframes only

- ADR/DL
- ADR/IDEAL
- CA-UNIVERSE
- Cullinet ADS
- IBM ADF II
- IBM AS
- IBM CSP
- Pansophic's GENER/OL
- Pansophic's TELON
- RCMS's Nomad 2
- Sage Software's APS
- Thorn EMI's CPG
- UFO

IBM PCs only

- ADR/IDEAL-ESCORT
- Ashton Tate's dBase IV
- Borland's Paradox
- Blyth Software's Omnis Quartz
- Compsoft's DeltaIV
- Limrose Software's PROGEN 4GL
- Microfocus's Sourcewriter
- Microft's Aspect
- Migent's Emerald Bay/ Eagle
- Progress Software Corp's Progress (marketed in the UK by Slinn Computing)
- Sapphire's Dataease IV

IBM System 3X

- Syon Ltd.'s Syon/2

Multi Environments

- Cincom's Mantis
- Cognos Powerhouse
- Deductive System's GENERIS
- Delta Software International's DELTA ADS
- Doric Computer System's INFO
- Information Builder's Focus
- Informix product set
- McDonald Douglas's PRO-IV
- Mimer Software's Mimer product set
- Oracle product set
- Parsoft's TODAY 4GL
- Rapid-Gen
- RTI's Ingres product set
- Sir Inc.'s SIR / DBMS (marketed in the UK by Pinpoint Analysis)
- Software AG's ADABAS and NATURAL product set

ICL mainframes only

- ICL Quick Build product set

DEC machines only

- Admins Inc.'s V32 (marketed in the UK by Celerity Software)
- Cortex's Application Factory
- Digital's COBOL generator
- Digital's Rally
- Digital's Teamdata
- Sybase product set

Apple Macintosh's only

- Acius Inc.'s 4th Dimension
- Borland's Reflex

Hewlett Packard only

- Hewlett Packard's Rapid / 3000
- Infosys Ltd.'s Genasys / 3000

UNISYS only

- Unisys Infoexec
- Unisys Linc

- Unisys Mapper

Unix only

- Care Business System's Empress

- Unify Corp.'s ACCELL

A.2   BY CATEGORY OF PRODUCT

The categories used are based on those defined in the Institute of Data Processing Managers report on Fourth–Generation Systems.

Application Builders-mainframe

- ADR / IDEAL
- CA-UNIVERSE
- Care Business System's Empress
- Cincom's Mantis
- Cognos Powerhouse
- Cortex's Application Factory
- Cullinet ADS
- Digital's Rally
- Hewlett Packard's Rapid / 3000
- ICL QuickBuild product set
- Informix product set
- McDonald Douglas's PRO-IV

- Mimer Software's Mimer product set
- Oracle product set
- RTI's Ingres product set
- Sir Inc.'s SIR / DBMS (marketed in the UK by Pinpoint Analysis)
- Software AG's ADABAS and NATURAL product set
- Sybase product set
- Synon Ltd.'s Synon /2
- Unify Corp.'s ACCELL
- Unisys Infoexec

Application Builders-PC

- Acius Inc.'s 4th Dimension
- ADR/IDEAL-ESCORT
- Ashton Tate's dBase IV

- Borland's Paradox
- Borland's Reflex
- Blyth Software's Omnis Quartz

373

- Compsoft's DeltaIV
- Limrose Software's PROGEN 4GL
- Microft's Aspect
- Migent's Emerald Bay / Eagle

- Progress Software Corp's Progress (marketed in the UK by Slinn Computing)
- Sapphire's Dataease IV

COBOL Generators and other language generators

- ADR/DL
- Delta Software International's DELTA ADS
- Digital's COBOL generator
- Doric Computer System's INFO(C)
- Microfocus's Sourcewriter

- Pansophic's TELON
- Parsoft's TODAY 4GL (C)
- Rapid-Gen (Assembler)
- Sage Software's APS
- Thorn EMI's CPG (Assembler)

Transaction Processor Builders

- Admins Inc.'s V32 (marketed in the UK by Celerity Software)
- IBM ADF II
- IBM AS
- IBM CSP

- Infosys Ltd.'s Genasys/3000
- Pansophic's GENER/OL
- UFO

End- User Products

- Digital's Teamdata
- Information Builders Focus
- RCMS's Nomad 2

- Unisys Linc
- Unisys Mapper

5th Generation

- Deductive Systems GENERIS